Temporary and Tactical Urbanism

Temporary and Tactical Urbanism examines a key set of urban design strategies that have emerged in the twenty-first century. Such projects range from guerrilla gardens and bike lanes to more formalised temporary beaches and swimming pools, parklets, pop-up plazas and buildings and container towns.

These practices enable diverse forms of economic, social and artistic life that are usually repressed by the fixities of urban form and its management. This book takes a thematic approach to explore what the scope of this practice is, and understand why it has risen to prominence, how it works, who is involved, and what its implications are for the future of city design and planning. It critically examines the material, social, economic and political complexities that surround and enable these small, ephemeral urban interventions. It identifies their short-term and long-term implications for urban intensity, diversity, creativity and adaptability.

The book's insights into temporary and tactical urbanism have particular relevance in the context of the COVID-19 pandemic, which has highlighted both the need and the possibility of quickly transforming urban spaces worldwide. They also reveal significant lessons for the long-term planning and design of buildings, landscapes and cities.

Quentin Stevens is an Associate Professor and Associate Dean of Research and Innovation in the School of Architecture and Urban Design at RMIT University in Melbourne. He studied temporary uses of urban spaces in Germany as an Alexander von Humboldt Fellow, and currently leads an Australian Research Council-funded project examining temporary and tactical urbanism in Australia and internationally. His publications include *The Ludic City* (2007), *Loose Space* (2007), *Activating Urban Waterfronts* (2020) and numerous journal articles.

Kim Dovey is a Professor of Architecture and Urban Design at the University of Melbourne and Director of the Informal Urbanism Research Hub (Infur-). His research on social issues in architecture and urban design has included investigations of urban place identity, creative clusters, transit-oriented urban design and the morphology of informal settlements. His books include *Framing Places* (1999/2008), *Fluid City* (2005), *Becoming Places* (2010) and *Urban Design Thinking* (2016).

Temporary and Tactical Urbanism
(Re)Assembling Urban Space

Quentin Stevens and Kim Dovey

Routledge
Taylor & Francis Group
NEW YORK AND LONDON

Cover image: Quentin Stevens and Ha Thai

First published 2023
by Routledge
605 Third Avenue, New York, NY 10158

and by Routledge
4 Park Square, Milton Park, Abingdon, Oxon, OX14 4RN

Routledge is an imprint of the Taylor & Francis Group, an informa business

© 2023 Quentin Stevens and Kim Dovey

The right of Quentin Stevens and Kim Dovey to be identified as authors of this work has been asserted in accordance with sections 77 and 78 of the Copyright, Designs and Patents Act 1988.

All rights reserved. No part of this book may be reprinted or reproduced or utilised in any form or by any electronic, mechanical, or other means, now known or hereafter invented, including photocopying and recording, or in any information storage or retrieval system, without permission in writing from the publishers.

Trademark notice: Product or corporate names may be trademarks or registered trademarks, and are used only for identification and explanation without intent to infringe.

Library of Congress Cataloging-in-Publication Data
Names: Stevens, Quentin, 1969- author. | Dovey, Kim, author.
Title: Temporary and tactical urbanism : (Re)assembling urban space / Quentin Stevens and Kim Dovey.
Description: New York, NY : Routledge, 2023. | Includes bibliographical references and index. | Summary: "Temporary and Tactical Urbanism examines a key set of urban design strategies that have emerged in the twenty-first century. Such projects range from guerrilla gardens and bike lanes to more formalized temporary beaches and swimming pools, parklets, pop-up plazas and buildings, and container towns. These practices enable diverse forms of economic, social and artistic life that are usually repressed by the fixities of urban form and its management. This book takes a thematic approach to exploring what the scope of this practice is, and understanding why it has risen to prominence, how it works, who is involved, and what its implications are for the future of city design and planning. It critically examines the material, social, economic and political complexities that surround and enable these small, ephemeral urban interventions. It identifies their short-term and long-term implications for urban intensity, diversity, creativity and adaptability. The book's insights into temporary and tactical urbanism have particular relevance in the context of the COVID-19 pandemic, which has highlighted both the need and the possibility of quickly transforming urban spaces worldwide. They also reveal significant lessons for the long-term planning and design of buildings, landscapes and cities"-- Provided by publisher.
Identifiers: LCCN 2022009549 (print) | LCCN 2022009550 (ebook) | ISBN 9781032256542 (hbk) | ISBN 9781032256535 (pbk) | ISBN 9781003284390 (ebk)
Subjects: LCSH: Cities and towns. | Urbanization. | Public spaces.
Classification: LCC HT151 .S6544 2023 (print) | LCC HT151 (ebook) | DDC 307.76--dc23/eng/20220411
LC record available at https://lccn.loc.gov/2022009549
LC ebook record available at https://lccn.loc.gov/2022009550

ISBN: 978-1-032-25654-2 (hbk)
ISBN: 978-1-032-25653-5 (pbk)
ISBN: 978-1-003-28439-0 (ebk)

DOI: 10.4324/9781003284390

Typeset in Univers
by MPS Limited, Dehradun

Contents

List of Figures vii

List of Tables ix

Contributor Details xi

Acknowledgements xiii

    Introduction 1

1 Definitions 17

2 Interests 33

3 Practice 53

4 Assemblage 79

5 Creativity 103

6 Temporality 129

7 Capacities 149

8 Futures 167

Bibliography 187

Index 199

Figures

1.1	Vegetable car, Berkeley, 1983	18
1.2	Temporary/tactical projects	21
1.3	Parklet, San Francisco	23
1.4	Paris Plages	24
1.5	Diagramming the temporary/tactica	24
1.6	Temporary café, Potsdamer Platz, Berlin, 1991	28
4.1	Typical city beaches in Germany: Strandsalon, Lübeck and La Playa, Leipzig	81
4.2	Skybeach, Stuttgart, on the roof of the parking garage of the Galeria Kaufhof department store	82
4.3	Temporary and relocatable buildings, play equipment, and awnings, and south sea umbrellas, palm trees and a ship create a beach atmosphere. Bundespressestrand, Berlin	85
4.4	Demonstration by local gymnastics club. Strandleben, Vaihingen an der Enz	87
4.5	Public Viewing of World Cup soccer matches. Strandbar, Magdeburg	90
4.6	South Pacific atmosphere through extensive use of thatching. Strand Pauli, Hamburg	92
4.7	The six sets of actors that are thrown together to create city beaches	96
5.1	Photomontage emphasising the role of 'Creative Nomads' in temporary activation of unused urban sites	108
5.2	A concert in 2017 by Yalta Club on Kulturstrand, Munich	112
5.3	Conceptual diagram of the relationships among the various actors that are creatively assembled to enable temporary use of a site	114
6.1	Eight ways that time frames temporary uses	142
7.1	Graffiti mapping – Fitzroy, Melbourne	155
7.2	A field of differences for t/t urbanist projects	157
7.3	Capacity mapping – Inner-city Melbourne	160
8.1	Eight ways that time frames temporary uses	170

Tables

5.1	Key themes in temporary use literature	106
5.2	Key critiques expressed in temporary use literature	106

Contributor

Fauster A. Awepuga is an academic staff member at La Trobe University and a practicing planner at the Department of Environment, Land, Water and Planning (DELWP) in Victoria, Australia. He researches peri-urbanisation, informality, social practices and urban governance in postcolonial Africa. His doctoral dissertation expanded knowledge on power relations and emerging tensions on land and livelihood developments in expanding metropolitan regions across Sub-Saharan Africa.

Acknowledgements

We thank the contributing author Fauster Awepuga and the research collaborators and associates Jonathan Daly, Merrick Morley, Troy Innocent, Ha Thai, Marco Amati, Salvador Rueda, Pippa Chandler, Patricia Aelbrecht, Amanda Claremont, Matthis van Oostrum and Lucy Pike. We thank the valued input, critique and support from Karen Franck, Claire Colomb, Matthew Carmona, Julia Lossau, Elek Pafka, Robin Chang, Philipp Misselwitz, Klaus Overmeyer, Martin Klamt and Naomi Barun. We are also grateful to the many editors and referees of journals, book chapters and conferences. Quentin would like to personally thank Dagmar Meyer-Stevens, and Kim thanks Sandy Gifford.

This research was supported by funding from the Australian Research Council (DP180102964), the Alexander von Humboldt Foundation, the Bartlett School of Planning at University College London, RMIT University School of Architecture and Urban Design, Faculty of Architecture, Building and Planning at the University of Melbourne, and in-kind support from the Geographisches Institut at Humboldt University Berlin.

This book is an assemblage of many years of research into how open spaces are designed and managed. There are thus some intersections and disjunctions between the arguments presented here. Earlier versions of some of this material have previously been published in the following articles and book chapters:

Chapter 1: Definitions	Dovey, K. "Temporary/Tactical", in *Urban Design Thinking: A Conceptual Toolkit*, London: Bloomsbury, 2016.
Chapter 2: Interests	Stevens, Q. and Dovey, K., "Pop-ups and Public Interests: Agile Public Space in the Neoliberal City", in Arefi, M. and Kickert, C. (eds) *The Palgrave Handbook of Bottom-Up Urbanism*, Basingstoke: Palgrave Macmillan, 2018.
Chapter 3: Practice	Stevens, Q., Awepuga, F. and Dovey, K. "Temporary and Tactical Urbanism in Australia: Perspectives from Practice", *Urban Policy and Research*, Vol. 39 No. 3, 2021.
Chapter 4: Assemblage	Stevens, Q., "Throwntogether Spaces: Disassembling 'Urban Beaches'", in Mehta, V. and Palazzo, D. (eds) *The Routledge Companion to Public Space,* Abingdon: Routledge, 2020.
Chapter 5: Creativity	Stevens, Q. "Temporary Uses of Urban Spaces: How Are They Understood as 'Creative'?", *Archnet-IJAR International Journal of Architectural Research*, Vol. 12 No. 3, 2018.
Chapter 6: Temporality	Stevens, Q. "Temporariness Takes Command: How Temporary Urbanism Re-assembles the City", in Andres, L. and Zhang, Y. (eds) *Transforming Cities through Temporary Urbanism*, Cham: Springer, 2020.

Introduction

Quentin Stevens and Kim Dovey

Existing Knowledge on t/t urbanism
Outline of the Book

The rise of 'temporary' and 'tactical' urbanism is arguably the most transformative global innovation in urban design and planning in recent years. Such practices, which we will refer to collectively as 't/t urbanism', encompass a myriad of small, experimental design projects led by diverse actors that transform underutilised urban spaces. Such projects range from temporary 'pop-up' parks and container villages to less formal 'DIY' and 'guerrilla' gardens and bike lanes. The COVID-19 pandemic has highlighted both the need and the possibility of quickly transforming urban spaces worldwide. Exploiting the temporal and spatial interstices of the city has much potential to intensify urbanity. Such interim and interstitial practices are generally also incremental and tactical; they squeeze between and within larger-scale strategies. These practices can enable diverse, experimental forms of economic, social and artistic life that are usually repressed by the fixities of urban form and its management. They turn the city into a testing ground for new forms of thinking. The t/t urbanism movement heralds a more agile, innovative and resilient future for urban design and planning.

The short-term benefits of t/t urbanism projects are often apparent in their intensive usage and transformative imagery. But the complex and dynamic interactions between actors within these projects make their broader and longer-term problems and impacts harder to discern and articulate (Fabian and Samson 2016, Mould 2014). To date, there has been little systematic critical analysis of the varied assemblages of actors and interests within different t/t approaches, or of how they engage with the wider public interest (Pagano 2013, Groth and Corijn 2005). A range of benefits has been claimed for t/t urbanism, including the enhancement of urban intensity, community engagement, innovation, resilience and local identity (Ferguson 2014, Lydon and Garcia 2015, PPS 2018). But t/t urbanism also raises significant problems and questions. Critics link its entrepreneurial agility to the deregulated planning regimes, boom-bust cycles, austerity policies and inequities of neoliberal urban development

(Brenner 2015, Bragaglia and Rossignolo 2021, Tonkiss 2013). Avant-garde 'pop-up' urbanism can add value to private property and stimulate displacement and gentrification, while masking the failures of strategic planning and the decline of long-term state investment (Andres 2013, Colomb 2012, Kamvasinou 2015, Mould 2014).

This book aims to develop a broad critical analysis of the diversity of 'tactical' and 'temporary' urbanism approaches, and their longer-term consequences, building on ways of understanding the complex, dynamic relationships between people, places, practices and desires which we draw from assemblage thinking and Actor-Network Theory. Assemblage thinking emerges from the philosophy of Deleuze and Guattari (1987) and has been developed philosophically by DeLanda (2006) who raises the prospect of understanding the city as a 'space of possibility'. Assemblage thinking connects the actual city to the capacities for transformation that are embodied within it. Assemblage thinking is relational thinking; the identities of places, people and things are not fixed, but constituted by the connections, flows and alliances between them. Such an approach has been used to re-think the concept of 'place' as a socio-spatial assemblage (Dovey 2010). Assemblage thinking has also been adapted by Latour (2005), who has spawned Actor-Network Theory (henceforth ANT) with a specific focus on forms of non-human agency embodied in the material world. ANT theory transforms the study of the ways both human and non-human elements (built forms, policies, forces) act upon each other (Yaneva 2012, Farias and Bender 2009). Latour (2004) notes that insights come from examining the multiple, dynamic relationships among networks of actors: how actors 'enrol' other actors into relationships that give them agency within specific contexts; how these relationships emerge, stabilise and transform over time. While there are differences between assemblage and ANT approaches, the synergies are significant and well-suited to understanding the informal, the temporary and the tactical. Such approaches are revolutionising our understanding of the processes through which the public space of cities is shaped, managed and transformed.

Research into assemblages does not presume to identify specific cause-effect relationships that lead to fixed outcomes; it involves a critical empiricism where truth and value constantly develop relationally among actors drawn together around diverse, historically situated *matters of concern* (Färber 2014, Farias 2017, Farias and Bender 2009, Latour 2004, McFarlane 2011, Yaneva 2012). The assemblage concept of 'matters of concern' provides an innovative, nuanced framework for exploring how various public and private interests are dynamically conceived, constructed, aligned and transformed in design and planning practices that are defined as temporary and tactical. Matters of concern bring together a focus on the specific materialities of public space, the specific desires and interests of its users, and the issues of concern for researchers. They draw attention to the formal and informal relationships that develop among a wide range of actors, both human and non-human. In Chapter 2, we map out the five key matters of concern that frame t/t urbanism.

While most existing books and papers on t/t urbanism focus on case studies of its varied forms, this book takes a thematic approach to explore the scope and nature of this practice, and understand why it has risen to prominence, how it works, who is involved, and what its implications are for the future of city design and planning. The book aims to critically examine the material, social, economic, governance and political complexities that surround and enable these small, ephemeral urban interventions. We seek to understand the short- and long-term implications for urban intensity, diversity, creativity and adaptability; to identify and critique the divergent private and public values, benefits and impacts that are entangled in such projects. We identify the implications of t/t urbanism for the broader planning and design of urban public space, and for urban policy and theory. This relational approach can help to critically contextualise t/t urbanist practices and outcomes within the larger frame of neoliberal capitalism, situating this work within recent debates about the potentials and limits of both assemblage-based and traditional political-economic interpretations of urbanism (Brenner et al 2011, Dovey 2012, McFarlane 2011). We seek to better understand t/t urbanism's synergies with the neoliberal economy, as well as its capacities to incrementally transform the forms, uses and meanings of public space. Assemblage thinking will enable us to explore and connect the dynamics of city making across many different spatial, economic and temporal scales. This book provides new insights into how small, informal, temporary urban interventions reflect large, complex forces at play in cities, and how they might contribute to major, long-term changes in cities and in everyday public life.

Existing Knowledge on t/t urbanism

To help frame the context of our study of t/t urbanism and the questions we will explore, it is useful to situate this book within the recent and rapidly growing literature on t/t urbanism, in its various manifestations, and in relation to the broader literature on assemblage thinking and ANT.

Cataloguing Practice

There are now many practice-based books that document case studies of t/t urbanism as broadly defined and have varying degrees of theoretical depth. Three seminal contributions stand out as the most thorough, structured explorations of t/t urbanism. These works – *The Temporary City* (Bishop and Williams 2012), *Urban Catalyst* (Oswalt et al. 2013) and *Tactical Urbanism* (Lydon and Garcia 2015) – have also become somewhat emblematic of the different approaches in the United Kingdom, continental Europe and the United States, respectively.

Bishop and Williams's *The Temporary City* (2012) was the first substantial English-language account of temporary urbanism, when the practices and concepts as we now know them were still relatively new. Its survey focuses chiefly on the United Kingdom, with some examples from Europe and the United States. The material is loosely organised into three thematic sections: the socio-economic context and drivers for temporary urbanism, its different manifestations and ways that urban planning processes started to adapt to these practices. As an introduction to the theme, the book is well illustrated and covers a very wide range of topics and projects, but it does not address any of them in depth. It also documents a range of practices that do not involve physical changes to the urban built environment, including events, mobile stalls and markets, art installations, gardening, and pop-up shops in existing buildings, as well as relatively permanent new buildings like the ostensibly 'pop-up' shopping mall Box Park, which opened in London's Shoreditch in 2011 and which still stands a decade later, having also expanded to two other locations. Bishop and Williams raise many issues and questions that we seek to address in much greater depth in this book, including the temporal frameworks for understanding cities, public and private interests, gentrification, the creative industries, and the implications of temporary urbanism for planning practice. Their book draws on most of the key literature that was available at the time of its writing, but could not reflect on the great many temporary projects, impacts from them, and critical analyses that have developed in the ten years since.

Another early analysis of t/t urbanism was *Urban Catalyst: The Power of Temporary Use* (2013) by Oswalt, Overmeyer and Misselwitz. This was a much-delayed publication of the Urban Catalyst team's ground-breaking academic study of temporary uses, which examined five European cities from 2001 to 2003. Some of the case studies and several essays from the authors' partners in Vienna had been published earlier by Haydn and Temel in *Temporary Urban Spaces* (2006). Overmeyer had also published *Urban Pioneers: Temporary Use and Urban Development in Berlin* (2007), documenting over 100 open space projects in that city, primarily written in German as a guide for local practice and policy. The wider *Urban Catalyst* study is organised into three thematic sections: a typology of different ways temporary uses link to the long-term development of their sites; a set of short provocative essays and conversations by diverse contributors that explore different potentials of informal, temporary planning; and a range of practice tools for cultivating temporary uses. The book features both short and detailed case studies from across Germany and from several other cities in Europe, with many photographs of projects and detailed, annotated timelines and conceptual diagrams and maps. It is filled with high quality and original ideas, including several essays from US and UK academics. Like *The Temporary City*, *Urban Catalyst* raises several issues that this book aims to analyse in more detail: relevant social and economic contexts for t/t urbanism, the definition of temporariness, the costs and benefits of temporary uses and informality for different actors, the role of the creative industries, and the ways that temporary uses might modify traditional planning processes.

The third seminal introduction to this field is Lydon and Garcia's *Tactical Urbanism* (2015). This practice-oriented book built on the authors' own extensive project work and a series of online catalogues that documented case studies from North America, Latin America and Australasia (Street Plans Collaborative 2012a, 2012b, Steffens 2013, CDS and SPC 2014). *Tactical Urbanism* draws on a range of North American examples including 'Better Block', 'Park(ing) Day', The Project for Public Spaces and its 'Lighter, Quicker, Cheaper' strategy. It usefully contextualises these practices in two main ways: firstly by surveying many earlier temporary, low-cost ways of incrementally improving the liveability of urban spaces; and secondly by noting the influence of contemporary factors such as the global financial crisis of 2007 and the new forms of information technology. The latter part of Lydon and Garcia's book is a how-to guide outlining the key parameters of more tactical urban design practices.

Tactical Urbanism emphasises the ways that both the interventions themselves and the processes that generate them can potentially transform large, formal planning practices and physical environments; hence the subtitle: *Short-term Action for Long-term Change*. The most distinctive contributions lie in their emphasis on tactics: approaches that are 'initiated by citizens to bypass the conventional project delivery process and cut through municipal bureaucracy by protesting, prototyping, or visually demonstrating the possibility of change' and which 'exist along a spectrum of legality' (Lydon and Garcia 2015:12,8). This tacticality, and Lydon and Garcia's frequent invocation of the importance of 'forging' and 'building' relationships, circumventing rules, and innovating, all align well to our assemblage view of practice that focuses on the development of new models, connections, alignments and flows, and the breaking down of old ones.

There are many other books, journal issues and papers that have explored aspects of t/t urbanism – far too numerous to critique in detail here. Edited books include *Insurgent Public Space* (Hou 2010), *Now Urbanism* (Hou et al 2015), *The Informal American City* (Mukhija and Loukaitou-Sideris 2014), *Transience and Permanence in Urban Development* (Henneberry 2017), *The Handbook of Bottom-up Urbanism* (Arefi and Kickert 2019) and *Transforming Cities Through Temporary Urbanism* (Andres and Zhang 2020). Special journal issues include *Spontaneous Interventions* (*Architect* Magazine, August 2012), *DIY Urbanism* (*Journal of Urbanism* Vol. 7 No. 4, 2014), *Pavilions, Pop-Ups and Parasols* (*Architectural Design* #235, May/June 2015) and *Guerrilla Urbanism* (*Urban Design International* Vol. 25 No. 2, 2020). These works generally present short, discrete, disparate views by various authors on a range of urban planning and urban design practices, often focused on single case studies.

Critiquing t/t urbanism

The political critique of t/t urbanism was first established by Tonkiss (2013) and Brenner (2015). In her paper 'Austerity Urbanism and the Makeshift City', Tonkiss suggests that a good deal of what counts as t/t urbanism can be seen as a form of band-aid urban planning for cities in decline; makeshift solutions produced by neoliberal policies that enforce a reduced role for the state. Thus, t/t urbanism patches the gaps left by uneven development, as cities become more resilient and cover for the failures of the state. In his critique of a tactical urbanism exhibition at New York's Museum of Modern Art, Brenner (2015) suggests that while such projects are grounded in participatory democracy and ostensibly oppose the neoliberal order, they cannot subvert it. He argues that t/t urbanists are 'at risk of reinforcing the very neoliberal rule-regimes they ostensibly oppose'. He notes the tendency of t/t urbanism to privilege 'ad hoc mobilisations over larger-scale, longer-term, publicly financed reform programs'. In other words, the key problems with t/t urbanism are that it is small-scale and temporary with little role for the state; it is not part of a master plan to address global capitalism. These are important critiques, but they suggest a tension between tactics and strategies, temporary and permanent, citizens and the state – these are not binary relations. These tensions resonate with those between Marxist and assemblage thinking that played out in the journal *City* in 2011 (Brenner et al 2011, Dovey 2011, McFarlane 2011, Tonkiss 2011).

These earlier critiques have been followed by several more recent studies. *The Help-Yourself City: Legitimacy and Inequality in DIY Urbanism* by Douglas (2018) provides a fresh and biting critique of the field of t/t urbanism within the United States. The book's focus is on Do-It-Yourself, grassroots or 'guerrilla' actors and actions, although it also examines the professional expertise of some DIY urbanists, and the engagement of temporary and tactical urbanism within formal urban planning processes. Douglas focuses on the role of DIY urbanism in reinforcing social inequality, rather than ameliorating it; in this view, its chief actors are educated, wealthy, privileged white males, with superior access to places, resources and social capital. Douglas examines DIY urbanism within the specific US context of inadequacies in public planning processes and the provision of civic infrastructure. A large number of small DIY projects are studied but there is little examination of significant physical transformations of public spaces.

A further critique of t/t urbanism is based on broader theories of urban informality in cities of the Global South where agile and transgressive tactics in the temporary transformation of public space are widely regarded as a normal part of everyday urban life. Street vending in particular is fundamentally geared to the livelihoods of the urban poor (Brown 2006). Devlin (2018) is critical of much of the t/t literature as being constrained by Global North thinking. He makes a distinction between informality born of 'need' and of 'desire', linked respectively to the urban poor and the middle classes (Devlin 2018: 570). He criticises the ways t/t urbanism in the Global North is biased towards desire-based informality and implicitly denigrates need-based informality in public space. For Devlin, t/t urbanism has become framed as politically neutral and geared to neoliberal policies of deregulation: 'social justice and equity might not be anathemas, but they are not at the top of the list of priorities' (Devlin 2018: 576). He calls for greater attention to Southern urban theory as a means to better understand t/t urbanism in the Global North and argues that 'informality produced by the urban poor to meet day-to-day needs can be generative of an insurgent politics' (Devlin 2018: 582). This distinction can be useful as a framework for a critique of the legitimacy of t/t urbanism when it transgresses formal codes of governance. However, from an assemblage perspective, there is no dichotomy between desires and needs – a need can be understood as an intensive and compulsive form of desire.

The most recent study of t/t urbanism at the time of writing is Ferreri's *The Permanence of Temporary Urbanism: Normalising Precarity in Austerity London* (2021). This critique addresses the broad political, economic and cultural context of t/t urbanism, and the processes through which it is both produced and consumed. Ferreri's approach involves a longitudinal ethnographic case study, with a core focus on different actors' perspectives and their power relations within temporary use practices as they played out in the neoliberal context of East London from 2009 to 2016. While the focus is on the temporary occupation of vacant shops rather than transformations of shared urban space, Ferreri's study addresses four dimensions of temporary urbanism that also animate this book: the discourses that frame t/t urbanism; how it is organised; the experiences produced; and the role of city planners. She emphasises a shift over time 'from marginal ad-hoc and experimental practices still shrouded in imaginaries of illicit counter-cultures to celebration and appropriation by urban policymakers and planners' (Ferreri 2021: 9–10).

In this book, we share the interest of these authors in the diverse social and economic contexts and drivers of t/t urban interventions, the different ways these come together in concrete projects, and the ways t/t urbanism has changed design and planning practice. We also share a critical stance toward the creative and economic forces that are shaping contemporary cities generally, and t/t urbanism specifically. As urban designers, we seek to focus more strongly on the analysis of spaces, physical design changes to those spaces, and the roles of spatial contexts, materials and design approaches in shaping the outcomes and impacts. In contrast to most political critiques, we resist any reduction of the spatial to the social - assemblage thinking is a critique of the ways power is embodied in the spatial and material world (Dovey 2010).

Theorising Cities, Planning and Time

To complete this brief review of current research, we also find inspiration in two recent books that engage in a more broadly philosophical examination of temporality and urban change. Rather than an analysis of temporary urbanism, Madanipour's *Cities in Time: Temporary urbanism and the future of the city* (2017) is primarily a theorisation of three kinds of temporality in cities: instrumental, existential and experimental. These three frames provide the structure for a broad examination of the use and regulation of urban spaces and the development of built form. Madanipour explores the concept and role of time within cities, its impact on people's lived experience, memory and identity in cities, and how and why cities change over time. He explores and illustrates a wide range of time frames and practices for using, regulating and producing urban space. Although 'temporary urbanism' is mentioned frequently, the book's key insight lies in locating it within the broader dynamics of cities. Madanipour argues that instrumental processes accelerate change and generate temporariness; existential processes illustrate users' precarity, adjustment and resistance in the face of urban change; and experimental processes explore ways forward. Madanipour's analysis draws on relational thinking, exploring the relationships between people, time and identity – but not space. The book has much more to say about the temporality of the city than its spatiality.

A second relevant conceptual analysis is Beauregard's *Planning Matter: Acting with things* (2015). Drawing on Actor-Network Theory, this is a theoretical and philosophical enquiry into what urban planning is as an activity. Its focus is on developing a relational understanding of actors and agency in how cities are shaped. The book is organised around a critical exploration of a series of concepts that define and shape planning practice: action, things, places, morality, truth, the state, theory and modernity. Several of these themes parallel those of chapters in this book. While Beauregard's focus is on analysing planning events and activities, including the creation of plans, our attention is directed more to the physical outcomes of planning: their sites, materials, forms and impacts; how spaces are made, experienced and function. Beauregard examines how different understandings of time influence how planning processes are carried out: what is planned and who is involved. But his focus is on the long-term, permanent, progressive development of cities, not short-term, reversible transformations.

This book seeks to build on all these conceptual insights to develop a more open, dynamic, relational understanding of time in city planning and development, and to give more attention to the relationships between different timeframes and various spatial conditions.

Outline of the Book

Our aim in this book is to extend knowledge in the field of t/t urbanism by critically examining the diversity of these practices and understanding how they are entangled with distinctive sets of human actors, objects, intangible forces, ideas and interests, and the possibilities that these relationships enable.

Chapter 1 – Definitions – provides an overview and mapping of the diversity of practices, examples, theories and terminology related to temporary and tactical urbanism that have been set out in the studies discussed above. We note that this emerging field of practices is varied and difficult to define, but can be understood as an intersection of the temporary and the tactical. We explore the distinctions and interconnection between these two core concepts. This chapter maps a wide range of spatial and temporal scales of t/t practices and charts their varied progressions from informal and temporary toward more formal and permanent. We identify a range of other dimensions including creativity, mobility and mutability (adaptability).

Chapter 2 – Interests – examines the diverse range of interests – public and private, individual and collective – that shape t/t urbanism and are shaped by it. While temporary and tactical urbanism is often portrayed in terms of spontaneous forms of agency, there is a paradox that such projects often involve complex intersections between the agency of the state and that of citizens. We foreground five particular *matters of concern* related to t/t urbanism: urban intensity, community engagement, innovation, resilience and place identity. We highlight that temporary and tactical urbanism can be seen as well-adapted to the cycles of creative destruction that characterise neoliberal urban development, boom/bust cycles, austerity policies and neglected neighbourhoods; to place marketing, privatisation and gentrification. The chapter explores what the public interest in t/t urbanism might be. What new ideas, actors and possibilities does it bring into the design of public space? We tease out the paradox that while t/t urbanism is a key manifestation of Lefebvre's (1996) notion of the 'right to the city', it also raises crucial questions about power, agency and public interests.

Chapter 3 – Practice – is a critical, comparative study of recent practices of temporary and tactical urbanism in Australia. It discusses the distinctive ways temporary and tactical urbanism is defined and enacted in the Australian context, drawing on interviews with expert practitioners from the public, private and non-profit sectors. The findings reveal a range of ways that the various actor relationships forged through temporary and tactical urbanism link to broader interests and practices of urban planning and management.

Chapter 4 – Assemblage – involves a focus on the ways different actors and processes come together through the example of artificial 'city beaches' in Germany. Six different categories of actors are defined and examined: underused spaces, landscape elements, human actors, various forms of energy, administrative schemas and economic austerity. This Actor-Network analysis of city beach projects highlights the complex and dynamic assemblages of relationships and processes through which these various actors are brought together and diverse forms of power which stabilise or transform their relationships.

Chapter 5 – Creativity – examines how that concept has been defined and applied to temporary and tactical urban management and development approaches: in terms of creative production, consumption of creativity, and creative governance. These concepts are argued here to mesh together with a liberalisation of urban planning and governance. Creative planning for temporary use suggests transforming the aims and methods of planning itself to be more dynamic and more facilitative and to involve continual engagement with a wide range of creative actors. In this context, the focus of planning shifts away from permanent built outcomes and towards facilitating creative activity. Drawing on ideas in the earlier chapters, this chapter highlights the various creative actors who are engaged with temporary and tactical urbanism, what particular interests and abilities they bring, and how they interact with each other within the urban development process.

Chapter 6 – Temporality – explores how temporariness shapes the processes and outcomes of urban development, exploring various definitions, perceptions and roles for time in relation to the production and use of the urban environment. The analysis shows how temporariness defines, encourages and enables specific sets of relationships to the many actors, forces and interests that shape cities. These dynamics are explored in terms of various benefits and impacts that temporary urbanism can have for various actors and a variety of ways that it links to longer-term urban development.

This characterisation of temporary urbanism and its networks of interdependence links it to wider critiques of neoliberalism, modernist masterplanning, and historic preservation: broad social constructs that themselves each embody and sustain particular understandings of time, building and cities. Two paradoxical and countervailing dynamics that constantly influence the form of cities are highlighted. First, temporary urbanism, for all its claimed ephemerality and fluidity, constantly establishes new, durable relationships and has broad and enduring effects. Second, all urban spaces are more-or-less impermanent assemblages of materials, people, technologies, and concepts, which are constantly being adjusted to meet changing resources and needs.

Chapter 7 – Capacities – draws on assemblage thinking to investigate the concept of 'capacity' in both its theoretical and practical dimensions. Capacities are relational, at once the capacities of citizens to change the city and the capacities of the city to be changed. While capacities are neither simply properties nor forms of agency, they can be mapped as part of a more adaptive and agile practice of urban planning, where the pursuit of fixed future outcomes is replaced by an understanding of the city as a 'space of possibility' that is real even if not yet actual. Capacities embodied in the material city are only actualised in relation to the adaptive capacities of citizens, buildings, technologies, loose parts and policies. Capacities also have a temporal dimension; they expand and contract over time, geared to the rhythms of urban life, from traffic to seasons and political cycles.

In the concluding Chapter 8 – Futures – the book's various threads of analysis are drawn together to speculate on the future of t/t urbanism. The COVID-19 pandemic has opened up many opportunities for t/t urbanism and demonstrated the need for more agile, adaptive and resilient forms of public space. A great deal of public space in many cities has been reclaimed from car space for more productive, creative and convivial uses. Cities around the world have recognised the opportunity to mitigate the loss of public life during the pandemic by repurposing street space for people – but what comes next? What futures are possible for public space? Are the tactical transformations of cities during COVID-19 a temporary change before a return to car-dependent cities driven by real-estate markets within idealised masterplans, or are they a harbinger of a more agile urban realm? Perhaps one long-term legacy will be the realisation that unpredictable disruption will become the new normal. Perhaps the temporary and the tactical might emerge from the margins of the urban imagination to become the mainstay of a more agile urban planning and design.

References

Andres, L. (2013) Differential spaces, power hierarchy and collaborative planning. *Urban Studies* 50 (4): 759–75.

Andres, L. and Zhang, Y. (eds) (2020) *Transforming cities through temporary urbanism: A comparative overview*, Cham, Switzerland: Springer.

Arefi, M. and Kickert, C. (eds) (2019) *The Palgrave handbook of bottom-up urbanism*. Cham, Switzerland: Palgrave Macmillan.

Beauregard, R. (2015) Temporalities, in *Planning matter: Acting with things*, Chicago: University of Chicago Press, pp. 151–71.

Bishop, P. and Williams, L. (2012) *The temporary city*, New York: Routledge.

Bragaglia, F. and Rossignolo, C. (2021) Temporary urbanism as a new policy strategy: A contemporary panacea or a trojan horse? *International Planning Studies* 26 (4): 370–386.

Brenner, N. (2015) Is 'tactical urbanism' an alternative to neoliberal urbanism? MoMA Post: Notes on Modern and Contemporary Art around the Globe. Retrieved 7 April 2021 from http://post.at.moma.org/content_items/587-is-tactical-urbanism-an-alternative-to-neoliberalurbanism

Brenner, N., Madden, D. and Wachsmuth, D. (2011) Assemblage urbanism and the challenges of critical urban theory. *City* 15 (2): 225–40.

Brown, A. (ed) (2006) *Contested space: Street trading, public space and livelihoods in developing cities*. Rugby: ITDY.

CDS and SPC (CoDesign Studio and Street Plans Collaborative) (2014) *Tactical Urbanism Vol. 4: Australia and New Zealand*. Retrieved 7 January 2022 from http://tacticalurbanismguide.com/guides/tactical-urbanism-volume-4/

Colomb, C. (2012) Pushing the urban frontier: Temporary uses of space, city marketing, and the creative city discourse in 2000s Berlin. *Journal of Urban Affairs* 34 (2): 131–52.

DeLanda, M. (2006) *A new philosophy of society*, New York: Continuum.

Deleuze, G. and Guattari, F. (1987) *A thousand plateaus*, London: Athlone Press.

Devlin, R. (2018) Asking 'third world questions' of first world informality. *Planning Theory* 17 (4): 568–87.

Douglas, G. (2018) *The help-yourself city: Legitimacy and inequality in DIY urbanism*, London, Oxford University Press.

Dovey, K. (2010) Becoming Places: Urbanism/Architecture/Identity/Power, London: Bloomsbury.

Dovey, K. (2011) Uprooting critical urbanism. *City* 15 (3–4): 347–54.

Fabian, L. and Samson, K. (2016) Claiming participation: A comparative analysis of DIY urbanism. *Journal of Urbanism* 9 (2): 166–84.

Färber, A. (2014) Low-budget Berlin: Low-budget urbanity as assemblage. *Journal of Regions, Economy and Society* 7: 119–36.

Farias, I. (2017) Assemblages, in M. Jayne and K. Ward (eds) *Urban theory: New critical perspectives*, New York: Routledge, pp. 41–50.

Farias, I. and Bender, T. (2009) *Urban assemblages: How Actor-Network Theory changes urban studies*, New York: Routledge.

Ferguson, F. (2014) *Make_shift city: Renegotiating the urban commons*, Berlin: Jovis.

Ferreri, M. (2021) *The permanence of temporary urbanism: Normalising precarity in austerity London*, Amsterdam: Amsterdam University Press.

Groth, J. and Corijn, E. (2005) Reclaiming urbanity: Indeterminate spaces, informal actors. *Urban Studies* 42 (3): 503–26.

Haydn, F. and Temel, R. (eds) (2006) *Temporary urban spaces: Concepts for the use of city spaces*, Basel: Birkhäuser.

Henneberry, J. (ed) (2017) *Transience and permanence in urban development*, Oxford: Wiley.

Hou, J. (ed) (2010) *Insurgent public space: Guerrilla urbanism and the remaking of contemporary cities*, New York: Routledge.

Hou, J., Spencer, B., Yocom, K. and Way, T. (eds) (2015) *Now urbanism: The future city is here*, New York: Routledge.

Kamvasinou, K. (2015) Temporary intervention and long-term legacy: Lessons from London case studies. *Journal of Urban Design* 22 (2): 187–207.

Latour, B. (2005) *Reassembling the social. An introduction to Actor-Network Theory*, Oxford: Oxford University Press.

Latour, B. (2004) Why has critique run out of steam? *Critical Inquiry* 30 (2): 225–48.

Lefebvre, H. (1996) *Writings on cities*, (transl. E. Kofman and E. Lebas), Oxford: Blackwell.

Lydon, M. and Garcia, A. (2015) *Tactical urbanism: Short-term action for long-term change*, Washington, D.C.: Island Press.

Madanipour, A. (2017) *Cities in time: Temporary urbanism and the future of the city*, London: Bloomsbury.

McFarlane, C. (2011) Assemblage and critical urbanism. *City* 15 (2): 204–24.

Mould, O. (2014) Tactical urbanism: The new vernacular of the creative city. *Geography Compass* 8 (8): 529–39.

Mukhija, V. and Loukaitou-Sideris, A. (2014) *The informal American city: Beyond taco trucks and day labor*, Cambridge, MA: MIT Press.

Oswalt, P., Overmeyer, K. and Misselwitz, P. (2013) *Urban catalyst: The power of temporary use*, Berlin: DOM publishers.

Overmeyer, K. (ed) (2007) *Urban pioneers: Temporary use and urban development in Berlin*, Berlin: Jovis.

Pagano, C. (2013) DIY urbanism: Property and process in grassroots city building. *Marquette Law Review* 97 (2): 335–89.

PPS (Project for Public Spaces) (2018) *The lighter, quicker, cheaper transformation of public spaces*. https://www.pps.org/article/lighter-quicker-cheaper (accessed 28 July 2020).

Steffens, K. (2013) *Urbanismo Táctico 3: Casos Latinoamericanos*, The Street Plans Collaborative and Ciudad Emergente, Retrieved 7 January 2022 from https://issuu.com/streetplanscollaborative/docs/ut_vol3_2013_0528_17

Street Plans Collaborative (2012a) *Tactical urbanism Volume 1*, Retrieved 7 January 2022 from https://issuu.com/streetplanscollaborative/docs/tactical_urbanism_vol.1

Street Plans Collaborative (2012b) *Tactical urbanism Volume 2*, Retrieved 7 January 2022 from https://issuu.com/streetplanscollaborative/docs/tactical_urbanism_vol_2_final

Tonkiss, F. (2011) Template urbanism: Four points about assemblage. *City* 15 (5): 584–88.

Tonkiss, F. (2013) Austerity urbanism and the makeshift city. *City* 17 (3): 313–24.

Yaneva, A. (2012) *Mapping controversies in architecture*, New York: Routledge.

Chapter One
Definitions

Kim Dovey and Quentin Stevens

The Scope of t/t urbanism
Mutability/Mobility
Governance/Informality
Temporary/Permanent

Urban design – the shaping of public space – is the most permanent of built environment practices, much more than buildings and plans that are demolished or abandoned with economic and political cycles. It is also the case, however, that many aspects of urban form change on a temporary basis, and a great deal of the potential for urban intensity involves the exploitation of both the temporal and spatial interstices of the city. Such interim and interstitial practices are generally also incremental and tactical in the sense that they squeeze between and within larger-scale strategies. When one of the authors was a student at Berkeley in the 1980s, the Vegetable Car (Figure 1.1) was often parked on his street as a memorial to the first person to die in a car accident. Designed by an eco-activist group known as Urban Ecology, it was towed every few weeks to a new location in order to evade local by-laws about abandoned cars (Downton 2009: 95). This was an early version of what has become known as 'guerrilla gardening' and a precursor to 'Park(ing)' and the 'parklets' that emerged in nearby San Francisco in the early 2000s, which have since morphed into a formally authorised and long-term 'Pavements to Parks' program.

There is now a pervasive global trend toward the temporary and the tactical that has become one of the key urban design strategies of the twenty-first century. Such projects range from guerrilla gardens, crosswalks, parklets and bike lanes to more formalised temporary beaches and swimming pools, parklets, parkmobiles, instant plazas, pop-up buildings, food trucks, outdoor theatres and container towns (Haydn and Temel 2006). This emerging field of practices is difficult to define. As we noted in our

FIGURE 1.1 Vegetable car, Berkeley, 1983.
Source: Kim Dovey.

Introduction, it is variously termed 'temporary urbanism' (Bishop and Williams 2012), 'insurgent urbanism' (Hou 2010), 'urban catalyst' (Oswalt et al 2013), 'tactical urbanism' (Lydon and Garcia 2015), 'austerity urbanism' (Tonkiss 2013), 'sandpit urbanism' (Stevens 2015), 'DIY urban design' (Fabian and Samson 2016), 'bottom-up urbanism' (Arefi and Kickert 2019), 'pop-up urbanism' and 'guerrilla urbanism'. In this book, we will characterise this field of urban design practice collectively through a twofold concept at the intersection of the temporary and the tactical – 't/t urbanism'. This is a broad field of incremental urban transformations that fill interim periods of time and underutilized, interstitial urban spaces – the vacuums, *terrain vague* and smooth urban spaces of the city. They are often cyclic, taking advantage of the daily, weekly and seasonal urban rhythms that produce times of underuse and the economic downturns that yield cheap or vacant space. The idea of tactical urbanism links to the work of de Certeau where a tactic is an action that takes place within a context that may be antithetical – 'The space of the tactic is the space of the other' (de Certeau 1984: 37). Tactical urbanism is a poaching operation, a form of encroachment; tactics infiltrate strategic systems. But tactics are also productive in that they seek to discover and create potentials and possibilities out of latent capacities. Tactics are linked to what McFarlane (2011) calls tactical learning – the use of everyday practical knowledge as part of an engagement with the city as a learning assemblage.

The twofold concept t/t urbanism recognises differentiation and potential tensions within this cluster of practices. The term 'temporary urbanism' is most prevalent in Britain and Europe and involves a focus on time horizons and rhythms of change; on physical transformations and 'meanwhile' or 'interim' uses of spaces that are not intended to last more than a few years (Bishop and Williams 2012). 'Tactical urbanism' is the more common term in North America and involves a focus on self-organised spatial practices and social needs that are not well served by governments or the market, and a political orientation toward new forms of social agency in public spaces (Lydon and Garcia 2015, Devlin 2018). This is not a binary division since a good deal of the tactical (guerilla, DIY, insurgent) also characterises British and European projects. Likewise, the temporal dimension is fundamental to the Tactical Urbanism of Lydon and Garcia, whose book is subtitled 'Short-term action for long-term change'.

While this book's consideration of t/t urbanism is chiefly limited to the relatively planned, orderly, wealthy cities of the Global North, temporary uses and informal interventions in urban open spaces are also widespread in the less formal cities of the Global South. In some ways, t/t urbanism involves forms of learning from the high levels of informal urbanism embodied in those cities – the spontaneous DIY urbanism of informal settlements.

t/t urbanism often involves the design of semi-fixed elements of public space, which have long been recognised as central in human-environment studies (Hall 1966, Rapoport 1982), extending this adaptability to temporary buildings and landscapes as well as more mobile furniture and vehicles. While the focus of discussion in this book is on public space, such practices are also often initiated in quasi-public spaces, especially vacant lots and buildings. The temporariness often applies to urban codes and regulations such that different practices are permitted for a limited period of time. However, tactical urbanism also encompasses informal practices of guerrilla urbanism that operate without landowners' permission and outside state control.

While temporary transformations by definition do not last, they don't always revert to a space's pre-existing form, but may morph into something new. Many forms of transformation are cyclic in that the forms are temporary but there is a repetition or a refrain to which the city returns – informal trading is a good example. In many cases, a temporary transformation becomes permanent over time. Temporary/tactical urbanism operates within the existing urban infrastructure, adapting and transforming existing types such as carparks, containers, vehicles and trees; it works within, around and against existing practices and regulations. There is much to admire in many of these temporary projects – pioneering enterprise, social commitment, a spirit of adaptation, exploitation of new materials and technologies, and urban greening strategies (Bishop and Williams 2012). In Chapter 2, we will examine in detail the range of benefits and values associated with temporary and tactical projects in urban spaces. t/t urbanism is a call to understand the city as a place under constant revision with room to move and space for the unexpected; where temporary opportunities are taken with high levels of creative community engagement and design collaboration.

There is little that is new about temporary or tactical urbanism. Many of the issues, concepts and practices that frame contemporary urban design are relatively tactical and temporary, including the self-organised, smooth, informal, rhizomic, incremental and interstitial; urban drama, political resistance, graffiti, advertising, street trading and informal settlement (Dovey 2016). Traditional cyclic events such as the circus, farmers' markets, street fairs and community gardens are all temporary. What is new is the degree to which the focus on the tactical and temporary is becoming organised into the deliberate design of a four-dimensional city; its evolution in space and time. Bishop and Williams (2012) identify a range of economic, technological and social forces that have led to an expansion of temporary urbanism: spatial vacuums are produced by the downturn of investment cycles; new social media create marketing opportunities for pop-up events; flexible work patterns and community activism produce a more adaptive and opportunistic urban life. This is a movement that celebrates the city as a dynamic space of possibility and becoming rather than a static sense of being. The irony is that such approaches to urban design often succeed so well that the tactical becomes strategic and the temporary becomes permanent; incremental changes accumulate into wholesale urban transformation.

The Scope of t/t urbanism

The range of project types that might be considered temporary and/or tactical depends on the definition of the field. As we noted in the Introduction, many books on the topic provide extensive catalogues of cases, organising them around diverse sets of contexts, kinds of temporary activities, and specific material forms. The focus of this book is on those projects that involve a redesign of urban public space. Within this definition, temporary and tactical projects range from those that temporarily transform the image of the city to a range of projects that materially appropriate public or quasi-public spaces in various ways (Figure 1.2). Small projects can become bundled into

Container Market

Guerrilla Park (Rebar)

Projections

Guerrilla Crosswalk

Yarn Bombing

FIGURE 1.2 Temporary/tactical projects.

Source: Top and centre right: Kim Dovey
Centre left: Rebar – https://creativecommons.org/licenses/by/2.0/
Bottom left: Kristy Dactyl – https://creativecommons.org/licenses/by/2.0/
Bottom right: Pinkyjosef – https://creativecommons.org/licenses/by-sa/3.0/deed.en

larger-scale projects on vacant lots and post-industrial sites with varying levels of strategy and permanence (Bishop and Williams 2012, Oswalt et al. 2013).

At the smallest scale, many forms of temporary urbanism involve a change of image without changing the use of public space. Traditional forms include graffiti and advertising as well as spontaneous memorials and urban artworks. Yarn bombing is a guerrilla activity that is deployed to transform meanings and atmosphere, to decorate and soften the city in a temporary manner. Guerrilla signage such as stencils on the pavement showing where a creek once flowed can increase the transparency of the city. Nocturnal projections onto buildings are another common example. Guerrilla gardening involves a range of illicit tactics including the planting of trees and gardens in public spaces and the grafting of fruit-producing branches onto street trees to render them productive. Guerrilla bike lanes and crosswalks involve spontaneous inscriptions on roadways, undermining and augmenting the formal urban code. Chair bombing involves the design and placement of new public seating, often combined with paving and other furniture to create public living rooms.

Many forms of temporary urbanism are mobile in the sense that they are easily and quickly moved from place to place. The concept of the 'pop-up' is now a rather overused and misused term but effectively defines a temporary building or occupation that is supposed to pop-down again after a short period of time. The use of shipping containers involves a transfer of technology from transport industries to temporary urban design. Parklets are small parks that originated in San Francisco with the temporary appropriation of kerbside car parking bays with minimal designs of seats and artificial turf while feeding the meter. This was a tactic, developed by the design firm Rebar, to reclaim the city from cars, undermine the car parking strategies of local governance and play on the double meaning of 'park'. This tactic has grown and developed in two main ways. First, it became a global movement known as Park(ing) Day when people across the globe were encouraged to spontaneously appropriate parking spaces for the day. Second, it has developed into formally authorised programs – San Francisco's is known as 'Pavements to Parks' – where local residents or businesses can apply to develop and host a parklet on one or more parking bays which then becomes semi-permanent. These parklets are sponsored, funded and maintained by local businesses or residents; they often add value as outdoor seating or a change of image, but they remain legally public spaces – the required signage says 'all seating is open to the public' (Figure 1.3) (Thorpe 2020, Bela 2015). A variation of the parklet is the 'parkmobile' – an assemblage

FIGURE 1.3 Parklet, San Francisco.
Source: Kim Dovey.

of plants and seats that can be transported from place to place as an instant park, often sized to fit a parking bay.

The urban beach is a form of temporary urbanism that seeks to bring the atmosphere of the beach into the city during the summer months. Paris Plages is a waterfront freeway in Paris that is closed during August (when traffic is quiet) and its pavement is covered with sand (Stevens and Ambler 2010) (Figure 1.4). The urban beach can be augmented with temporary swimming pools, either floated into place or in shipping containers filled with water. Larger-scale t/t projects often occupy large post-industrial sites, vacant lots and buildings. These are often bundles of smaller projects and functions that include neighbourhood parks, community gardens/orchards, cafés/shops, artist studios, temporary cinemas, cultural facilities and exhibition spaces (Oswalt et al. 2013).

As a means of understanding this field of temporary/tactical urbanism, Figure 1.5 diagrams this range of urban design practices according to two primary axes. The horizontal axis represents the degree to which such practices are temporary and tactical (left) and the degree to which they can become permanent and strategic (right).

FIGURE 1.4 Paris Plages.
Source: Kim Dovey.

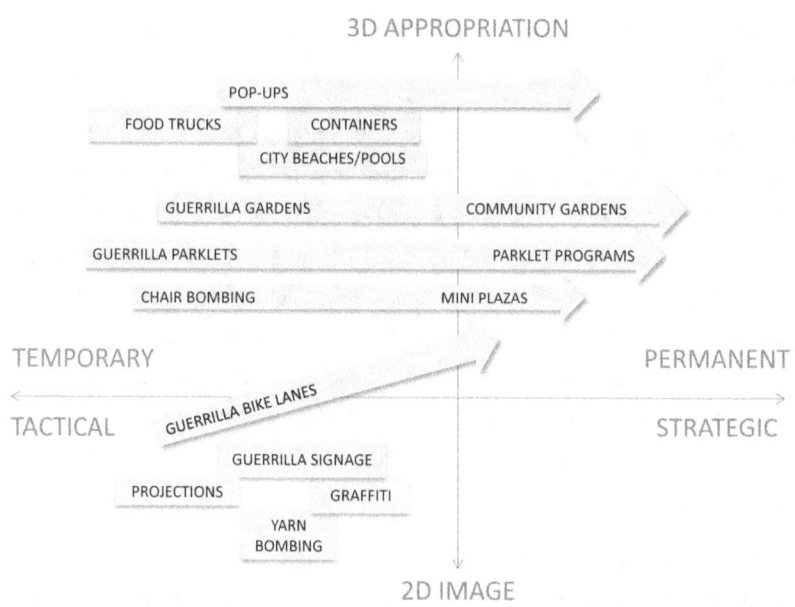

FIGURE 1.5 Diagramming the temporary/tactical.
Source: Kim Dovey.

The vertical axis distinguishes between practices that transform only the two-dimensional image of public space (such as wall projections, signage and graffiti) and those that also appropriate three-dimensional public spaces (through beaches, parks, containers and gardens) and thereby transform their usage. While all temporary/tactical urbanism begins on the left of the diagram, many such practices are in a process of becoming more permanent and strategic, represented by the arrows. This is particularly the case in North America and Australia, where tactics link to long-term strategies for the design, management and use of the public realm. The diagram thus distinguishes between those practices that may become cyclic or seasonal but not permanent (such as graffiti, food trucks, beaches and projections) and those that often embody the desire and potential to become permanent (such as parklets, gardens, pop-ups and bike lanes).

This range of practices embraces different forms of social and artistic expression that are otherwise repressed in the overdetermined city. By enabling greater use of under-utilised space, they make urban space more productive and get more value out of the same infrastructure. They add intensity to the city through greater diversity and adaptation of use and meaning plus a greater density of interaction.

Temporary/tactical urbanism enables a much higher level of creativity and innovation in urban design because it turns the city into a testing ground where new forms of thinking can be implemented without the danger of permanent failure. The temporary framework is a key to bypassing the formal planning processes that are necessary to secure approval for permanent change and build tolerance for innovative design. Because the change is temporary, a higher level of informality is seen as legitimate.

Temporary/tactical urbanism grants designers the freedom to fail by lowering costs and risks. Urban design is not a science and the city does not have the controlled conditions of a laboratory, yet our cities are littered with the permanent remains of failed urban design experiments based on flawed and inflexible thinking. A temporary framework enables us to increase the range of experimentation and speed up the learning process. The city is simply too complex and unpredictable to enable the approval of every smart idea that comes along. Temporary/tactical urbanism is a means of breaking down urban design to an incremental scale that enables us to circumvent the status quo; but again the irony is that it embodies a strategy to become the status quo. Temporary urbanism can stimulate markets, change the place identity of rundown neighbourhoods, reactivate vacant sites, refine innovations, demonstrate viability and stakeholder acceptance. There is spin-off value for developers as interim uses secure their sites, halt decay, reduce their land holding costs, add value, and pave the way for permanent projects (Bishop and Williams 2012).

Temporary/tactical urbanism also plays a key role in incrementally reclaiming the city back from the car. The freeway lining the River Seine that enables the Paris Plages beach during summer would never be built today, and the beach demonstrates what might have been possible if it had not been built. The success of the temporary beach calls the permanence of the freeway into question – why does and why should the car maintain a monopoly on this choice riverside space? Tactical urbanism then involves a testing of the legitimacy of the ways the city has been designed and what it might become. The power of temporary and tactical urbanism is that it shifts the ontology of the city from being towards becoming; it opens a space of possibility.

Mutability/Mobility

One framework for understanding temporary/tactical urbanism stems from the work of Latour (2005) and is generally known as Actor-Network Theory. This is an approach that treats the world as a complex human-environment assemblage where both human and non-human elements have agency. For Latour, anything that modifies a state of affairs is an actor, or to use the jargon, an 'actant'; just as people act, so trees shelter, gates open and close, timetables and traffic signals regulate flows. 'Every time you want to know what a non-human does, simply imagine what other humans or other non-humans would have to do were this character not present' (Latour 1992: 155). Actor-Network Theory removes intention from agency in order to look at the human-environment assemblage as an interactive network of both human and non-human actants (Bender 2010). A key form of non-human actant is the 'immutable mobile' – assembled technologies that are difficult to change but that can move easily from place to place and plug into different contexts where they recombine with other technologies and practices – automatic doors, traffic signals, mobile phones and food trucks are examples (Latour 1987). From this perspective, Guggenheim (2010:175) suggests that the city is in many ways the opposite of the immutable mobile – we can change it but we can't move it: 'The very idea of a city consists in an assemblage of mutable immobiles'. Mutability is the adaptability of the city, its capacity to reform and recombine into new forms of co-functioning.

Temporary and tactical urbanism exploits and demonstrates this mutability of the city, the micro-practices of everyday urban life, the city as a human-environment assemblage of affordances and semi-fixed elements, the network of actants.

Governance/Informality

Bishop and Williams (2012) argue that while policy and governance cannot directly create many forms of temporary urbanism, they can play a key enabling role: producing conservation codes that protect post-industrial shells, publishing databases of vacant properties, leasing state-owned properties for temporary use, and providing seed funding for events and organisations. Bishop and Williams also call for more flexible forms of urban planning that incorporate temporary projects – alternatives to the traditional masterplan that favour incremental development without a fixed end-state, with small grain adaptability and short time cycles. Such planning promotes general visions rather than idealised end-states; it aims to be implementable through flexible phasing, an open time frame that can respond to changing conditions.

Temporary/tactical urbanism is at once a violation of rules and a production of new rules; it involves a double movement of both informalizing the formal city and formalising the informal city (Christiaanse 2013, Sassen 2013). There are interesting interconnections with the formalisation of informal settlements; both are forms of relatively informal urbanism that fill the interstices of uneven urban development with adaptive small-scale projects. While one adds vitality to the poorer quarters of overdetermined rich cities of the Global North, the other remains a permanent feature of poorer cities in the Global South. A growing body of research is seeking to explore how t/t urbanism in the Global North might learn from the diversity and long experience of informal urbanism across the Global South (Devlin 2018, Lara-Hernandez et al 2020, Andres and Zhang 2020, Andres et al 2021). There are important differences between these contexts, which shape the aims, conduct and impact of temporary and tactical interventions in the respective urban settings. A key disparity that frames the distinction between 'developed' and 'developing' countries is the relative deficiency of formal processes for creating and managing urban spaces in the Global South. Due to the absence of alternatives and the paucity of rights and resources, informal urbanism there may not be temporary gap-filling, but 'permanently impermanent' (Andres et al 2021). Informal urbanism in the Global

South often involves survival; '"tactics" more of necessity than of choice' (Bermann and Marinaro 2014: 410).

Temporary/Permanent

Another key question that emerges here is the degree to which temporary urbanism is a temporary function of economic downturns or the harbinger of more enduringly dynamic urbanism. Is this just a matter of artists and activists collaborating with out-of-work architects and urbanists to fill the gaps created by capital markets as an interim between permanent projects? We suggest t/t urbanism is both filling gaps and driven by new markets. On the one hand, it is clear that temporary urbanism is geared to the failures of market capitalism; particularly high rates of vacancy and dereliction. It is a response to the polarising effects of neoliberal urbanisation that turns the city into islands of luxury in a sea of leftover space; as Sassen (2013:116) puts it: 'informal activity is not the failure of regulation or a return to older modes … it is part of advanced capitalism.' Opportunities are also created by major geopolitical ructions. Soon after the fall of the Berlin Wall, a temporary open-air cafe was set up near Potsdamer Platz with scattered wall segments as the key attraction (Figure 1.6). A hammer and chisel could be hired from the pop-up van to souvenir a piece of the wall

FIGURE 1.6 Temporary café, Potsdamer Platz, Berlin, 1991.
Source: Kim Dovey.

and contribute to its demolition. A slightly more long-lasting example nearby involved the struggle for reuse of the massive former East German parliament building, formally occupied for just 14 years, and hosting various temporary uses for another 16 years before its eventual demolition (Oswalt et al. 2013: 288–303).

The demand side of temporary urbanism is linked to the ways it creates a word-of-mouth 'buzz' based on the demand for the new and unique. A pop-up event gains symbolic capital because one needs to catch it before it pops down – lack of enduring supply creates demand. Urban events are increasingly used to generate brand identity for both places and products; it can become difficult to distinguish creative temporary urbanism from a camouflaged marketing campaign. The term 'pop-up' is used as marketing discourse to create buzz around the idea of the temporary – such popups often don't pop-down.

Oswalt et al (2013) outline a range of processes through which temporary uses are implemented, co-exist with other uses, and then may or may not become permanent in different ways. A temporary project may simply occupy an underutilized site during an interim period of vacancy with little long-term impact. The same bundle of forms and functions may then flow from site to site, following the gaps of the property market – the temporary becomes permanent but mobile. The temporary can fire the urban imagination and become an impulse for other uses that utilise similar sites or tactics. If the temporary use is successful, it may be permitted to co-exist with its replacement and operate in synergy with the long-term use. In some cases, the temporary use displaces the existing use and becomes permanent. This is a rhizomic global urbanism that spreads primarily through websites; a temporary use in one site or city may become permanent in another.

The temporary and the tactical are forms of urbanism that augment the permanent and the strategic, and also have a tendency to themselves become more permanent and strategic. They are particularly useful in filling temporal and spatial vacuums, taking advantage of opportunities produced by politics and markets. They represent a key cutting edge of the democratising movement broadly known as the Right to the City (Bela 2015, Lara-Hernandez et al. 2020). The temporary and tactical often emerge as self-organised guerrilla tactics and can produce a very makeshift aesthetic image (Figure 1.6). While it may be difficult to defend the lack of design quality in many cases, temporary and tactical urbanism is self-organised, improvised and irregular by definition. Design quality emerges from a culture of creativity that will determine that poor designs will be very temporary. The larger questions remain: how to plan for the unplanned, how to regulate for difference, how to design for the unpredictable and how to organise for self-organisation.

References

Andres, L., Bakare, H., Bryson, J., Khaemba, W., Melgaço, L. and Mwaniki, G. (2021) Planning, temporary urbanism and citizen-led alternative-substitute place-making in the Global South. *Regional Studies* 55 (1): 29–39.

Andres, L. and Zhang, Y. (eds) (2020) *Transforming cities through temporary urbanism: A comparative overview*, Cham, Switzerland: Springer.

Arefi, M. and C. Kickert (eds) (2019) *The Palgrave handbook of bottom-up urbanism*. Cham, Switzerland: Palgrave Macmillan.

Bela, J. (2015) User-generated urbanism and the right to the city, in J. Hou, et al. (eds), *Now urbanism: The future city is here*, New York: Routledge, pp. 149–64.

Bender, T. (2010) Reassembling the city, in I. Farias and T. Bender (eds), *Urban assemblages*, London: Routledge, pp. 303–23.

Bermann, K. and Marinaro, I. C. (2014) 'We work it out': Roma settlements in Rome and the limits of do-it-yourself. *Journal of Urbanism* 7 (4): 399–413.

Bishop, P. and Williams, L. (2012) *The temporary city*, New York: Routledge.

Christiaanse, K. (2013) Preface, in P. Oswalt, K. Overmeyer and P. Misselwitz (eds), *Urban catalyst: The power of temporary use*, Berlin: DOM Publishers, pp. 6–7.

de Certeau, M. (1984) *The practice of everyday life*, Berkeley: University of California Press.

Devlin, R. (2018) Asking 'third world questions' of first world informality: Using Southern theory to parse needs from desires in an analysis of informal urbanism of the global North. *Planning Theory* 17 (4): 568–87.

Dovey, K. (2016) *Urban design thinking: A conceptual toolkit*, London: Bloomsbury.

Downton, P. (2009) *Ecopolis*, Dordrecht: Springer.

Fabian, L. and Samson, K. (2016) Claiming participation – A comparative analysis of DIY urbanism in Denmark. *Journal of Urbanism* 9 (2): 166–84.

Guggenheim, M. (2010) Mutable Immobiles, in I. Farias and T. Bender (eds), *Urban assemblages*, London: Routledge, pp. 161–78.

Hall, E. T. (1966) *The hidden dimension*, New York: Doubleday.

Haydn, F. and Temel, R. (eds) (2006) *Temporary urban spaces: Concepts for the use of city spaces*, Basel: Birkhäuser.

Hou, J. (ed) (2010) *Insurgent public space: Guerrilla urbanism and the remaking of contemporary cities*, New York: Routledge.

Lara-Hernandez, J. A., Coulter, C. and Melis, A. (2020) Temporary appropriation and urban informality: Exploring the subtle distinction. *Cities* 99, article 102626.

Latour, B. (1987) *Science in action*, Cambridge, MA: Harvard University Press.

Latour, B. (1992) Where are the missing masses? Sociology of a door, in W. Bijker and J. Law (eds), *Shaping technology/building society*, Cambridge, MA: MIT Press, pp. 225–58.

Latour, B. (2005) *Reassembling the social. An introduction to actor-network theory*, Oxford: Oxford University Press.

Lydon, M. and Garcia, A. (2015) *Tactical urbanism: Short-term action for long-term change*, Washington, D.C.: Island Press.

McFarlane, C. (2011) Assemblage and critical urbanism. *City* 15 (2): 204–24.

Oswalt, P., Overmeyer, K. and Misselwitz, P. (2013) *Urban catalyst: The power of temporary use*, Berlin: DOM publishers.

Rapoport, A. (1982) *The meaning of the built environment: A nonverbal communication approach*, Beverly Hills: Sage.

Sassen, S. (2013) Informal economies and cultures in global cities, in P. Oswalt, K. Overmeyer and P. Misselwitz (eds), *Urban catalyst*, DOM Publishers, pp. 105–16.

Stevens, Q. (2015) Sandpit urbanism, In B. Knudsen, D. Christensen and P. Blenker (eds), *Enterprising initiatives in the experience economy: Transforming social worlds*, New York: Routledge.

Stevens, Q. and Ambler, M. (2010) Europe's city beaches as post-Fordist placemaking. *Journal of Urban Design* 15 (4): 515–37.

Thorpe, A. (2020) *Owning the street: The everyday life of property*. Cambridge: MIT Press.

Tonkiss, F. (2013) Austerity urbanism and the makeshift city. *City* 17 (3): 313–24.

Chapter Two
Interests

Quentin Stevens and Kim Dovey

Urban Intensity
Community Engagement
Innovation
Resilience
Place Identity
Researching t/t urbanism
On Planning for Uncertainty
Assemblage

Temporary and tactical urbanism are often praised for bringing innovation and agility to urban design practices that are typically constrained by context, convention, regulation, high cost, long timelines and complex stakeholder roles and needs. Such urbanism typically involves the rapid mobilisation of new constellations of urban actors, resources and spaces to quickly address a range of previously unmet desires. As our discussion in Chapter 1 indicated, these ostensibly spontaneous public space projects often involve complex intersections between the agency of the state and that of citizens; there is rarely a simple binary between bottom-up and top-down, informal and formal, temporary and permanent, tactical and strategic. Temporary projects are often strongly linked to the long-term transformation of urban property values and consumption patterns. Tactical urbanism has ironically become a new form of top-down strategic planning – by both the state and private interests. Temporary urban interventions can serve as vectors of gentrification and neoliberal planning, or they can be reactions to it.

This chapter explores the various claimed public benefits of a more agile, tactical urbanism. It also explores the paradoxes, entanglements and potential duplicity of such urbanism in the context of neoliberal urban planning regimes, through a critical examination of the range of interests that such projects might serve and the positive and negative impacts they can have. As the 'tactical' side of t/t urbanism's definition highlights, short-term and low-cost adaptations of the urban fabric often involve a circumvention of conventional urban planning rules and approaches. Such agile open space projects embrace a wide variety of forms, functions, scales and durations. They range from relatively regulated artificial beaches, floating swimming pools, pop-up buildings, outdoor theatres and container villages, to more informal projects such as instant plazas, unsanctioned guerrilla gardens and parklets. Their functions include consumption, recreation, public art, performance, community engagement and creative production.

We noted in Chapter 1 that the t/t urbanism focused on in this book is responding to conditions in already highly-developed cities that are subject to rapid change: increases and decreases in urban density; rising social diversity; economic volatility; or decline and shrinkage. These kinds of agile open space projects in the Global North often seek to do more than just provide space to meet current needs. As the neoliberal state cuts taxes and deregulates, the pressure increases to deliver better public spaces with fewer resources and to adapt more rapidly. At the same time, the vitality of urban public space is seen in connection with economic development and the production and exchange of new ideas that help drive a knowledge economy. Conventional urban development forms and planning tools are often considered inadequate to address these challenges (Oswalt et al. 2013). Agile open space projects are generally incremental and interstitial, emerging between large-scale and long-term strategies, and filling interim periods of time and underutilised urban space, particularly during economic downturns. Different stakeholders may have quite different views about the temporariness of these new forms and uses of spaces. Tactical urbanism can blend into long-term strategies; some pop-ups never pop down. Other projects are terminated or relocated even though their sponsors, managers and users wish to see them continue. The variety of uses and locations of temporary open space interventions, and the diversity of actors who are involved in developing them, illustrate the rich scope of rights, interests and desires of citizens in urban public space (Lydon and Garcia 2015, Haydn and Temel 2006, Hou 2010).

The benefits that are argued to flow from t/t urbanism are many and interlinked. We summarise them here in terms of five key values: urban intensity, community engagement, innovation, resilience and place identity. In each case, there is also a downside; a danger that public interests cannot be easily presumed. t/t urbanism mobilises and empowers particular urban actors; it unleashes particular flows of desire in public space with some clear public benefits. But there are also crucial questions about power, agency and public interests that are much less explored. What follows first argues the case for each of these five benefits, followed by what are seen as their potential dangers. What are the prospects that temporary and tactical transformations of public space might reproduce or even exacerbate the urban problems they seek to address? Our interest in exploring such contradictions lies in developing more critical forms of t/t practice and a more rigorous critique of such projects.

Urban Intensity

Temporary and tactical urbanism is argued to increase the intensity of open space use. This concept of intensity can be difficult to define (Dovey and Pafka 2014), but here means an increase in both the volume and the variety of uses and users. t/t urbanism is opportunistic in seeking out underutilised public spaces and redesigning them for a greater volume and variety of people, activities, and experiences. t/t urbanism introduces new uses into existing public spaces, and it produces new forms of public life in spaces that were not previously accessible. A good example is the replacement of low-intensity car parking with high-intensity parklets. By accommodating more uses and users within existing public spaces, temporary urbanism embodies a more efficient use of limited space, infrastructure and other resources. This addresses the challenge of rising densities and demands for economic efficiency and environmental sustainability (Nemeth and Longhorst 2014, Oswalt et al. 2013). In this context, tactical greening or renaturalisation of urban spaces is also a form of intensification because of its focus on improving ecological performance. t/t urbanism also explores and harnesses the underutilised capacities of the city by expanding the physical scope of public spaces, to bring people and activities to vacant and underutilised spaces that were closed off or privately owned. These include empty parking lots, rooftops, infrastructure easements, vacated and ruined buildings, waste sites and wild landscapes.

Intensification means a diversification of public space designs, as well as their uses and users. The most expansive survey of temporary urban uses, in Berlin, classified over 100 open space projects into four main activity categories: culture, gardening, food and playing sports (SenStadt 2007). Other studies have noted a range of uses including consumption, open space, active recreation, art and performance, community engagement and creative production (Haydn and Temel 2006, Hou 2010, Lydon and Garcia

2015). While good public space design has always catered to a multiplicity of functions, tactical urbanism tends to address existing inequities in public spaces and services, to meet underrecognised and underserved needs by spontaneously providing new amenities, such as street furniture, cycle lanes and pedestrian crossings (Fabian and Samson 2014). Vacant, derelict sites often offer the potential to accommodate exploratory, experimental and divergent activities that may be specifically excluded from formal public spaces. By expanding the range of functions of public space, t/t urbanism encompasses the desires of a greater variety of citizens and provides greater social equity. It cuts across the constraints of any 'one right way' of designing public space and creates a field of expression for differences in social class, culture and ethnicity.

Finally, tactical open space interventions can increase intensity by enabling richer mixes of activity in both time and space. They can overcome the physical boundaries and legal controls that typically delimit and separate different uses and user groups in public spaces, often in the name of protecting amenity and preventing conflict (Valverde 2005). Agile urbanism can overcome the monotony and inflexibility of more conventional, top-down, long-term urban development. It can intensify urban life by enabling synergies both among short-term, informal uses and between them and the formal city (Loukaitou-Sideris and Mukhija 2014, Oswalt et al. 2013).

The other side of this argument for a more intensified city is to ask: why is it that so much urban space is underutilised? Why is the state not engaged in such intensification and diversification? To what degree do t/t projects fill the gaps created by the failures of a more permanent and strategic urban planning process? The boom/bust cycles of capitalist urban development produce uneven development pockmarked with sites that remain vacant for long periods. The neoliberal economic consensus that has prevailed globally since the 1970s involves a focus on economic growth as the goal of urban planning. Neoliberalism embodies regimes of inter-city competition, tax-cutting and deregulation, where the state retreats from investment in cities; it seeks instead to negotiate the private production of quasi-public space that couples public access to private control. Tactics for temporarily filling urban voids can be seen as well-adapted to the cycles of creative destruction that characterise neoliberal urban development. To what degree then might t/t urbanism be understood as austerity urbanism – band-aid urban planning for cities in decline (Tonkiss 2013)?

There are further questions that might be raised about t/t urbanism's claims to appeal to a greater diversity of users. To what degree is this simply a switch to a different range of uses and users? t/t urbanism can be integrated with practices of privatisation, gentrification and displacement, whereby some categories of users (consumers, creative actors, potential investors) are seen to add value to underutilised land, while others are subtly marginalised. Temporary commercial activities that are enabled by relaxed regulations can undermine the sustainability of local businesses as they privatise public space. New functions that emerge under the umbrella of creative innovation can disrupt the amenity of existing users and initiate a subtle displacement of previous functions. In Chapter 5, we explore in detail these Janus-faced aspects of creative practices and 'creative destruction' within t/t urbanism and its discourse. The activations of t/t urbanism have been criticised for encroaching on vacant, wild and derelict urban spaces that have unrecognised uses and values – the city's 'terrain vague' (Kamvasinou and Roberts 2014, Solà-Morales 1994). Such sites have long been recognised as sites of homeless refuge, urban memory, childhood imagination and wild flora and fauna (Barron 2014, Carr and Lynch 1968, 1981). t/t interventions have been intentionally deployed in such spaces to displace such socially marginal and illicit activities (Douglas 2014, Tonkiss 2013).

Community Engagement

t/t urbanism can produce high levels of community engagement. Engagement is a very broad term that embraces a range of roles people have in leading, facilitating, shaping and experiencing t/t projects. Many studies have pointed to the wide range of actors involved, from community groups, artists and activist designers to landowners, entrepreneurs and varied branches of government (Hou 2001, Haydn and Temel 2006, Lydon and Garcia 2015, SenStadt 2007). Such engagement ranges from self-organised to state-led, from politically neutral citizen groups to unsanctioned, politically charged guerrilla urbanism by anonymous agents, from commercial enterprise to community volunteering (Hou 2001, Finn 2014). Three specific aspects of engagement are brought to the fore in the rhetoric and practice of t/t urbanism.

First is the engagement of new actors. A range of individuals are drawn into these production processes who have little or no prior experience with the development and management of urban open space. DIY urbanism emphasises the empowerment of ordinary citizens in creating public space (Ferguson 2014, Finn 2014, Lydon and Garcia 2015). It has been suggested that t/t urbanism establishes niche sites and opportunities for those who are excluded from mainstream society, such as refugees and counter-cultural drop-outs (Urban Catalyst 2001). t/t urbanism also provides engagement opportunities for migrants and others who are moving between social roles and for whom there is no established niche. t/t urbanism can also serve as a professional incubator for start-up enterprises and those seeking to introduce new spaces, ideas and activities into the wider society. This bottom-up engagement is often facilitated by initiatives from local governments to provide advice and liaison services, such as one-stop shops and fast-tracking for necessary permits (Bishop and Williams 2012, SenStadt 2007).

A second feature of engagement is that these varied actors bring with them new ideas, entrepreneurial skills, social networks and resources to the processes of social engagement (Colomb 2012, Stevens 2015, Stevens and Ambler 2010). New non-government agencies emerge to facilitate such actors and projects, which then produce new working relations, site users, developers, artists and designers – all of which increase the breadth and depth of citizen involvement (SenStadt 2007, Oswalt et al. 2013). When t/t projects succeed in producing community benefits, they gain broad community support, and this can lead in turn to official sanctioning and long-term changes to regulatory codes and processes (Lydon and Garcia 2015, Pagano 2013).

A third distinctive feature of community engagement with t/t projects is that it changes relations between production and consumption. At varying levels, t/t projects encourage ordinary citizens who visit them to become 'prosumers', who are actively involved in the co-production and management of the space, promoting it to other potential users, and through their performances as they make use of the space (Toffler 1980, Richards and Wilson 2006). In principle, such co-creation should enhance environmental fit (Lynch 1981).

However, there is a case for critiquing the ways that such opportunities and obligations for community engagement fit with the agendas of both the neoliberal state and predatory markets geared to privatisation and exploitation. To what degree has a user-engagement model become a user-pays model in which the state retreats from the production of public space while communities fill the gap in a makeshift manner that we might call 'sweat without equity'? To what extent does community engagement become the end for which the design of public space is the means – where the design quality, durability and sustainability of public space are sacrificed for the ideals of citizen participation? To what degree are private interests camouflaged as public interests? Expansions of community engagement are not always transparent or socially equitable. The opening up of public space to individual entrepreneurial initiative can be a form of uneven development that facilitates some desires better than others. Some new actors become engaged while others become disengaged.

Innovation

Large-scale, permanent urban design projects are time-consuming and expensive, which means that innovation is both risky and very slow (Dotson 2016). t/t urbanism accelerates creativity and innovation within urban development by reducing both risk and cost (Bishop and Williams 2012). t/t urbanism is incremental and fast. It is generally low cost and low-tech, operating at a small scale with simple construction methods and moveable and malleable elements. Creative open space ideas can thus easily be developed, tested and revised in practice both by designers and through co-design involving end-users. The city becomes a laboratory for urban experimentation. Design creativity is stimulated through a focus on underutilised, degraded and problematic urban sites where there is less danger of damage. It is also stimulated through the new activities that are introduced into those sites and through the range of creative practitioners involved (Angst et al. 2009).

t/t urbanism enables an iterative testing of how creative solutions can best be implemented, managed and made financially viable. Much tactical urbanism focuses on processes rather than outcomes; on ways that citizens can bypass local government bureaucracy and conventional project delivery processes, and on how such practices might be brought into the mainstream (Lydon and Garcia 2015). The rules and relationships that frame t/t projects are negotiated across a broad scope of conditions, including lease arrangements, uses, permits, rents, guarantees, insurances and the provision of utilities and services (SenStadt 2007). Much of this experimentation involves t/t urbanism testing formal codes; testing the boundaries between permitted and proscribed practices and forms. t/t projects often transgress existing codes in a manner that provokes a response from the state, which then enforces, or adapts by tolerating non-conformity or turning a blind eye. Increasingly, local governments respond by engaging creatively with such processes of enabling innovative open space outcomes (Bishop and Williams 2012, Kamel 2014, SenStadt 2007). The innovation is both bottom-up and top-down.

t/t urbanism enables experimentation with a wider range of forms and functions than permanent urban design projects that require larger budgets and face larger risks. They can cater to smaller and more specialised audiences. The public has a higher tolerance of unconventional and controversial projects when they occupy marginal spaces that were previously unused and when they are of limited duration (Bishop and Williams 2012, Kamvasinou 2011).

The idea of the city as a laboratory in which we can test ideas within a temporary framework is appealing but also has limitations and drawbacks. It raises questions around whether existing urban spaces are insufficient and boring, and whether existing placemaking tools are actually inadequate. As we argue further in Chapters 5 and 6, t/t urbanism may merely find creative ways of circumventing existing controls, without necessarily producing innovative, better outcomes or benefitting underserved groups. Does this toleration of non-conformity and rule changes – liberalisation – undermine certainty for other, larger, longer-term investment decisions and undermine faith in the role and rules of planning? Might these innovations ignore community needs and standards regarding use, aesthetics, safety and durability? To what degree does rapid, ephemeral transformation surrender public space to a cycle of fashion, novelty and gimmickry? There is a case to be made that a minimalist design of public space is the framework that creates the greatest openness of access and appropriation for the widest gamut of citizens – a design that neither prescribes nor proscribes particular uses or users. Such an argument suggests that the role of the state is to create the minimum formal framework for a robust and convivial public space; protecting rights of access and use without overdetermining forms or functions. What is the danger that t/t urbanism is engaged in creative ways of privatising and appropriating public space through a production of novelty rather than enduring public interest? Is t/t urbanism a backdoor way of getting approval for something that would not otherwise be approved – where no case needs to be made for public interests beyond the fact that it is innovative?

Resilience

The idea of the resilient city is often invoked in terms of the capacity of cities to adapt to shocks and stresses in a manner that preserves and protects the core vitality and identity of the place. Resilience thinking involves a focus on complex adaptive systems, where the parts adapt to each other in unpredictable ways – outcomes cannot be determined in advance but rather emerge from practices of adaptation and self-organisation (Johnson 2001, Walker and Salt 2006). Key properties of resilient systems include the diversity and redundancy of parts, such that each performs a multiplicity of functions – no single part is crucial to success, so the system can adapt by moving around forms, functions and flows. Rigid hierarchical systems by contrast are fragile, in that any single dysfunction can collapse the entire system. The diversification of actors, place types, locations and outcomes outlined above all demonstrate the potential of t/t urbanism to rapidly and flexibly adapt spaces to unforeseen changes and localised opportunities and challenges. These factors enhance urban resilience in the face of uncertain futures (Lydon and Garcia 2015, Greco 2012).

Temporary schemes do not require the major 'sunk' investments in large, fixed projects that generate inertia. Temporary and flexible forms allow easy reconfiguration and redeployment as conditions change. Their technologies and designs allow ready replication and adaptation to new sites and to changing social, economic and environmental contexts. Resilient systems are distributed through networks rather than being strictly hierarchical. In contrast to the inflexible hierarchies of top-down planning and management, t/t urbanism involves a broader distribution of know-how, social connections and resources for urban placemaking (Radywyl and Biggs 2013). In contrast to conventional public and private-sector real-estate development, t/t urbanism can be sustained by a broader and more flexible mix of resources, most importantly the 'sweat equity', discretionary spending power and political support of local communities. Resilience thinking suggests strong two-way interconnections between scales – from individuals to institutions, and from sidewalks to neighbourhoods – where micro- and macro-scale activities and forms are each informed by the other. t/t urbanism is fundamentally an activity of connecting urban processes both vertically and horizontally, forging new kinds of partnerships, and finding new ways of engaging with external influences (Dobson and Jorgensen 2014, Greco 2012, SenStadt 2007).

The term 'tactical' in particular implies seeking innovations that respond to local resistance. Greater inclusion and collaboration can reduce conflicts and uncertainties. t/t interventions enhance resilience by improving the overall sensitivity of urban planning and design. These projects draw various actors' attention to sites that were boring, lifeless and unloved, to social groups that were underserved and disengaged, and to control mechanisms that were overly inflexible and restrictive. They help to announce and to test opportunities and possibilities. Individual t/t projects are thus argued to operate as catalysts for long-term improvements to both cities and urban planning processes (Lydon and Garcia 2015, Oswalt et al. 2013). We explore in Chapter 6 a range of different trajectories that small, temporary projects can follow within the context of longer-term urban development processes.

While t/t urbanism can increase resilience, not all kinds of resilience in cities are necessarily positive. There are parts of cities that are seriously dysfunctional, where a spiral into poverty, dereliction or crime, or toward regulation, uniformity and sterility, require transformational change. Such neighbourhoods can be deeply resistant and resilient to such change. New public infrastructure may be vandalised, crime may be displaced from one public space to the next, and both rich and poor communities may resent and oppose any attempt at change. The key task may be to overcome resilience. Here, we also see an echo of the problems outlined earlier in relation to neoliberal planning. To what degree does t/t urbanism become the means of filling the gaps left by the withdrawal of the state from urban planning and investment? To what degree are the boom-bust cycle of capitalism, the exodus of the manufacturing industry from rich Western cities and exclusionary forms of zoning and place management the very disasters to which the city needs to adapt? In some cases, t/t urbanism is produced by policies of austerity that force cities in decline to become more resilient (Tonkiss 2013, Färber 2014). In the context of adaptation to climate change, many examples of t/t urbanism – from cycle lanes to urban orchards – are driven by green imperatives. Yet, such t/t projects alone cannot effect the necessary transformation to low-carbon cities that also needs to be driven on a much larger political and urban scale.

Place Identity

The final dimension we will discuss concerns the contribution of t/t urbanism to place identity and urban character. t/t urbanism has a metamorphic capacity to renew and transform the image of derelict public spaces and neighbourhoods. Public space produced by the state often becomes identified with top-down control, regularity and uniformity – a law-and-order image of the city, lacking in vitality and character (Nemeth and Longhorst 2014). t/t urbanism by contrast brings informality and irregularity; it signifies a multiplicity of differences that emerge unpredictably from bottom-up appropriations of the 'right to the city' (Lefebvre 1996). t/t urbanism is a form of creative placemaking (Krauzick 2007). The production of place identity through t/t urbanism is generally emergent rather than imposed. It often signifies the dynamism of insurgency, resistance and change that is introduced through social and political differences (Sandercock 2003).

Studies of place identity and urban character show that conceptions of place range from a relatively closed, stable and deeply rooted sense of place to a more open and dynamic sense of place, where a diverse mix becomes essential to its character (Dovey 2013). t/t urbanism shifts the balance toward more open, multiple and dynamic conceptions of place. The typically provisional and ephemeral nature of t/t urbanism challenges the grounding of identity in a single authorised history and its preservation. Temporary projects can question, re-evaluate and enrich local identity, and inform future development by engaging critically with the historical legacy of places. Even where heritage controls ensure a fixity of built form, the provisional and ephemeral nature of temporary projects enables the city to embody more than one story.

t/t urbanism thus enables the city to encompass both preservation and change, to embody the tensions between history and progress, singularity and multiplicity. It enables more transparent forms of placemaking in the sense that one can read the values and concerns of citizens from the form of the city. One key way that t/t projects aid the production of a new place identity is through their nurturing, engagement and empowerment of local actors and resources; 'It is through this involvement in the creation and management of their city that citizens are most likely to identify with it and, conversely, to enhance their own sense of identity and control' (Jacobs and Appleyard 1987: 120). Because t/t interventions often occur in the most marginalised spaces, they engage with the contradictions and uneven power relations that generate social and spatial marginality. The city becomes twofold — both formal and informal, top-down and bottom-up, permanent and temporary, strategic and tactical. t/t projects provide opportunities for the re-negotiation of urban identity between marginalised social groups and those who typically exercise control over urban spaces, memories and character. These projects are spatial performances that can transform the image and the social interpretation of both formal and informal urbanism (Rios 2014). Tactical urbanism, as an iterative process characterised by high social engagement, innovation and rapid adaptation, also contributes to 'building self-reflexive awareness of a coherent group identity and defining member roles and self-organising practices' (Radywyl and Biggs 2013:162). Constructing new communities of interest in this way underpins the extension and resilience of place identity across time and space.

While t/t urbanism can have a powerful impact on urban character and place identity, this is not always positive. A key concern lies in questions of design quality. While a large proportion of t/t urbanism emerges under conditions where the state has abrogated responsibility for quality, there are many parts of great cities where a consistently high-quality design of architecture, landscape, street furniture, signage, paving and the shaping of public space – often minimalist and underdetermined – makes a crucial contribution to the vitality, accessibility and multiplicity of public life, and to the construction of urban character. t/t urbanism has the potential to lower the bar in this regard – shoddy public seating, dead plants in planter boxes, rusty shipping containers and bad public artworks can be too readily accepted if they are free and temporary.

A second concern is that the powerful impact that t/t urbanism has on place identity can become subsumed into place marketing. t/t urbanism often creates a buzz and adds a value to urban sites that is relatively easily capitalised. Pop-up urbanism can be a form of place marketing that enhances private property values. Such projects often facilitate the privatisation of public space through advertising and commerce (Biddulph 2011, Rios 2014). Transformations of place identity under new regimes of t/t urbanism can become a cheap and superficial form of rebranding for derelict public spaces; a replacement for the investment and design thinking that might integrate sites of disadvantage with the larger city, and a means of colonising disinvested land for an elite clientele. While t/t urbanism can add significant depth to urban character and place identity, these new values also become available for reappropriation, reduced to a brand and privatised.

Researching t/t urbanism

Having explored some of the critiques that might be applied to existing t/t projects, we now suggest both a research agenda and a conceptual rethinking of this field. We begin with three key dimensions for future research into t/t urbanism. The first area for further enquiry would be to carefully study its varied physical forms, sites and morphological contexts. Where does t/t urbanism emerge and why? What particular forms of urban space are seen as ripe for intervention, and what are the forms of intervention that take place? What is the materiality of t/t urbanism, and how is it geared to technologies of instant transformation, such as shipping containers and synthetic turf? To what degree is it formally innovative? How are t/t designs adapted to local morphology and history?

The second focus is a more rigorous study of the processes of developing, regulating, constructing and managing t/t projects, and the range of actors and roles involved in them. To what degree are these transformations authorised by the state or transgressive? How are design and development decisions shaped by existing urban design and planning codes, or by financing and leasing arrangements? How are planning regulations relaxed, circumvented, broken or revised? What kinds of informal and tacit codes emerge, and with what effects? How do various participants understand the temporariness and benefits of a t/t project, and how and why might these views shift over a project's lifetime? Which project development pathways lead to more efficient, equitable, innovative, resilient and engaging outcomes? Public interests lie as much in knowing 'how' as in knowing 'what'.

Third, such research needs to investigate the outcomes of t/t projects both during and after their execution. Who benefits from such interventions? What specific activities and meanings do these projects give rise to? Public interests need to be evaluated rather than deduced or presumed. What is the impact of t/t projects on everyday urban life? This requires examining the new users, uses, perceptions and interpretations that temporary projects introduce, as well as recognising the invisibility of prior uses and users that they displace. What are the political impacts? How do t/t projects change the state's approach to the permanent and strategic? To what degree does t/t urbanism become the harbinger of gentrification?

These three approaches to understanding t/t urbanism - in terms of form, process and outcome - need to be applied across a broad range of cases to rigorously compare and contrast international practice in this field. While a comparative approach has been attempted within Western Europe (Urban Catalyst 2001, Oswalt et al. 2013), the spread of t/t urbanism through the United Kingdom, North America and Australasia, and a growing awareness of parallels to practices in the former Soviet Bloc and the developing world, make international comparisons possible. We noted in Chapter 1 that the twin concepts of Temporary Urbanism and Tactical Urbanism reflect a divergence between practices in European and North American practices, which in turn reflect different economic, political, developmental and urban contexts. In Chapter 3, we will examine t/t urbanism in Australia, and identify the specificities of that context. Further work is needed to identify the global scope of such practices; to better understand the forms, processes and impacts of t/t urbanism, what insights are transferrable and the consequences of local differences; and to be able to predict the pathways, opportunities and obstacles that bottom-up urbanism may encounter within varying physical, economic, institutional and social milieu.

On Planning for Uncertainty

Earlier in this chapter we explored various theoretical critiques that can be applied to t/t urbanism, to unpack the different interests and impacts, revealing both public benefits and dangers. We now address the deeper research questions that are opened up: how to plan for the unplanned; how to design for the undesignated; how to expand and protect public interests while enabling self-organisation and spontaneity. How are we to understand the affinities between a more agile public space and neoliberal economic regimes? The challenge lies in a fundamental rethink of urban planning and design in both research and practice. The ideal of rational urban planning working systematically toward master plans with fixed outcomes that drove the urban planning profession from its inception has little scope for the high levels of adaptation, informality and uncertainty that prevail in t/t urbanism. Yet, if the structures and certainties of comprehensive rational planning are weakened, how are public interests to be protected?

In unpacking the relationships between t/t urbanism, social needs, uncertainty and neoliberal capitalism, it is useful to note the important distinction between capitalism and markets. This distinction derives originally from the economic historian Braudel (1981–1984), for whom the economy can be understood as an interconnected triad of capitalism, markets and everyday material life. Markets and capitalism both involve entrepreneurial activity. But while markets emerge from the bottom up to fill the material desires of everyday life, capitalism is a top-down system involving private ownership of the means of production and a global division of labour. Capitalism requires an alliance with the state to ensure a free flow of capital, a deregulated economy and a hands-off approach to urban development. In the current era, it is the multinational neoliberal regime that keeps this system intact (Harvey 2007), ensuring that economic growth dominates other public interests in urban development. Neoliberalism involves a privatisation of the production of public space. Indeed, public space becomes a zone for profit-seeking, and much of the space thereby produced becomes 'quasi-public' – publicly accessible but privately controlled. Profit-making need not be excluded from t/t projects, but the difficult tensions between markets and capitalism need to be recognised and effectively managed. The privilege of using public space for private profit needs to be grounded in a critical understanding of public interests. The distinction between markets and capitalism is crucial here because the challenge of t/t urbanism – of planning for innovation and uncertainty – is one of enabling markets while resisting capitalism.

Assemblage

In Chapter 1, we briefly reflected on Latour's Actor-Network Theory, complex human-environment assemblages, mobility and mutability as conceptual tools for understanding t/t urbanism and its distinctive capacities to change the city and to itself be changed. Another closely related framework that can be useful for researching t/t urbanism is what might be called an assemblage approach, based on the work of Deleuze and Guattari (1987). Assemblage involves a rethinking of cities in ways that prioritise the connections between buildings, places, projects and people over things-in-themselves; differences over identities; co-functioning over particular functions (Dovey 2010, Chapter 2). Assemblage thinking involves understanding the morphogenetic processes through which places emerge, based on a philosophy of transformation rather than one of fixed forms and identities. There are several ways in which assemblage thinking can contribute to the critique of t/t urbanism.

First, assemblage engages with the concept of public interests in a direct and creative manner through a conception of urban life as an assemblage of flows of desire. Desires – for shelter, territory, security, aesthetic pleasures, views, privacy and profit – are productive forces that produce the city as they also become a product of it. Collective desires congeal into shared interests, either formally or spontaneously. Public interests do not pre-exist waiting to be satisfied; rather, they emerge through urban life and collective action. Thus, t/t urbanism is a means of directly engaging with and expanding public interests in an experimental manner.

t/t urbanism cuts across authorised narratives and practices of everyday urban life; it expresses and practices the right to the city in creative ways, expressing a claim over public space that does not wait for the state to determine where the public interest lies. By constructing dialectic images and spatial practices where authorised and unauthorised codes intersect, t/t urbanism changes the way in which public interests are conceived and constructed.

Second, assemblage thinking allows us to contextualise urban design within the larger frame of neoliberal capitalism without reducing the city to economic conditions. Neoliberalism is the embodiment of contradictory ideals; an open and deregulated economy within a notional framework of democracy and social justice. The neoliberal city embodies a reduction of urban design values to consumption and economic growth. While t/t urbanism has synergies with the neoliberal economy, it can also be a potent antidote. In filling the gaps and papering over the cracks produced by the creative destruction of capitalism, t/t legitimates this larger order. Yet, t/t also violates the urban order, expanding capacities for the use and meaning of public space. These two actions operate at different scales; assemblage thinking connects them.

Third, assemblage thinking is a form of critical urbanism that valorises both top-down and bottom-up practices of power. It provides a useful framework through which to rethink questions of urban informality. t/t practices are relatively informal, yet they emerge within the formal city with its existing morphology and regulatory codes. t/t urbanism is experimental with regard to these formal codes of governance; it pushes the boundaries of what is possible in public spaces in terms of both built form and spatial practice. The raison d'etre of urban codes lies in some notion of public interests such as safety – codes are congealed and formalised public interests – yet they often overdetermine outcomes. t/t urbanism unleashes desires in a temporary manner that enables a reassessment of the relations between formal codes and informal practices.

Finally, assemblage opens up questions of urban capacity and possibility – how can we better understand the diverse possible futures – environmental, social, economic, aesthetic – that are embodied in an existing city but not yet actualised? We often speak about the development capacity of a site or a neighbourhood as if it were fixed and waiting to be filled like a cup. Yet, cities embody a much more complex set of capacities for transformations of form, function and vitality. Assemblage thinking opens up the city as a space of possibility, not just a site for design speculation, but for a rigorous testing of what works and what does not. The capacity for change is discovered and produced through t/t experimentation in the city as a living laboratory.

At its best, t/t urbanism represents a relatively free market in the production of public space, where the drivers of innovation lie in a mix of market-based competition (some t/t designs are simply far better than others) and local creative networks and industries. t/t urbanism produces and embodies the emergence of new and more agile forms of urban governance; less rigid structures that allow room for creative experimentation and unpredictable outcomes. We need to learn more about what these practices are: how they work to enable and produce urban intensity, engagement, resilience, innovation and place identity; how they work to expand and protect public interests; how and why they fail. In the end, the value of temporary and tactical urbanism is that it exposes and forces a creative engagement with one of the great dilemmas of urban design: How to organise the city while also enabling and enhancing its self-organising capacity, how to plan for the unplanned and how to govern spontaneity.

References

Angst, M., Klaus, P., Michaelis, T., Müller, R. and Wolff, R. (2009) *Zone*imaginaire: Zwischennutzungen in Industriearealen*, Zürich: Vdf Hochschulverlag.
Barron, P. (2014) Introduction, in P. Barron and M. Mariani (eds), *Terrain vague: Interstices at the edge of the pale*, New York: Routledge.
Biddulph, M. (2011) Urban design, regeneration and the entrepreneurial city. *Progress in Planning* 76: 63–103.
Bishop, P. and Williams, L. (2012) *The temporary city*, New York: Routledge.
Carr, S. and Lynch, K. (1968) Where learning happens. *Daedalus* 97 (4): 1277–91.
Carr, S. and Lynch, K. (1981) Open space: Freedom and control, in L. Taylor (ed) *Urban open spaces*, New York: Rizzoli.
Colomb, C. (2012) Pushing the urban frontier: Temporary uses of space, city marketing, and the creative city discourse in 2000s Berlin. *Journal of Urban Affairs* 34 (2): 131–52.

Deleuze, G. and Guattari, F. (1987) *A Thousand Plateaus*, London: Athlone.

Dobson, S. and Jorgensen, A. (2014) Increasing the resilience and adaptive capacity of cities through entrepreneurial urbanism. *International Journal of Globalisation and Small Business* 6 (3/4): 149–62.

Dotson, T. (2016) Trial-and-error urbanism: Addressing obduracy, uncertainty and complexity in urban planning and design. *Journal of Urbanism* 9 (2): 148–65.

Douglas, G. (2014) Do-it-yourself urban design. *City and Community* 13 (1): 5–25.

Dovey, K. (2010) *Becoming places*, London: Routledge.

Dovey, K. (2013) Planning and place identity, in G. Young, et al. (eds), *The Ashgate research companion to planning and culture*, London: Ashgate.

Dovey, K. and Pafka, E. (2014) The urban density assemblage: Modelling multiple measures. *Urban Design International* 19 (1): 66–76.

Fabian, L. and Samson, K. (2014) DIY urban design: Between ludic tactics and strategic planning, in B. Knudsen, D. Christensen and P. Blenker (eds), *Enterprising initiatives in the experience economy: Transforming social worlds*, New York: Routledge.

Färber, A. (2014) Low-budget Berlin: Towards an understanding of low-budget urbanity as assemblage. *Journal of Regions, Economy and Society* 7: 119–36.

Ferguson, F. (2014) *Make_shift city: Renegotiating the urban commons*, Berlin: Jovis.

Finn, D. (2014) DIY urbanism: Implications for cities. *Journal of Urbanism* 7 (4): 381–98.

Greco, J. (2012) From pop-up to permanent. *Planning* 78 (9): 15–16.

Harvey, D. (2007) *A brief history of neoliberalism*, Oxford: Oxford University Press.

Haydn, F. and Temel, R. (eds) (2006) *Temporary urban spaces: Concepts for the use of city spaces*, Basel: Birkhäuser.

Hou, J. (ed) (2010) *Insurgent public space: Guerrilla urbanism and the remaking of contemporary cities*, New York: Routledge.

Jacobs, A. and Appleyard, D. (1987) Toward an urban design manifesto. *Journal of the American Planning Association* 53 (1): 112–20.

Johnson, S. (2001) *Emergence: The connected lives of ants, brains, cities and software*, London: Penguin.

Kamel, N. (2014) Learning from the margin: Placemaking tactics, in V. Mukhija and A. Loukaitou-Sideris (eds), *The informal American city: Beyond taco trucks and day labor*, Cambridge: MIT Press.

Kamvasinou, K. (2011) The public value of vacant urban land. *Municipal Engineer* 164 (3): 157–66.

Kamvasinou, K. and Roberts, M. (2014) Interim spaces, in P. Barron and M. Mariani (eds), *Terrain vague: Interstices at the edge of the pale*, New York: Routledge.

Krauzick, M. (2007) *Zwischennutzung als Initiator einer neuen Berliner Identität?* Berlin: Universitätsverlag der TU Berlin.

Lefebvre, H. (1996) *Writings on cities*, Oxford: Blackwell.
Loukaitou-Sideris, L. and Mukhija, V. (2014) Conclusion: Deepening the understanding of informal urbanism, in V. Mukhija and A. Loukaitou-Sideris (eds), *The informal American city: Beyond taco trucks and day labor*, Cambridge: MIT Press.
Lydon, M. and Garcia A. (2015) *Tactical urbanism: Short-term action for long-term change*, Washington, D.C.: Island Press.
Lynch, K. (1981) *Good city form*, Cambridge: MIT Press.
Nemeth, J. and Longhorst, J. (2014) Rethinking urban transformation: Temporary uses for vacant land. *Cities* 40: 143–50.
Oswalt, P., Overmeyer, K. and Misselwitz, P. (2013) *Urban catalyst: The power of temporary use*, Berlin: DOM publishers.
Pagano, C. (2013) DIY urbanism: Property and process in Grassroots City building. *Marquette Law Review* 97 (2): 335–89.
Radywyl, N. and Biggs, C. (2013) Reclaiming the commons for urban transformation. *Journal of Cleaner Production* 50: 159–70.
Richards, G. and Wilson, J. (2006) Developing creativity in tourist experiences: A solution to the serial reproduction of culture? *Tourism Management* 27: 1209–23.
Rios, M. (2014) Learning from informal practices: Implications for urban design, in V. Mukhija and A. Loukaitou-Sideris (eds), *The informal American city: Beyond taco trucks and day labor*, Cambridge: MIT Press.
Sandercock, L. (2003) *Cosmopolis II: Mongrel Cities in the 21st century*, London: Continuum.
SenStadt (Senatsverwaltung für Stadtentwicklung Berlin) (ed) (2007) *Urban pioneers: Temporary use and urban development in Berlin*, Berlin: Jovis.
Solà-Morales, I. (1994) Terrain vague, in C. Davidson (ed), *Anyplace*, Cambridge: MIT Press.
Stevens, Q. (2015) Sandpit urbanism, in B. Knudsen, D. Christensen and P. Blenker (eds), *Enterprising initiatives in the experience economy: Transforming social worlds*, New York: Routledge.
Stevens, Q. and Ambler, M. (2010) Europe's city beaches as post-Fordist placemaking. *Journal of Urban Design* 15 (4): 515–37.
Toffler, A. (1980) *The third wave*, New York: Bantam Books.
Tonkiss, F. (2013) Austerity urbanism and the makeshift city. *City*, 17 (3): 313–24.
Urban Catalyst (2001) *Analysis report Berlin study draft*, Berlin: Technische Universität Berlin.
Valverde, M. (2005) Taking land use seriously: Toward an ontology of municipal law. *Law, Text, Culture* 9: 34–59.
Walker, B. and Salt, D. (2006) *Resilience thinking: Sustaining ecosystems and people in a changing world*, Washington, D.C.: Island Press.

Chapter Three
Practice

Quentin Stevens, Fauster Awepuga, and Kim Dovey

  Literature and Conceptual Framing
  The Scope of Existing Practice
  Definitions
  Benefits and Impacts
  Contexts and Models
  Scope of Actors
  Collaboration
  Future Directions
  Conclusion

While temporary and tactical urbanism has emerged as a significant global movement in urban design and planning in recent years, it has been little studied in Australia. This chapter draws on interviews with expert practitioners to examine the emerging scope of 'temporary' and 'tactical' urbanism within Australia; the diverse constellations of actors, interests and contexts that shape them; and their wider implications for the planning and design of urban public space. As we noted in Chapter 2, academics and advocates have argued that this area of practice promises to increase the agility and innovation of planning and design, broaden civic engagement, and enhance the character, diversity and resilience of open space. Designers and activists have also sounded warnings about a proliferation of low-quality urban design in times of austerity, and the co-opting of t/t urbanism to further neoliberal deregulation, privatisation and gentrification. To date, there has been little systematic critical analysis of the varied assemblages of actors and interests engaged within different t/t approaches, or their broader and longer-term benefits and problems.

To explore and critique Australian practice in t/t urbanism, this chapter draws on a set of interviews undertaken in 2019 and early 2020 with ten expert practitioners from the public, private and non-profit sectors, based in Melbourne, Sydney and Perth. These interviews thus reflect on t/t urbanism prior to its significantly expanded deployment for transforming and repurposing public spaces in response to the COVID-19 pandemic. Interviewees G1 and G2 were local government planners who had both implemented and facilitated t/t urbanism. The majority of interviewees, C1 to C7, were private-sector consultants who had led t/t urbanism projects for government, commercial and community organisations. These consultants represented a range of roles and disciplines: placemaking consultants; consultants who enabled and facilitated community-led placemaking by others; experts in design, planning and transportation engineering; and non-government place managers. This sampling itself highlights the generally arms-length nature of planning through temporary and tactical projects. Interviewee A1 was an academic who had undertaken action research in t/t urbanism with a range of government and community stakeholders. The interviews explored five key aspects of recent practice, which are outlined in the literature review below. The first is the definitions of 'temporary' and 'tactical' urbanism, and their differences. The core of the interviews explored t/t urbanism's perceived range of benefits and impacts; the influence of local political, economic and policy contexts and particular models of practice; and the scope of different actors involved in these projects. This last theme precipitated further discussion around the particular kinds of collaboration that t/t urbanism enabled and fostered. Finally, the interviews probed the potential longer-term impacts of t/t urbanism on Australian planning and urban development.

Literature and Conceptual Framing

The international literature on t/t urbanism has grown rapidly over the past decade. It has explored a range of interconnected questions about t/t urbanism's scope, factors that have prompted and shaped its development, and its positive and negative impacts on places, communities and planning practice. Many analyses highlight the varying definitions of t/t urbanism, embracing a range of ideas, actions and projects, often involving grassroots actors and circumventing formal planning and regulations (Bishop and Williams 2012, Bragaglia and Rossignolo 2021, Hou 2010). Iveson (2013) identifies a range of 'vectors' across which these practices vary, including temporary/permanent, public/private, collective/individual and legal/illegal. We argued in Chapter 1 that the uses of specific terms by practitioners and in policy are significant because they link to particular contexts, practices, built forms, and impacts, and distinct values, theories and antecedents. 'Temporary urbanism' and 'tactical urbanism' in particular have diverging definitions.

In Chapter 2, we noted that t/t urbanism projects' varied aims and their wider and longer-term potential benefits and negative impacts can be summarised in terms of five broad matters of planning policy: urban intensity, community engagement, innovation, resilience, and place identity. t/t practices have been hailed as critical instruments for enlivening and rejuvenating vacant and underutilised urban spaces (Hou 2010, Groth and Corijn 2005). t/t's rapid, flexible, small-scale actions are claimed to encourage hands-on participation in activating places and broaden the range of actors involved (Douglas 2018, Iveson 2013). t/t urbanism is seen to increase agility and innovation in urban planning and design because it is relatively unconstrained by short-term financial or political motivations (Andres 2013). It enables rapid adaptation to changing circumstances, and encourages creativity, enabling field testing of new approaches with minimal economic and political risk before implementing more permanent changes. These actor engagements and innovations also enhance the resilience of open spaces and local communities (Lydon and Garcia 2015, PPS 2018, Oswalt et al. 2013, Bishop and Williams 2012). The projected benefits outlined above all resonate with calls from Australian policy-makers, planners and designers to make cities smarter, more innovative and more resilient (DPMC 2016, PIA 2016). The intensification, engagement and creativity of t/t urbanism also combine to enhance or transform the distinctive identity of individual places (Douglas 2018, Madanipour 2017, Oswalt et al. 2013). The geographical differences between 'temporary' and 'tactical' urbanism, and the strong focus of research on case study analyses, underscore that these practices, and their intended and actual impacts, need to be understood within specific local political, economic and policy contexts (Douglas 2018, Pagano 2013, Groth and Corijn 2005). This chapter thus seeks to extend the very limited existing analyses of t/t urbanism within Australian cities (CDS and SPC 2014, Iveson 2013), to identify similarities and differences in contexts, aims and outcomes.

Many studies internationally have emphasised the wide range of actors engaged in producing t/t urbanism, and particularly the engagement of non-professional local citizens, artists, activists and community organisations, who bring creative ideas, approaches and networks (Groth and Corijn 2005, Hou 2010, Lydon and Garcia 2015).

The suggested benefits of such actors' involvement in 'grassroots' t/t projects include 'opportunities for social inclusion, reflection and engagement' (Sandler 2020: 146), developing a sense of belonging and place identity through increased local connections and social interaction, enhancing community resilience and asserting citizens' rights (Andres et al. 2021, Iveson 2013). Bragaglia and Rossignolo (2021) distinguish between different types of t/t urbanism practice, involving different key promoters and networks of actors. These range from autonomous, oppositional practices involving only marginal actors, to institutionalised top-down strategies seeking to engage and align local residents, civil society and the private sector. The latter forms of community engagement help to test residents' reactions to urban change and make them active promoters of it, and build consensus, community attachment and value. There are numerous critiques of the unequal power relations that shape non-professional actors' interactions within t/t projects with more powerful local governments, landowners, investors and entrepreneurs (Douglas 2018, Andres 2013), suggesting that grassroots engagement is associated with a neoliberal withdrawal of government investment in urban spaces (Brenner 2015, Mould 2014, Tonkiss 2013). Bragaglia and Rossignolo (2021: 14) conclude that t/t urbanism may be 'inextricably Janus-faced ... simultaneously look[ing] towards two different horizons, that of the just city and that of the creative (and often neoliberal) city'.

The final key theme of concern is the longer-term dynamics between t/t projects and urban planning. The assemblages of actors involved in particular t/t projects clearly shape the interests that those projects serve and the impacts they can have. Little is known about how recent t/t urbanism in Australia might influence broader practice. Existing research suggests that t/t projects, which are ostensibly temporary and tactical, can produce outcomes that are formal, strategic and enduring, shaping larger and longer-term political agendas, policies, planning practices and built environments (Iveson 2013, Lydon 2015, Pagano 2013). Some scholars note an evolving legitimisation, legalisation, formalisation and institutionalisation of t/t urbanism (Fabian and Samson 2016, Henneberry 2017). Mould (2014) suggests this institutional control undermines t/t urbanism's essential potential to enhance innovation, community participation and local identity. Some researchers contend t/t urbanism has been co-opted by government, business and privileged social groups to further neoliberal deregulation, privatisation and gentrification, enabling rapid appropriations of urban spaces that would otherwise require lengthy, formal, more participatory processes of design, approval and implementation. This ostensibly tactical, grassroots tool may in fact be sharpening the inequalities within urban space (Bishop and Williams 2012, Douglas 2018, Tonkiss 2013). As t/t urbanism is still very new in Australia, little is known about if and how it might influence formal practices of urban space planning, development and management in the future.

The Scope of Existing Practice

To provide a sense of the extent of Temporary and Tactical Urbanism in the Australian context, we conducted an extensive online search in 2019, which identified just sixty-six projects dating from 2010 to 2019. Twenty of these projects were identified in the sole published review of practice in Australia and New Zealand (CDS and SPC 2014). Twenty-four projects were created in the five years after that publication's release. Fourteen of these projects appeared in 2015, the year immediately following its release, which was also when the 'handbook' Tactical Urbanism, by a leading US practitioner and co-author of the Australia/NZ study, was released free online (Lydon and Garcia 2015). It appears that these publications helped to inspire a relative flurry of activity.

The 66 cases fall into three broader categories in terms of their forms and functions. The most numerous projects (32 examples, 48%) were those primarily focused on temporary greening of underused urban spaces. This included both temporary parks and gardens installed on vacant parcels of private or government-owned land (which were often community-led or focused on community engagement), and parklets installed onto urban street edges as either political actions or demonstration projects. The next most common type of temporary urbanism (14 cases) we have dubbed 'urban infrastructure'. This ranges from temporarily providing additional seating in public areas, playground equipment, sports facilities, sculptures, and improved pedestrian infrastructure. Seating was also one component within a large number of other t/t projects such as greening. The third distinct category was temporary commercial uses (12 cases), including markets, outdoor cafés, retail pop-ups in open spaces, and food trucks. The remaining eight examples involved some combination of these three formats – a mix of greenery, public amenities and food. These three categories of t/t urbanism in Australia strongly parallel the most expansive existing survey of temporary urban uses, in Berlin, which classified over 100 open space projects into four main activity categories: gardening, sports, food and culture (Overmeyer et al. 2007).

In terms of geographical distribution, the 66 identified examples of t/t urbanism were predominantly located in Australia's two largest cities, Melbourne (40%) and Sydney (25%), with six cases in Adelaide (9%), a total of eight in Australia's other three mainland capital cities, and seven in five smaller regional cities in Queensland and Victoria. One other temporary intervention type was also common throughout Australia: Park(ing) Day, a worldwide annual event held on the third Friday of every September, now in its 17th year, which creates approximately 1000 temporary parks in 35 countries (Thorpe 2020).

The results and analysis of the interviews presented in this chapter are organised around the five themes outlined in the literature review above. Since there are significant divergences in how this field is defined, we begin by reflecting on the ideas we mapped out in Chapter 1, by looking at how the interviewed practitioners characterise 'temporary' and 'tactical' urbanism and related terms such as 'DIY' and 'guerrilla' urbanism. We proceed to discuss the perceived benefits and impacts of these practices. The following section investigates the influence of local morphological, political and economic forces and existing planning and policy contexts. We then discuss the range of actors, agents and collaborations that shape t/t urbanism. The chapter ends by exploring the interviewees' views on the potential future directions of t/t urbanism in the Australian context.

Definitions

Our definition of this field as 't/t urbanism' in Chapter 1 emphasised that definitions of this area of practice are imprecise and contested (Iveson 2013). The ways the field is defined frames its subsequent critiques, and also reflect different actors' aims in promoting these practices (Bragaglia and Rossignolo, 2021). Interviewees provided varied definitions that mostly focused on public space projects done quickly with small budgets and activities conducted to test ideas and obtain community participation or feedback. However, many practitioners tended to be wary of definitions. One consultant noted that existing definitions of t/t activities were 'woolly' (C5); for another, they are limiting, and attention needed to focus on doing rather than judging and categorising:

I think the moment something is labelled and put in a box, the easier it is [for it] to be dismissed or misunderstood, it tends to create a shorthand for what people think your intent is. (C3)

Interviewees generally agreed on a distinction between 'Temporary' and 'Tactical' urbanism. These broadly reflect the differing overseas uses of the terms, as discussed in Chapter 1. 'Temporary Urbanism' is a more common expression in Britain and Europe, which focuses on physical transformations of space that have limited time horizons. 'Tactical urbanism' has more currency in North America and has a stronger emphasis on the 'bottom-up' nature of spatial practices and new forms of social agency that develop through them. There were variations among the interviewees' views on the implications of these two terminologies for Australian practice. Several considered 'Tactical Urbanism' in Australia to mainly be a top-down tool used by local governments to seek and test community response to urban space proposals, as an outcome in its own right, relating it to terms such as 'provocative', 'catalyst', 'awareness raising', 'experimentation', 'vision', as well as 'consultation' and 'community relationship building'. Tactical urbanism was also seen to include local governments strategically using temporary actions to build community support for larger, longer-term development strategies. A1 used the compound term 'temporary-tactical' to describe projects that sought stakeholders' responses to ideas that could then be made more permanent and scaled up. Several interviewees associated 'Temporary Urbanism' with ad hoc, interim, gap-filling, short-term or 'meanwhile' activities such as pop-up shops and temporary parks prior to site redevelopment. C3 argued that t/t urbanism should be primarily defined by its intent rather than its duration. C1 highlighted that one project they had managed had been in place for a full decade; 'it's absolutely temporary, but it's certainly not short-term'. C5 similarly referred to an open space development being 'temporary relatively speaking... it could last for 15 years because it's a 15-year buildout - project'. These views nevertheless all confirm an understanding of temporary urbanism as operating within the interstices between higher-value, longer-term formal investments and developments in urban spaces (Oswalt et al. 2013).

Other terms used to describe this area of practice also illuminate different contexts and objectives that shape particular actions, including variations in their duration, publicness, who participates in them, and how they align to official policies and strategies (Iveson 2013, Bragaglia and Rossignolo 2021). Interviewees discussed five distinct terminologies: *guerrilla urbanism, informal urbanism, grassroots urbanism, DIY* (Do-It-Yourself) *urbanism* and *austerity urbanism*. While interviewees' views on these parallel practices varied, all generally agreed that the first three terms embraced elements of unauthorised, illegal, adversarial activities. A1 explained *guerrilla urbanism* as a community response to frustrations of things not happening fast enough and difficulties faced by citizens in getting permission from councils to do things. C2 suggested that guerrilla urbanism is generally 'small scale', 'asymmetric warfare' which bears a 'military connotation'. But even the rare international research that acknowledges this connection (Lydon and Garcia 2015) does not portray guerrilla urbanism as being in direct conflict with strong, centralised planning, regulation and enforcement. That inference certainly does not reflect the close rapprochement between residents and local government that appears to generally characterise t/t urbanism in Australia. For Australian practitioners, guerrilla urbanism appears synonymous with DIY urbanism (Iveson 2013). People 'just go and do it' (A1) in pursuit of their rights as citizens, to try to bring about a 'democratisation of public space' (C2). More strategically, guerrilla urbanism was also seen as having a longer-term potential for 'changing mindsets' (C6) and inspiring broader changes in public policy. Cited examples of guerrilla urbanism included residents' self-initiated gardens on their front nature strips and in public spaces that were deemed to be 'dead'. Though interviewees were less familiar with the terms *informal urbanism* and *DIY urbanism*, they likened these to guerrilla urbanism, in terms of claiming citizens' rights in urban spaces. These activities emerge from:

> a shared feeling [among communities] that something needed to be done to improve that place, and that it wasn't happening from a local government ... [so] rather than whinge, or lobby ... let's do something ourselves and let's engage positively and make it happen ourselves. (G2)

Nevertheless, many Australian 'DIY' cases generally still involve close cooperation with, and involvement of, government actors. Genuinely bottom-up, 'guerrilla' urbanism was considered rare in Australia, although it was deemed valuable because of its potential to democratise both public spaces and planning practices and to change mindsets.

The term *austerity urbanism* is generally associated with neoliberal policies of budget cuts and the retreat of the state from spending on public services (Tonkiss 2013, Douglas 2018). C2 noted that austerity urbanism arose in circumstances where communities had to step in, in 'desperation', to provide for themselves where the state had withdrawn. C1 suggested that in Australia, natural disasters such as fires and earthquakes also created circumstances where communities needed to regenerate their local places with few resources. C4 suggested there is not much truly bottom-up, informal urbanism in the context of Australia's economy, because:

> we haven't really had to; we've got an incredibly well-managed public domain... the community believes it's the councils generally that are responsible for that... you don't have to get too involved. It's not like what happened after 2008 [the Global Financial Crisis] in America, where local governments were going broke and there was no way to improve the public domain. (C4)

Conversely, another practitioner noted of one Australian local government with a very small rate base, 'they see placemaking as a way of handing over some of the responsibilities ... They just see it as lightening their load' (A1). C1 saw the ongoing economic decline of Australian regional towns as a driver of t/t urbanism: 'they're trying to regenerate, and they've got no money. This is the other thing with tactical urbanism, [when] there is no money, [t/t urbanism is] quicker, lighter, cheaper'. This last phrase is a mantra of the New York-based consultancy Project for Public Spaces (PPS 2018). Our interviews show that while the economic advantages of t/t urbanism are seen to be a driver of t/t urbanism in Australia, the movement is less defined in terms of austerity here than in the United States, the United Kingdom or continental Europe.

The limits to what could be considered t/t urbanism were also explored, and three key criteria emerged — the amount of planning, intent and duration of the project. A1 contended that projects that require significant amounts of planning and design to make them work do not qualify as temporary or tactical. Two of the consultants concurred that practices that were 'corporate' or 'developer-driven' did not qualify:

> We question the legitimacy of still calling those actions tactical or guerrilla, because they are... a corporate client presenting a piece of urban infrastructure as if it was done by the community. ... it's a bit of window dressing... When they try, in that moment between purchase and eventual development [of a site]... to do things that allow for community benefit... I wouldn't deem them tactical or temporary or DIY urban responses at all. I would suggest that's a corporate response. (C2)

> I think there's been an... intersection between the world of marketing and branding and the idea of temporary [urbanism] as either window dressing or corporate marketing, at a level that isn't really about experimentation or engagement or diversity. (C3)

G1 contended that many 'pop-up' activities can no longer be defined as temporary or tactical because they have become more-or-less permanent – they don't pop down. These responses show that t/t urbanism as a field of practice has contested boundaries (Douglas 2018). They also infer a co-opting of the aesthetic and processes of t/t urbanism in Australia by commercial interests to facilitate developer approvals, gentrification and displacement.

Benefits and Impacts

Interviewees identified a wide range of benefits of t/t projects, which reflects the diverse aims of their supporters, and also shows that variants of t/t urbanism can flexibly align to a variety of short-term and long-term governance objectives and strategies. Many interviewees suggested that t/t projects provided new amenities, services, infrastructure and job opportunities that were otherwise lacking. They were seen to provide health, environmental and lifestyle benefits by promoting walking. Practitioners particularly emphasised the community engagement benefits pursued through Australian approaches to t/t urbanism (also discussed further under '*Actors*'). This implies perceived shortcomings in existing relationships and planning processes for urban space development within Australian cities, and highlights that much of t/t urbanism's innovation lies in processes, not just physical outcomes. Innovative, small-scale projects were felt to galvanise community engagement in local government planning and development activities and to develop new relationships among actors. One consultant noted that even when the public only played a relatively passive role as end-users, experimental t/t urbanism projects were:

> a great way to raise awareness around that way of living... Because there's an increasing lack of trust between the community and government when it comes to developers and... to anything new. For them to be able to see and hear and feel the space and to see how... people respond, that's the real magic in tactical urbanism... also to be able to measure the impacts of your idea... and do before-and-after analysis of the success or

otherwise of that intervention... and because they could say to [the community], 'look, this is temporary, see what you think', it's a lot less confronting to people. (C5)

t/t urbanism is thus seen to have been deployed by Australia's public- and private-sector property developers and managers to pursue innovation in the face of community indifference and opposition to change. Government planner G1 also noted the advantages of testing and demonstrating new possibilities to decision-making councillors, who are 'usually pretty risk-averse'. The experimental, less confrontational, evidentiary and adjustable aspects of temporary 'pop-up' projects have led to them becoming a popular tactic for local governments as a component within their larger urban development strategies (Bragaglia and Rossignolo 2021). As the same planner described it:

tactical urbanism is around delivering urban change that has a coordinated vision or direction, but through quicker implementation than normal capital projects... For me, it's very different to guerrilla urbanism or doing things *ad hoc*... those things are done by people who are not in a position to deliver long-term change... the problem for me with pop-up or guerrilla stuff is that it just happens for that moment and then disappears, and it's not delivering any long-term change... Most of the people want to see something change in the longer term. (G1)

Although the practitioners interviewed are among Australia's leading advocates of t/t urbanism, they identified a range of criticisms and shortcomings that align with international experience, which indicate various ways that t/t urbanism might need to be regulated to further the public interest. A1 expressed cynicism around ostensibly temporary, pop-up projects that may be top-down, and may not be flexible, experimental or participatory. Consultant C3 indicated that t/t urbanism's claimed benefits for economic development should be seen as serving four broad areas of impact: it increases urban intensity by bringing public spaces into more productive use; increases resilience and adaptability by facilitating changes in the use of space; transforms place identity from negative to positive; and increases community engagement by drawing people into new relationships of production, decision-making and consumption. However, gentrification was frequently mentioned as a negative counter to this economic development narrative. t/t projects were seen to contribute to rebranding; a transformation of place identity that also facilitates broader redevelopment, leading to the displacement of marginalised groups by middle-class residents and consumption venues. Interviewees suggested property developers often propose using temporary urbanism to deliver required community services, to help secure approvals and funding for development projects. Sometimes these promises were not fulfilled. Local politicians were, similarly, alleged to have used t/t projects to secure votes for their re-election, producing quick and eye-catching outcomes, but implementing minor and sometimes low-quality infrastructure. Local governments were seen to sometimes use temporary urbanism as a way of reducing capital works and maintenance expenditures, and to 'avoid doing strategy' (C4). One planner expressed concern that some emerging practices adopted by councils to achieve 'quicker, lighter and easier' results risk producing sub-standard outcomes and reducing overall investment budgets. One consultant suggested that the low-budget, 'DIY' appearance of tactical urbanism potentially limited community ambitions for improving the public realm:

> the biggest shortfall of tactical urbanism is… there can be an acceptance that's good enough and we can't strive for more than that… an acceptance around tactical interventions being permanent solutions… the biggest danger… is the disregard for the value of good urban design… It's not just about the soft programming. You've got to get the physical aspects of design right as well. (C5)

Some interviewees noted local business owners' concerns about t/t projects. These included negative impacts such as parklets occupying parking spaces and reducing the visibility of their shopfronts; and a perception that new public spaces can attract undesirable uses and users (G2).

Some practitioners suggested that not all the aims of t/t urbanism are being achieved, particularly environmental resilience and social justice. While enhancing community engagement is a key aspiration of tactical urbanism, interviewees suggested that in Australia, marginalised groups including the poor, indigenous, young and older people and ethnic minorities are not effectively involved:

> the twin pillars [that are] missing in placemaking are social justice and ecological justice… I think tactical urbanism is going to have to redefine itself with community, community governance and sharing economies (C1)

These criticisms regarding the accountability and inclusivity of t/t urbanism processes in Australia corroborate international research findings that t/t urbanism discourse and practice often serve those who already have resources and power (Bragaglia and Rossignolo 2021, Douglas 2018, Mould 2014).

Contexts and Models

While t/t urbanism is not a recent phenomenon in Australia, its early practices were largely considered radical and illegal; tactical in the sense of finding ways around the constraints of existing power relations. Several interviewees suggested that the more recent growth of t/t urbanism in Australia was partly a response to the gradual retreat in governments' role in service and infrastructure provision, including the neoliberal privatisation and deregulation of public assets – a parallel to the UK experience with austerity urbanism (Tonkiss 2013):

> After the GFC [the Global Financial Crisis of 2007-08], across the world, there was limited money for government investment or capital investment and so that then opened councils to look at quicker ways to implement things... and you look at the Project for Public Spaces - they talk about lighter, quicker, cheaper - and I guess that type of thing, which probably wasn't palatable to councils [previously], [councils] started to look at that. (G1)

In this context, some interviewees expressed concerns about t/t urbanism being linked to diminished investment in the public realm, lower design quality, and a lack of long-term vision. Other interviewees argued that it is growth in community expectation and engagement, rather than financial austerity, that has driven t/t urbanism practice in Australia:

> I think [t/t urbanism] originally stemmed from the UK following the GFC. Governments just had no money and the community had to come up with clever ways... But in Australia, I think it's more about just frustration with red tape... and the community just saying, well, we'll lead the way and we'll show you how we think it can be done. (C5)

Government planner G2 suggested that in Australia, t/t urbanism was responding to 'this incredible change in community engagement over the last 20 years', and how to address increasing community expectations regarding the public realm:

> there was a community expectation that local governments would do a whole bunch of things... but they couldn't... because of lack of resources. But they still felt that they needed to be, that [it] was their space. And it wasn't until... local citizens stepped into that space and started to do it... that maybe dispelled that notion that it's not for local governments to [do] ... Local governments... sometimes can feel burdened by the overwhelming creativity and ideas within their community, and the expectation that that drives for the local government to have to deliver on those... Community engagement... has been poorly designed... [it's] been a forum for a collection of ideas from the community and a false sense, a false promise, that when you give your idea to a local government that that local government is going to act on that idea. (G2)

Interviewees identified a range of other contextual factors they felt were driving t/t urbanism in Australia. Urban intensification in inner-city areas led to property developers seeking to create amenities and character to attract apartment buyers, 'trying to create a temporary community' (C7). C2 remarked:

> I would be hard pushed to think of interesting projects that aren't within areas that have been gentrified... you don't see many tactical urban responses in greenfield sites in the [city periphery], although perhaps that's where they're wanted more than anywhere.

t/t urbanism in Australia was noted to have developed through a transfer of ideas from other countries, including the United Kingdom, United States, Brazil and Mexico, with increasing numbers of local councillors travelling to learn about and replicate ideas from t/t projects overseas. Several interviewees across Melbourne, Sydney and Perth mentioned the influence of Park(ing) Day, a now-global initiative where temporary parklets are installed on street-side car-parking spaces for one day. C7 noted that social media had made it far easier for Australian urbanists to maintain awareness of, and participation in, such small-scale, short-term actions overseas. Interviewees in Perth suggested that t/t urbanism there had been initiated by local community organisations, comprised of local businesses, landowners and residents, who had coalesced around common interests in proactively activating and reshaping their local public realm. Many of the residents brought with them professional expertise in planning, design and public relations. The success of the first such group led to a wider 'Town Team Movement' in 2014, which in turn facilitated many more local groups across Perth and throughout Australasia. This Town Teams Movement had taken its name and core inspiration from the recommendation of an independent review commissioned by the UK government in 2011 into the future of retail high streets and town centres (Portas 2011). That review focused narrowly on supporting Business Improvement Districts and on the view 'that once we invest in and create social capital in the heart of our communities, the economic capital will follow'. The Town Teams Movement more broadly pursues placemaking, with a focus on community-led 'doing' in collaboration with local governments. Local governments are increasingly supporting this model (G2).

While there is strong evidence of international influence, interviewees also noted that t/t urbanism in Australia is increasingly defined by local conditions and conventions. The emergence of parklets, food trucks and pop-ups was seen to respond to conditions shared with the United States, such as overcoming the limitations of low density and single-land-use zoning. In particular, t/t practices and projects in Australia were seen to be shaped by the need to reduce the large amount of underutilised space allocated to roads and car parks, plus the need to reduce the profusion of regulations restricting possible uses of public space. The four interviewees from Perth particularly highlighted that city's sprawl and car dependence, its indoor focus, 'leftover spaces' between buildings and low pedestrian amenity. This was the only significant difference interviewees identified between the three Australian city contexts.

Several interviewees noted the value of t/t projects for long-term planning and urban development. G1 emphasised the opportunity to demonstrate and test new ideas before making major capital works investments – to use the city as a testing ground. They noted the value of the capacity to adjust or cancel capital projects when stakeholders were opposed or problems became evident. C5 also noted that community-led projects had different liability thresholds, and this enabled local government to test different regulatory and performance parameters. These are pragmatic operational, risk management benefits of community engagement as seen from the perspective of governments and developers.

Interviewees with experience collaborating on t/t projects from both community and local government sides noted the development of a 'nexus' in Australia between community-led and state-led initiatives. One respondent noted: 'we don't always agree on everything, but that's healthy I think. And we have some pretty robust debates' (C5). Sometimes local government initiated the processes and guidelines, and then 'flipped' the process, inviting businesses and community groups to develop t/t projects themselves. In other instances, the community approached the council, who then gave them a grant and participated in a community-led process. The short-term, small-scale, flexible nature of t/t urbanism was seen to enable the citizen-state planning nexus to remain dynamic and emergent. Consultant C6 highlighted that the 'doing' of t/t urbanism shifted actors' mindsets about roles and relationships:

> shifting that mindset [of] 'from government' and 'from the community'... to get people to understand that this is about you doing something... a mural or parklets or greening or guerrilla urbanism.

There was a general sense that t/t practice in Australia is continually being reshaped and localised, through the engagement of planners, consultants, citizens and academics; these practices are increasingly normalised within local councils and state government agencies that manage significant amounts of underused urban land.

Scope of Actors

Interviews showed that the actors and roles involved in Australian t/t urbanism are diverse. Future developments in planning practice and policy will need to take this into account and manage participants' different ambitions, expectations and resources, and the power relations between actors, to identify and serve broad long-term public interests. Professional actors identified by interviewees included urban planners, architects, landscape architects, urban designers; carpenters, gardeners or others with the skills to actually build small-scale t/t interventions; local council staff across many other departments including engineering, maintenance and transport; academics and their students; and private consultants working either for-fee or *pro bono* (C7). Interviewees also mentioned a wider range of non-professional actors, including state and local politicians, business and property owners, community groups and social organisations (indigenous groups, non-profit organisations, churches, street traders), local residents and artists, and philanthropists. Consultant C5 highlighted the advantage of having all these actors engaged:

> you don't need to be a planner or urban designer to get great tactical urbanism outcomes on the ground. And in fact, sometimes it's better that you're not, because they think more freely... They are just so liberal in their thinking... [they] just think more creatively around how you can get stuff done, and challenge you as a professional to think, well, why can't we do that? (C5)

A government-sector planner emphasised a different strength that community members brought:

> They were strong leaders, and doers as well. Not ideas people, but people willing to actually take the next leap from having a great idea to actually doing the hard yards and implementing something... Lots of people have great ideas, but not many people are willing to actually do. (G2)

t/t urbanism was seen to engage actors who brought new ideas and skills to shaping places. However, local practice perhaps does not benefit as much from these actors as it does in the United Kingdom and the United States. Most t/t projects in Australia are driven by local councils, who provide funding, sites and materials, and appoint professional staff members as place managers. This top-down emphasis predates the worldwide explosion of government-led open space interventions during the COVID-19 pandemic. Local government place managers in turn either engage directly with community groups, or contract consultant placemakers. Interviewees were asked to characterise the emergent discipline of Placemaking. For one planner, placemaking is about 'creating a sense of community' (G1). Short-term pop-up projects are predominantly a means to that end, by enhancing public engagement:

> the aim is... to build a community now, so we're not building this [permanent] 30-million-dollar structure and hoping the community just comes to it and it all works. We're actually trying to build a community from day one and build it into it... Placemaking is having a vision of where the community wants to get to in the future, and then doing the pieces that create that sense of place... It's about listening to community, identifying opportunities for the community to do bottom-up stuff and allowing that to happen. (G1)

A consultant who had created and managed t/t projects for several government agencies confirmed this top-down strategy of placemaking through network-building:

> I would say placemaking is very much within the remit of organised, legislated, council-delivered, and in partnership with [property] development. I think placemaking is the approved version of tactical urbanism… [to be] a caretaker or a synthesist, someone who is able to view networks and be able to say, 'You're doing an interesting thing, and you're doing an interesting thing. You guys should have a cup of tea'. (C2)

Interviewees noted that residents and business owners with expertise in art, marketing and urban planning played crucial roles in creating awareness and getting their communities engaged in the planning, construction and activation of t/t projects. Media agencies such as local newspapers were noted to be influential actors who can promote and advocate for t/t projects. Four different interviewees from across government, private practice and academia all mentioned 'Town Teams', an Australian-founded movement of formalised local groups that bring together businesses, community leaders and other interested parties, who can then strategize about initiatives such as t/t urbanism and engage with councils (Town Team Movement 2020). International critiques highlight that these kinds of key involvements of the creative industries and non-government actors align neatly to neoliberal agendas for urbanism: solutions that are low-cost and precarious; creating marketable imagery, beautification and public activation that facilitates gentrification; and shifting responsibility and resourcing of the public realm away from accountable, long-term forms of governance (Douglas 2018, Tonkiss 2013, Mould 2014). Professional actors including academics and t/t consultants were seen as instrumental in providing training and developing knowledge for other actors. Interviewees mentioned the influence of specific facilitating initiatives and organisations, including Park(ing) Day, the Better Block Foundation (2019), and the US-based Street Plans Collaborative (Lydon and Garcia 2015), and visits from experts such as the latter's founder, Mike Lydon. While the Australian-founded Town Teams Movement has strong parallels with these overseas organisations, it has its own charter, models, and priorities that reflect local contexts and actors.

Two interviewees highlighted the role of 'nature' as an actor in t/t urbanism by creating conditions of possibility, as an inspiration and as a stakeholder. C1 was directly motivated to work on t/t urbanism by thinking in Deep Ecology. This interviewee also pointed to the deployment of temporary uses in the reconstruction of Marysville, Victoria and Christchurch, New Zealand as illustrations of the influence of natural disasters such as fire, drought and earthquakes on the activation and reconstruction of urban spaces. Interviewee A1 emphasised the role of t/t urbanism in developing synergies and reciprocities between different actors, including Nature:

> The point of [a t/t project] is to attract all the stakeholders of the place, including Nature. I mean the non-human. Nobody speaks about them as an actor, but they're very much an actor of place. You can't get them to fill out a survey or whatever, but you can see how temporary activation brings certain species back and what happens, so they do have a voice in that way. (A1)

Collaboration

Interviewees noted that t/t projects promote engagement and the development of new relationships and collaborations between diverse actors. These networks develop both within local government and between government, external professionals, the private sector and local residents. In some t/t projects, collaboration has been enabled by specific individuals who already have personal, professional or place-based links across different stakeholder groups. One parklet project was proposed and crowd-funded by a local resident as a demonstration project in front of a café:

> the guy who was funding it, he was good friends with the café owner, and his partner worked with the [local government], in the activation team, so it was very easy for them to get across the line. (C7)

Town Teams appear to be broad, durable, legitimated networks that can draw in additional collaborators, including local governments, university researchers and students. Careful, incremental cultivation of their relationship with local government appears to be key in such initiatives achieving empowerment and legitimacy. One consultant involved with a Town Team emphasised that:

> our relationship with [the local council's] really important... we really need to work as a team, to the extent where we meet with their exec team on a monthly basis. We meet with their CEO; we have coffee catch-ups on a regular basis. It's a lot of mutual respect there. (C5)

External funding was another factor that encouraged local collaboration on t/t projects, sometimes through unexpected channels:

> The RAC [Royal Automobile Club] is being very generous, so we've got $50,000 in grants for Town Teams… [The RAC] are a member-based organization. It's funny that they're a motoring group that are promoting community and placemaking, but that shows you the breadth of opportunities for government agencies or other corporates to get involved. [The RAC] were sponsors of our first conference. (C6)

For another interviewee, this example also shows that a range of t/t projects provided the RAC with an opportunity to engage with a broad range of stakeholders across local communities:

> They've traditionally been associated with cars… They're trying to rebrand themselves as being more forward thinking and more about cycling and pedestrians… to reposition themselves. (C5)

In line with international experience (Bragaglia and Rossignolo 2021, Douglas 2018, Fabian and Samson 2016), several interviewees indicated that collaborations on t/t projects can be vexed by asymmetrical power relations between different stakeholders:

> The people who are able to be in that [influential] role generally are of a particular demographic. They have more capacity, they're usually better educated, they are financially stable. They are super confident… whereas those that have the least capacity are always the ones that miss out. [The influential actors] shouldn't be setting the agenda. It's not fair and we need to have more equity geographically as well as demographically. (C4)

> I would say it tends to be people that don't have to work full-time, people who are really engaged in place… People that aren't [just] surviving [paying] their mortgages. (A1)

Another consultant suggested that while the first t/t project in their city was started in 'a very white middle-class area', t/t practice was starting to become more widespread in multicultural neighbourhoods (C6). These asymmetries suggest a need for mechanisms that can ensure equity in decision-making and resourcing within informal, non-government modes of urban space development, especially if these new modes engender long-term changes in practice.

Future Directions

The interviewees identified several ways that t/t practices in Australia are changing. This emphasises a need for ongoing research to track and understand shifts both locally and abroad in actions, actors, locations and resources, to help governments, communities and other actors remain responsive to new trends and challenges. Tactical urbanism was seen to have evolved from unsolicited and illegal activities to solicited, legitimised practices, with councils, property owners and developers increasingly leading or endorsing t/t urbanism as an innovative placemaking activity. The increase in the breath of actors and practices engaged in t/t urbanism was seen to enhance the development of knowledge and further innovation. Some consultants noted that the growing experience of government-based professionals with t/t urbanism was enabling new thinking and more openness:

> [There is] a generational change in planners and the planning system... they seem to have a much greater understanding of the need for the system to allow for and encourage the diversity of small-scale activity... I suspect that will bubble up over time through the planning system. (C3)

> they've opened up environments to allow communities to respond without too much regulation... [Professionals] who have often come through... either university, design school or community engagement or community development education, who had come through and who've worked in tactical urbanism kind of practices... [are] genuinely changing the culture of those large institutions and I think it's unstoppable. (C2)

Both the local government planners interviewed had been key actors in implementing pioneering t/t projects in their respective cities. Each had then been hired into more senior management roles at other local councils where they introduced related strategies and practices. Local planner G2 noted that 'a lot of other local governments now are trying to follow, and they're trying to figure out what works for them and their context'. These changes appear to parallel Mould's (2014) analysis that subversive tactics are becoming, or giving way to, formalised urban development strategies. Interviewees expressed some concern that this general mainstreaming of t/t urbanism can lead to institutional acceptance of a smaller budget for public space and of temporary solutions as permanent:

> My nervousness was that you start either watering down the budget or watering down the outcome, because instead of actually doing proper landscape projects, you're just astroturfing. (G1)
>
> A decade ago there was one parklet there, and today there's [still that] one parklet there. Now [Temporary Urbanism]'s being accepted as a permanent solution really. (C5)

In terms of policy, interviewees noted various ways that t/t practice is being normalised by state and local governments and by professional designers. Regulations are becoming friendlier toward t/t urbanism, and academics are building a knowledge base and lending the practice legitimacy. These changes could have both positive and negative implications. Formalising t/t activities risks defeating the core aim of t/t urbanism as an avenue for a broad range of actors to initiate and engage in placemaking without the restrictiveness of standard land-use and development practices. This might introduce laborious, bureaucratic procedures into t/t urbanism, co-opting it into formal planning and statutory regulations (Groth and Corijn 2005). There are also optimistic views that t/t urbanism can be accepted and used in positive ways within Australia (CDS and SPC 2014) and can have a range of positive impacts on the five key issues we discussed in Chapter 2: urban intensity, community engagement, innovation, resilience and place identity.

Like practice overseas, Australian t/t urbanism is also developing from informal to more organised practices through consultancy services. One local government planner noted that 'there are firms now that specialise in pop-up design and consultancies around how to do it… it's become an industry now' (G1). One pioneering consultant who was interviewed has had former staff leave and found six different new placemaking consultancies. Through mediating organisations like the Town Teams Movement, practice is also being formalised and commercialised through the development of formal training, online resource hubs, and peer-to-peer learning.

Conclusion

This review of practitioner views on temporary and tactical urbanism in Australia over the past ten years has identified a range of project types, modes of practice and kinds of uses. It has also explored a range of spatial and governance contexts, a diversity of actors, processes and values that drive such projects, and a range of public benefits and impacts that they can provide. The findings raise a number of questions that recommend further research.

Several interviewees emphasised that local practice is distinguished by local economic, spatial and governance contexts. In terms of t/t urbanism's physical manifestations, the locations, densities and pace of urban development and redevelopment within Australian cities are clearly different to both Europe and America. Future research could more closely examine specific physical and process models of t/t urbanism that relate to local conditions, such as Melbourne's recent profusion of parklets, which has been shaped by the city's distinctive street profiles, liberal hospitality regulations, and increasingly streamlined, facilitatory permitting regimes. These prospects will be taken up further in Chapter 8. The widespread and extended adoption of t/t urbanism approaches during the current COVID-19 pandemic indicates they will likely have long-term impacts on the future of Australian planning and urban development, even when individual temporary urbanism projects might not endure. Lydon and Garcia (2015) argue that the key goal of tactical urbanism's short-term actions is to achieve long-term changes in the mindsets and procedures of planning and governance. Our interviewees highlighted a broader 'generational' and 'cultural' change in the perspectives of Australian local governments and landowners toward t/t urbanism, a growing knowledge base, and continual transfers of ideas and expertise both into and within Australia. Further research should explore if, and how, t/t urbanism is contributing to a wider re-thinking of local practices of placemaking and place management.

The distinctive nature of t/t urbanism in Australia, which is mostly pursued through government-led, consultant-guided modes rather than guerrilla initiatives, suggests a need for research to focus on understanding how exactly short-term, 'pop-up' initiatives fit within larger-scale, long-term urban development schemes, and within specific formal planning processes and instruments; what kinds of desirable innovations temporary and tactical tools might bring to these; and how procedurally those changes in practice can happen. It particularly suggests a need to understand how formal planning and design processes can ensure that t/t urbanism serves public interests, by examining how these new modes of placemaking produce new inflections in age-old questions about who contributes and who benefits. Future developments in planning practice and policy will need to learn how to manage the different ambitions, expectations and resources among t/t urbanism's participants, and the asymmetrical power relations between them, to identify and serve broad public interests (Iveson 2013). Tactical urbanism in Australia may not reflect government austerity, but we still need to examine what role it might play within the neoliberal privatisation, deregulation, place marketing and gentrification of our cities. How can t/t urbanism be a suitable instrument for meeting longer-term community needs? Can decision-making about our future cities be temporary and tactical? Such questions link to practical issues of resourcing and risk management, but also to normative questions of inclusion and equity. Another set of critical questions surround how t/t urbanism influences the various time frames of planning, as an activity that is fundamentally oriented toward long-term futures, and how the contributions, impacts and benefits of t/t urbanism are distributed across time. We explore these issues further in Chapter 6.

References

Andres, L. (2013) Differential spaces, power hierarchy and collaborative planning: A critique of the role of temporary uses in shaping and making places. *Urban Studies* 50 (4): 759–75.

Andres, L., Bakare, H., Bryson, J., Khaemba, W., Melgaço, L. and Mwaniki, G. (2021) Planning, temporary urbanism and citizen-led alternative-substitute place-making in the Global South. *Regional Studies* 55 (1): 29–39.

Bishop, P. and Williams, L. (2012) *The temporary city*, New York: Routledge.

Bragaglia, F. and Rossignolo, C. (2021) Temporary urbanism as a new policy strategy: A contemporary panacea or a trojan horse?. *International Planning Studies* DOI: 10.1080/13563475.2021.1882963

Brenner, N. (2015) Is "Tactical urbanism" an alternative to neoliberal urbanism?. *MoMA post: Notes on modern and contemporary art around the globe*. Viewed 7 April 2021. http://post.at.moma.org/content_items/587-is-tactical-urbanism-an-alternative-to-neoliberal-urbanism

CDS and SPC (CoDesign Studio and Street Plans Collaborative) (2014) *Tactical Urbanism Vol. 4: Australia and New Zealand*. Viewed 12 June 2019, http://tacticalurbanismguide.com/guides/tactical-urbanism-volume-4/

Douglas, G. (2018) *The help-yourself city: Legitimacy and inequality in DIY urbanism*, London: Oxford University Press.

DPMC (Department of Prime Minister and Cabinet) (2016) *Smart cities plan*, Canberra, Commonwealth of Australia.

Fabian, L. and Samson, K. (2016) Claiming participation – A comparative analysis of DIY urbanism in Denmark. *Journal of Urbanism* 9 (2): 166–84.

Groth, J. and Corijn, E. (2005) Reclaiming urbanity: Indeterminate spaces, informal actors and urban agenda setting. *Urban Studies* 42 (3): 503–26.

Henneberry, J. (ed) (2017) *Transience and permanence in urban development*, Oxford: Wiley.

Hou, J. (ed) (2010) *Insurgent public space: Guerrilla urbanism and the remaking of contemporary cities*, New York: Routledge.

Iveson, K. (2013) Cities within the city: Do-it-yourself urbanism and the right to the city. *International Journal of Urban and Regional Research* 37 (3): 941–56.

Lydon, M. and Garcia, A. (2015) *Tactical urbanism: Short-term action for long-term change*, Washington, D.C.: Island Press.

Madanipour, A. (2017) *Cities in time: Temporary urbanism and the future of the city*, London: Bloomsbury.

Mould, O. (2014) Tactical urbanism: The new vernacular of the creative city. *Geography Compass* 8 (8): 529–39.

Oswalt, P., Overmeyer, K. and Misselwitz, P. (2013) *Urban catalyst: The power of temporary use*, Berlin: DOM Publishers.

Overmeyer, K., et al. (2007) *Urban pioneers: Temporary use and urban development in Berlin*, Berlin: Jovis.

Pagano, C. (2013) DIY urbanism: Property and process in grassroots city building. *Marquette Law Review* 97: 335–89.

PIA (Planning Institute of Australia) (2016) A new era for national city planning. Viewed 12 June 2019. https://www.planning.org.au/documents/item/7874

Portas, M. (2011) The Portas review: An independent review into the future of our high streets. London: Department for Business Innovation and Skills. Viewed 22 October 2020, https://www.gov.uk/government/publications/the-portas-review-the-future-of-our-high-streets

PPS (Project for Public Spaces) (2018) *The lighter, quicker, cheaper transformation of public spaces*. https://www.pps.org/article/lighter-quicker-cheaper (accessed 28 July 2020).

Sandler, D. (2020) Grassroots urbanism in contemporary São Paulo. *Urban Design International* 25 (2): 137–51.

The Better Block Foundation (2019) Better Block. Viewed 11 November 2020. https://www.betterblock.org

Thorpe, A. (2020) *Owning the street: The everyday life of property*, Cambridge: MIT Press.

Tonkiss, F. (2013) Austerity urbanism and the makeshift city. *City* 17 (3): 312–24.

Town Team Movement (2020) Town Team Movement. Viewed 6 November 2020. https://www.townteammovement.com/

Chapter Four
Assemblage

Quentin Stevens

Vacant Land
Landscaping and Furnishings
Human Actors
Energy
Concepts
Austerity
What Brings the Beach Together?

Cities and their open spaces are generally planned to endure. But in recent decades, urban design practice and research have given increasing attention to open spaces that are, instead, very temporary and malleable. Alongside permanent open spaces that are funded and managed by governments and private landowners, there have recently emerged a range of impermanent, more-or-less-public spaces that are facilitated by other actors. This chapter, inspired by Latour's (2005) Actor-Network Theory, considers these 'actors' in the widest possible sense, including not just persons with financial, material and legal control, but the many non-humans that also have agency in transforming urban spaces. The chapter examines the diverse plurality of materials, people and intangible forces that dynamically come together to shape open spaces today. It illustrates these through one particular new temporary space type that is very widespread in Germany, and which also occurs in many developed countries: artificial 'city beaches' on formerly industrial riverfronts (Stevens 2011, 2015, Stevens and Ambler 2010).

This account emphasises the constant actions that are necessary to create, maintain or transform the relationships between the various actors that constitute these spaces. City beaches foreground the dynamically constructed, performed nature of many open spaces, because they are typically packed away each autumn, and re-created using new, limited capital the next year. Some beach projects change site, size, form or managers between years; some don't reopen. This dynamic, opportunistic, throwntogether nature of city beaches reflects wider trends in open space design, planning and management that have arisen in the context of de-industrialisation and growing local participation. These approaches are messy, and constantly evolving to take tactical advantage of shifting, localised resources and opportunities (Franck and Stevens 2007, Hou 2010, Lydon and Garcia 2015). I draw here on Doreen Massey's (2005) conception of places as 'throwntogether' to emphasise that non-human objects and forces, like people, have their own trajectories (or 'aims'), and that city beaches highlight the nature of all places as the result of continuing acts of conflict, negotiation and alignment among these actors.

The archetypal German city beach is a low-key, temporary, independent hospitality venture on the ex-industrial riverfront of a large city, with sand, palm trees, thatched huts where drinks are sold, deck chairs and a pool (Figure 4.1). The city beach concept originated in the French city of St Quentin, France, in 1995, although it first became widely known through *Paris Plage* in 2002, a big-budget project developed by the city government on a temporarily closed section of a northern-riverbank freeway.

This chapter examines in turn six distinct categories of actors that have come together to constitute various city beach settings in Germany and the various ways that they are constelled, and explores the ongoing efforts required to bring and hold them together as places.

Vacant Land

The city beach concept presented in *Paris Plage*, with its riverside view and southern exposure, has undergone translation to a variety of empty urban sites. Many city beaches temporarily occupy spaces on Germany's extensive ex-industrial urban riverfronts. These spaces have presented themselves as available through the departure of former uses. Vacancy requires that rapid large-scale redevelopment is somehow precluded, whether by economic conditions or inadequate infrastructure. In Hamburg, a string of city beaches opened on the north bank of the Elbe River in St. Pauli, a historic port area long made redundant by larger-scale shipping. Seasonal flooding kept this area free from urban redevelopment. A long, narrow strip of land between Berlin's East Side Gallery (the remnant section of the Berlin Wall) and the

FIGURE 4.1 Typical city beaches in Germany, with portable pools, decking, deck chairs, potted palm trees, and surfboard props. Strandsalon, Lübeck (top) and La Playa, Leipzig (bottom).

Source: Quentin Stevens.

Spree River was for many years a prime city beach location because it was unviable for major development until the city approved knocking a gap in the Wall. Such former port spaces are often disconnected from their cities, and action is typically required to improve pedestrian access, through the agency of new bridges and access stairs; by demolishing the walls of ports and factories; and through new signs, maps and place identities that reconnect these sites into people's image of the city.

One vivid illustration of a newly created alignment of underused urban spaces with this new spatial concept is Stuttgart's *Skybeach* (Figure 4.2). Its creator had seen *Paris Plage* in 2003, but no river runs through Stuttgart's centre. After seeing an aerial photograph of a downtown department store, he connected the beach concept to the previously unused, elevator-accessible top level of its parking garage, with its excellent inner-city views, quietness and sunshine, and to the popularity of rooftop bars. This new association of city beaches with parking garages was itself subsequently translated to the rooftops of 19 other garages in 14 other German cities. The little-used rooftop of a Frankfurt department store parking garage was linked to the lift that ended at the second-top parking level by a wide, temporary scaffolded

FIGURE 4.2 Skybeach, Stuttgart, on the roof of the parking garage of the Galeria Kaufhof department store, adjacent to the city's main pedestrian axis, Königstraße.

Source: Quentin Stevens.

staircase. This newly assembled pathway connected the city's pedestrian shopping street to the rooftop sunshine and views of its skyscrapers. Large banners and flags improve city beaches' local visibility. Maps on many beaches' websites help visitors to find their way down minor alleys and truck routes to access their ex-industrial waterfront sites.

Only half of Germany's city beaches occupy waterfront sites, even though most city beach operators and users feel water frontage or views are essential (Stevens 2011). Several other kinds of cheaply available vacant sites attract numerous beach projects: underused public parks and plazas, sections of the former Berlin Wall 'death strip' without river frontage, railway easements, and inland industrial areas. All these sites offer plentiful low-rent space, flexibility regarding construction and operation, and few conflicts with neighbours. Indeed, city beaches are often stimulated by other low-rent leisure and creative activities nearby, including nightclubs, performance venues and artists' studios. Beaches are easily 'plugged into' available spaces among these emerging creative milieux.

New city beaches sometimes form larger precincts in the ample space around the pioneering projects in larger cities, including 'Costa Hamburgo' in St Pauli on the port authority's carpark and Dresden's 'Elbiza'. On both ex-urban waterfronts and downtown garages, vacant open spaces provided physical, representational, functional and historic contexts that helped produce a new sense of place, linking local residents and visitors to water, sun, and escapist leisure, and facilitating further new, escapist leisure settings.

Landscaping and Furnishings

The development of city beaches has also been influenced by a palette of landscape elements that are readily available, cheap, light, collapsible and relocatable, yet welcoming and comfortable. In Berlin, sandy ground was already apparent before the first city beaches, revealed as the city's geological substratum by building demolitions (Schulz and Abele 2011). In pre-existing outdoor beach volleyball venues, underused sandy areas were reimagined by the city beach concept. For some city beaches, construction-grade sand is donated or rented cheaply by building supplies businesses, who collect it after the project ends and sell it for concreting.

Sand is a disorderly, unfixed material that invites people to adjust it to make themselves comfortable, and which encourages initiative, playfulness and creativity in its use (Franck and Stevens 2007, Stevens 2009). Yet maintaining sand's role as a leisurely beach environment demands work from beach managers, who must constantly remove cigarette butts and smooth and replenish the sand. Specialist suppliers have developed proprietary mixes of two grain sizes that combine appearance and comfort without clinging to shoes and street clothes (David 2010). Because sand is also annoying for prams, high heel shoes, keeping tables and chairs level, and waiters, it is often confined to small patches surrounded by decking, more for looking at than touching. One sixth of all 'beaches' have no actual sand, but other elements combine to sustain the necessary atmosphere.

'City beaches' are also defined by loose, shifting assemblages of small, easily transportable items, especially potted palm trees, beach umbrellas, collapsible swimming pools, and portable cabins (Stevens 2011). Palm trees are a key scenographic element, invariably placed framing the beach's entrance. Transportability, cost, sub-zero-winters and a need to minimise permanent shade dictate that palms are typically small and rented. Some hire firms provide low-maintenance synthetic ones. Only 25% of beaches provide access to swimming; pools and rivers often just offer ambience. Cabins include thatched huts, market kiosks and trailers, shipping containers, and portable toilets, all easily rented, transported and repositioned. Most are necessarily confined to sites' rear boundaries, to form visual and acoustic barriers to surroundings, to screen back-of-house functions, and to keep beaches open to views and sun. Sail roofs, tents, buildings with openable facades and awnings, and large umbrellas allow rapid reorganisation, relocation and disassembly (Stevens 2011) (Figure 4.3).

Deck chairs are ubiquitous on city beaches, even though they are rare on real beaches, having been imported from cruise ships. They thus connect to Europeans' preconceptions and memories of the Mediterranean. While at real beaches, people often sit or lie on the sand on towels or on rented sun lounges in their swimwear, deck chairs on city beaches enable their many short-term visitors in street clothes to relax, put just their feet in the sand, and sit comfortably, so they can see and be seen. This furniture combines city comforts with informal, escapist appearances. Deck chairs also forge relationships between beach operators and drink, food and cigarette vendors, who provide free, pre-branded ones.

FIGURE 4.3 Temporary and relocatable buildings, play equipment, and awnings, and south sea umbrellas, palm trees and a ship create a beach atmosphere. Bundespressestrand, Berlin.
Source: Quentin Stevens.

Beach atmosphere is also created by 'tropical' cocktails (sold from thatched huts), music, lighting, heat lamps, and props including surfboards, anchors, rowboats, paddles, life preservers, lighthouses, cargo chests, pirate flags, fishing nets and shells. Equipment that supports activities that attract beach patrons also forces other elements into city beach landscapes: volleyball pitches, children's playgrounds, sandcastle-building tools, dance floors and stages. Children's sand play with buckets and spades demonstrates city beaches as unfixed, 'do-it-yourself' landscapes. Beaches' managers and their users are constantly reorganising, removing, or adding deck chairs and umbrellas, to optimise escapist atmosphere, patron capacity, social arrangements, activity needs, views, sun angle and weather. This is a post-Fordist 'co-production' of a comfortable leisure environment and experience (Richards and Wilson 2006, Stevens and Ambler 2010).

Human Actors

Despite strong consistencies in city beaches' formats, these spaces involve diverse human actors. Several early German city beaches were developed by artists, stimulated by government funding for new ideas for open spaces. These artists introduced creativity to seemingly prosaic issues and processes around the design and management of open spaces, challenging expectations and sometimes circumventing regulations (Stevens 2015). Their craft involved negotiating with various other people, and with the unfamiliar media of public spaces and landscaping materials, to realise these projects. Peter Arlt (n.d.) notes his 1999 Berlin beach *Bad Ly* 'contribute(d) to the mobilisation of new and different forces'.

Most German beaches are commercial ventures. A shortage of summer income at indoor bars and restaurants, vacant sites, the city beach concept, and support and encouragement from local governments have combined to attract hospitality entrepreneurs, who then gather an idea, a site, funding, permits and equipment. They must transfer their existing relationships with public bureaucracy, neighbours and patrons, and develop new ones. Their interests inevitably influence their beaches' clientele and openness. The innovation and challenges of both artistic and commercial city beaches bring together a wide range of actors from the creative industries; people with creative, technical and organisational expertise, who are nonetheless new to the processes of urban placemaking. They are compelled to develop new practices, discover new spatial potentials, and also to creatively navigate bureaucratic, regulatory and financial relationships (SenStadt 2007). Such actors include 'culturepreneurs' from the fields of media, marketing, entertainment and environmental design (Lange 2011).

Other German city beach projects have attracted involvement from non-profit organisations and local community groups, highlighting that such innovative, risk-taking open space projects are not always motivated or shaped by profits. These citizen initiatives generally emerge in cities small enough for community actors to maintain strong contacts in local government, but large enough to support, deliver and warrant such ambitious projects. The protagonists of these projects emphasise the importance of existing organisations and strong engagement and trust, to draw in the many other necessary actors. They also note that city beach projects help to build these relationships (Stevens 2015). Similarly, the novel requirements of city beach projects help to establish new cross-department working relationships within local governments (Stevens 2011). Several of these beaches were consciously developed for and by local organisations, as mechanisms for drawing their communities together and facilitating social interaction in public spaces (Figure 4.4). Notably,

FIGURE 4.4 Demonstration by local gymnastics club. Strandleben, Vaihingen an der Enz.
Source: Quentin Stevens.

community beach spaces recognise children and teenagers as members of the public, who are in some cases negotiators, builders, and performers, not just passive consumers of adult-determined environments (Stevens 2015). France's city beaches, including *Paris Plage*, are mainly free to access, being publicly funded by governments of inland cities. In an age of increasing austerity, these governments are seeking to change the historical relationship between the French summer, seaside atmosphere, a vacation exodus to the coast, and reduced local business revenues.

Whether city beaches are public- or private-led, their novel spaces, experiences and use programs bring together very diverse user groups. These users all have an important role in continually performing the beach space and its atmosphere, with their sunglasses, bare feet, sunbathing bodies, swimwear and shovels (Stevens and Ambler 2010). The continual production of beaches draws together the desires and skills of their employees, artists and designers, sponsors and suppliers, legislators and bureaucrats, and changing financial conditions, weather, and surrounding events. Beach staff and visitors constantly rearrange and perform the city beach's flexible assemblage of sand, props and atmosphere, according to different tastes and activities, financial conditions, weather, and surrounding events. They pack them away, extend or compress them, and also redeploy them to new locations. City beaches' intangible atmosphere relies on the labour of entrepreneurs with backgrounds in theatre, music, media, and advertising, and constant reinforcement from local citizens passionate about sports, yoga and dancing. Participatory events and changing themes maintain novelty and keep visitors engaged (Gale 2009).

Despite the strong formal similarities among city beaches, differences among the human actors that initiate and run them precipitate differences in the other social actors that are drawn to these spaces, and the actions and social relationships that these spaces afford. Avant-garde artist-led beaches, as performative experiments with no pre-ordained social objective, are intentionally very open to users and activities. They challenge social expectations. They respond creatively to regulations, often circumventing them. The non-profit-run *Bristol Urban Beach* engaged local service providers and sought to attract performances and activities led by diverse local community members, with the aims of encouraging broad community participation and interaction and strengthening community institutions; not because this would maximise patrons and profits (Mean et al. 2008). On publicly-funded and community-run beaches, numerous vigilant, uniformed security guards and support staff ensure child safety and cleanliness, and there are often bans on smoking and alcohol. By contrast, on Germany's commercial beaches, there are few staff beyond waiters, ubiquitous cigarette and alcohol advertising on banners and furniture, extensive decked, roofed dining areas, and posted controls and bag checks to prevent patrons from bringing their own food and drinks. The most common form of social interaction is staff asking visitors what they want to drink. Children only visit most German city beaches accompanying their parents.

While city beaches all involve temporarily throwing together similar spaces, furnishings, aesthetics and creative energy, different cases have evolved through quite different groups of human actors, linking to different constellations of personal and collective aspirations, obligations, responsibilities and risks. These in turn are linked to different financing arrangements and management approaches (Stevens and Ambler 2010). These links are not fixed. Temporary city beach projects also involve dynamic and varied flows and combinations of initiative, creativity, authority and risk-taking among human actors. These factors all affect the publics and publicness of the spaces that emerge. Yet beaches' human actors remain somewhat interchangeable.

Sometimes entrepreneurs operate beaches under contract for local governments. One short-term artist-initiated and city-financed beach was subsequently revived by a local residents' association. The atmosphere and activities it had stimulated provided a durable nexus for continuing it with quite different actors, funding and labour. These shifts in motivations and responsibilities thus reflect a wider development dynamic of the city beach concept: ideas first created and explored by artists with public funding were adopted and translated by numerous entrepreneurs who tested the profitability of various formats, sites, services and clienteles, and were then adapted by local residents, who optimised their social benefits (Stevens 2015).

Energy

Alongside the various constellations of individual people, objects and spaces that give life and form to city beaches, there are also several kinds of broader intangible actors that stimulate these projects, and influence how, when and where they arise, and which other actors acquire agency in shaping them. Prime among these intangible actors are the various flows of energy that erratically circulate through cities, including creative energy, excitement, and weather. Attention to these energies highlights the dynamism of the actor relationships that usher projects like city beaches into existence, and the forces that can drive them apart.

City beaches first emerged where creative individuals were immersed in urban milieux, like Berlin's, that were latent with creative energy (SenStadt 2007, Lange 2011). These milieux enabled rapid transfers and cross-fertilisations of new ideas, skills, customers, and further contacts, bringing new knowledge and unconventional approaches to the development of urban spaces. Under such conditions, the enthusiasm, imagination and initiative for creating city beaches could spread, from artists to individuals in the hospitality and entertainment industries, and to city planners and untrained residents. New ideas also keep transforming the relationships between the various actors that produce city beaches. This is evident from the diverse ways that city beaches have acquired sites, materials, equipment and funding; the shifting roles of local governments in relation to temporary uses like city beaches (from regulation to toleration to facilitation); and the emergence of mediating agencies that link other actors together (as discussed further in Chapter 5). Such innovations bring complexities and risks that can be hard to channel.

Furthermore, energy and relationships built around single projects do not necessarily endure (Mean et al. 2008).

The spread, form and success of city beaches have also been precipitated by short bursts of energy and excitement, in particular Germany's hosting of the Football World Cup in the exceptionally warm summer of 2006 when large crowds visited city beaches to watch games on outdoor televisions (Figure 4.5), and the many would-be entrepreneurs among them became smitten with replicating the idea. The World Cup and the new, very profitable concept of 'public viewing' essentially drew in and created entrepreneurs. Several avant-garde artist- and community-led city beach projects were stimulated by local, regional or European events and funding schemes with unrelated purposes, including campaigns to clean up Germany's rivers, catholic pilgrimages, and horticulture competitions (Stevens 2015).

Weather is also a fluctuating form of energy. Increasingly warm European summers, especially 2006's '100-year-summer', had helped prompt the growth of city beaches, but Germany's unpredictable, uncontrollable, often-rainy summers cause major operational difficulties and influence profitability, often causing closures. Weather

FIGURE 4.5 Public Viewing of World Cup soccer matches. Strandbar, Magdeburg.
Source: Quentin Stevens.

requires city beach assemblages to be highly adaptable. It forces beach operators to provide weather protection for guests that is adjustable, moveable and demountable, including buildings with openable facades and awnings, sail roofs, and tents with transparent or openable sides. Operators consider rain protection as a more essential element of a city beach than having access to a river or lake. Beaches provide large numbers of umbrellas and deck chairs that can be quickly reoriented or stored away in response to rain and the quotidian passage of the sun and clouds. Fickle weather also requires beach operators to provide weather forecasts on their websites and post daily updates about their opening hours on their web pages and social media. This energy flow also conditions the hiring conditions of beach service staff and entertainers, who typically have flexible or no contracts, so that they can be called in to work or declined work according to changing weather. When the sun comes out, staff, deck chairs and umbrellas, and music must all spontaneously materialise (Stevens 2011).

Concepts

The city beach as a concept is more enduring than any specific project, site or operator. The *Paris Plage* exemplar was rapidly translated in turn by artists, entrepreneurs, and community organisations, which have each had to adapt it to a diversity of German sites and work with different materials, funding and legislation (Stevens 2015). Many projects have been inspired by people seeing a city beach, and then seeking sites, funding and clientele to create one. One month after *Paris Plage* appeared, the first German commercial beach, *Strandbar Mitte*, found a south-facing waterfront site within a run-down, former-East-Berlin park, a prohibition (as with *Paris Plage*'s site) on permanent construction, an operator who already had a theatre and clientele there, and sand exposed by building demolitions (Stevens and Ambler 2010, Schulz and Abele 2011). The pre-existing concept connected these. Its 2002 appearance in Berlin linked it to an abundance of other vacant sites, underemployed creative entrepreneurs, tourists, and a government receptive to new ideas. The idea spread quickly to other major cities and then smaller German towns (Stevens 2011). Some entrepreneurs purchased franchises to *Skybeach's* successful rooftop concept; others merely copied elements.

The materials, design and programming of individual beaches have been shaped around several distinct themes that connect them to specific desired clienteles: white-plank cruise-ship chic; Mediterranean resort town; laid-back 'castaway' driftwood; and

FIGURE 4.6 South Pacific atmosphere through extensive use of thatching. Strand Pauli, Hamburg. Source: Quentin Stevens.

'South Pacific native' bamboo and thatch (Figure 4.6). Beaches' names help anchor these themes. Six beaches on parking garages play on the word 'deck'. Eight sites are called 'Island', although none actually are. Many names evoke the Mediterranean (del mar, sol, plage, playa), tropics (cabana, coco, Copa, 'Baykiki'), or deserts (oasis, dune, Sahara, Casablanca, Zanzibar). The surrounding industrial waterfront aesthetic also influences city beach décor, introducing shipping containers, 44-gallon drums, dock cranes and graffiti.

Use programs are also important in enlivening and differentiating city beaches' atmospheres. Yoga classes and children's playgrounds attract early-morning female patrons. Free wireless internet attracts students and creative workers. Dance floors and free Salsa lessons attract couples and singles. Community-run beaches host social and educational activities, and even religious services. Entrepreneurs with backgrounds in event management and the arts bring live music, poetry readings, debates, and exhibitions to their beaches. Germany's hosting of Football's World Cup in the warm summer of 2006 gave rise to beaches hosting 'public viewing' - watching sports and films on large outdoor screens - which financed a major expansion. Many of these activities have very tenuous links to sandy beaches. Playing sport is another major use: predominantly volleyball, but also beach soccer, boules, minigolf and canoeing.

The broader concept of temporary use (*Zwischennutzung*) is a force that has both facilitated and shaped opportunities for various people and landscape materials to appropriate land for city beaches (and other projects). It configures time as both a constraining and an enabling factor. It establishes terms for new actor agreements on rents and responsibilities, reducing financial overheads and risks, valorising new uses as experiments with planning regulations, and quashing local resident and commercial opposition to such projects by circumscribing their impacts (Polyak 2016). Such reimagining allows *Strandbar Mitte* to still claim temporariness in its 17th year of operation. The concept of temporary use will be addressed in detail in Chapter 6.

The flexibility of the city beach concept has allowed beaches to move to new sites. Düsseldorf's first beach operator relocated onto a moored boat in nearby Cologne when his original harbour-front location was developed for an international hotel. Munich's *Kulturstrand* has occupied six different locations. Some 70% of their staff time was spent acquiring relevant permits. They ultimately negotiated with the city to rotate annually between four sites (David 2010).

Numerous other administrative concepts have also shaped the possibilities of city beaches. Beverage companies minimise operation costs by supplying beach operators with drinks on consignment: they deliver, take no up-front payment, and earn only from drink sales. Some beaches have a *Minimumverzehr*, a minimum-purchase scheme, where patrons must pre-purchase on entry a voucher that is valid for food and drinks. Existing German building code provisions for temporary 'flying buildings' allow beaches exemptions from many time-consuming and expensive requirements and approval processes that would otherwise thwart such low-budget initiatives. Instead, performance-based regulations – related to levels of inebriation, noise, light and waste – shape city beaches as events, optimising the usability of their sites. Two Berlin projects, *Bad Ly* (1999, Peter Arlt) and *Badeschiff* (2004 onwards, Susanne Lorenz) were able to place swimming pools and beaches on urban sites without obtaining planning permits or meeting normal health and safety requirements, by defining them as temporary art projects, and not charging entry fees (Stevens 2009, 2015).

Austerity

The lure of money is one of the factors that has encouraged some entrepreneurs to pursue profits by assembling whimsical beach atmospheres out of degraded urban spaces, cheaply rented furnishings and casually employed staff, and by circumventing expensive regulatory requirements. But city beaches are not necessarily profitable, and investment finance is often very limited. Money also has a great influence on city beaches through its absence. An absence of market demand and financing to redevelop Germany's extensive urban brownfields has created spatial opportunities for new users and uses with small budgets and short time horizons. Landowners often provide sites for little or no rent, or even pursue tenants, to help advertise their site, to facilitate repairs, or just to cover holding costs (SenStadt 2007). Operators' lack of initial capital shapes beaches by encouraging a 'Zero-Euro Urbanism', requiring new practices of renting, donations and making-do, inputs of sponsorship, and inputs of sweat equity and creativity from operators and from local residents (Müller et al. 2015). Market weakness also means that city beaches' operations (their admissions policies, use programs, noise levels, employment) remain strongly conditioned by their financial dependence on local governments, through grants, loans, rent-free land, free services and tax reductions.

Emphasising operators' power to shape city beaches also ignores operators' and staff's dissatisfaction with economic conditions and outcomes they cannot control. A lack of existing profitable business opportunities and stable employment requires individuals with media or hospitality backgrounds to work in a quite different sector, designing and managing landscapes. This low-budget entrepreneurship is in part an effect of the social circumstances of German cities' economic crisis and the atmosphere and practices of austerity that follow from it (Färber 2014). City beaches are more numerous in German cities with high unemployment. To focus on operators' control also ignores the temporary and fragile nature of the relationships constituting these beaches. Premises must remain rapidly vacatable on the occasion of flooding or property sale. The vicissitudes of weather easily bring financial ruin. Low-income customers require that most city beaches forgo admission charges. A shortage of conventional urban development funds and customer receipts has also drawn arts and social funding into these open space projects, especially in smaller and poorer cities (Stevens 2015).

What Brings the Beach Together?

This analysis of the diverse actors that shape city beaches brings into focus four broad insights into the contemporary production of public spaces that are in marked contrast to much waterfront redevelopment literature, which foregrounds the impact of large multinational corporations and architecture firms, long-term planning, partnership contracts, and sophisticated land-forming and construction techniques (Marshall 2001).

First, successful spaces can be throwntogether by extremely diverse and distributed sets of agents and mechanisms, including materials, sites, and contextual conditions (Figure 4.7). City beaches and other public spaces can be stimulated, created, managed and supported through entrepreneurship from the private sector, the public sector and/or diverse community actors.

Second, city beaches exemplify an exploratory, experimental attitude toward placemaking. City beaches are both tangibly and metaphorically 'sandboxes': physical and social milieux that are open and unstructured, gathering together a diversity of elements that can easily be manipulated to serve different roles, and which thus encourage playful, collaborative exploration of possibilities and learning, and foster new approaches (Stevens 2015). While they use a palette of simple materials, they innovate through new kinds of actors, sites, timeframes, new funding and management approaches and programming (Lydon and Garcia 2015). They re-imagine and re-purpose previously underutilised urban spaces to discover varied new uses and benefits. These outcomes in turn produce other changes, by financially underwriting culturepreneurs' other ventures, enhancing German social cohesion during the World Cup, and stimulating the cleaning up of waterways and the gentrification of former harbours.

The third distinctive characteristic of city beaches is their variability. They illustrate the dynamic relationships and processes through which actors are brought together to constitute spaces, and the variable power relations which produce stability or change in these relationships and these spaces. These projects embrace impermanence. They demonstrate the potential flexibility of public spaces that can transform from hour to hour (with the sun, rain and human visitors), from day to day (with seasons, programs, new local ideas and events) and from year to year (with changes in equipment, budget, site, landlords and operators). They show how even loose furnishings can significantly modify a space's atmosphere and functionality.

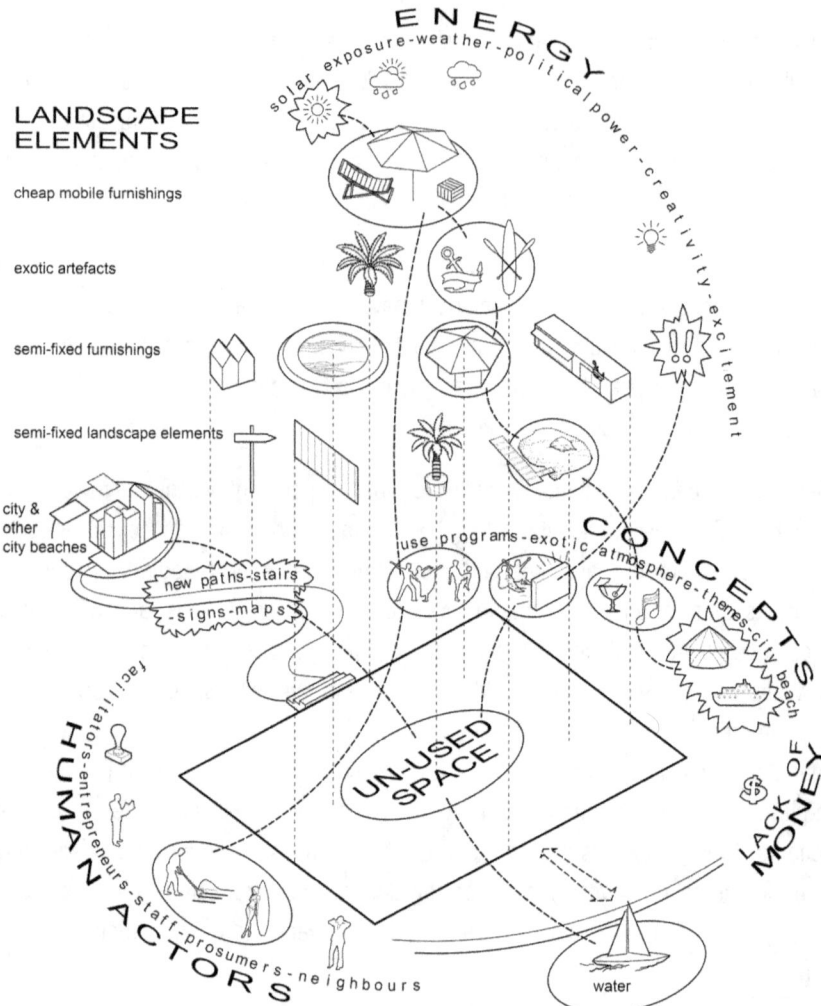

FIGURE 4.7 The six sets of actors that are thrown together to create city beaches. Dashed lines illustrate four ways different actors temporarily assemble other actors, clockwise from the top:

- sunshine draws together staff, prosumers, and activities such as sunbathing that perform the beach.
- The excitement of the World Cup draws together unused spaces and the new activity of Public Viewing.
- specific city beach themes draw together exotic atmosphere, landscape elements, exotic artefacts and mobile furnishings.
- New paths, stairs, signs and maps draw together cities, unused spaces and waterfronts.

Source: Image by Quentin Stevens and Ha Thai.

They encourage various actors to modify and extend the setting, its uses and even its location. The combination of the city beach's robust and transferable central concepts and components and its extremely variable details is surely fundamental to its success. The flexible and dynamic approaches of city beaches and other temporary uses, as post-Fordist, 'just-in-time' open spaces, seem well-suited to recent economic uncertainties (Tonkiss 2013). Their short cost-recovery timeframes limit their need for fixed relationships to sites, capital, robust landscape design, or to popular enthusiasm, political will, regulatory certainty, or capital. They harness the fluid, short-term availability of all these factors. Nothing is tied down, and every element can be rapidly exchanged or re-purposed in response to changing needs.

Fourth, the conditions outlined above raise an open question about the diverse, exploratory and varying publicness of these and other throwntogether urban spaces. The human relationships that produce city beaches may seem particularly transient. But the success of city beaches as public spaces rests on the ongoing, active involvement of a wide range of actors. These include beach users, who are typically 'prosumers' actively engaged in the performative co-production of the space and its uses and meanings (Richards and Wilson 2006). They include community organisations, creative industry synergies, cross-departmental working within government, and close citizen-city government relationships. These projects illustrate the important role of existing social and business networks and associations, and also the role of the beach projects in initiating and strengthening such connections. The community organisers of Vaihingen's *Strandleben* (Figure 4.4) highlight that the assemblage that produced it did not exist beforehand. Trust developed through the process of making the space, through detailed discussion and negotiation over rights and responsibilities between the council, the community association and organisers (Gassner et al. 2011). Community-based facilitators of city beach projects, representing residents, youth, churches and arts organisations, maintain open communication, engagement, and trust with local government and with the many other people necessary to produce these beach spaces, including beach users.

Constellations of human actors and beach sites have also evolved at a wider geographic and economic scale. City beach projects also link to each other, amassing and sharing resources, interests, and processes. The large number of city beaches in Germany has subsequently shaped other industries, which rent potted palms and sand, print deck chair logos, and structure beverage consignment contracts. Some musicians and dancers tour German beaches. Sets of beaches are also assembled by individual entrepreneurs. As the city beach concept quickly became stable, replicable and transferrable, professionalisation and systematisation began developing in the operation of private-sector city beaches. This networking and stabilisation are evident in the emergence of eleven chain operators, and of franchises. Five companies in Berlin run fourteen beaches between them. Both *Hexenkessel und Strand* and *Freiluftrebellen* expanded by one new beach each year, harnessing past profits and contacts and existing equipment and staffing. Three regional monopolies are based around the Rhine port cities Mannheim and Düsseldorf. In ten cities, sites already developed into beaches were acquired or revived by different operators in later years, applying new branding and management approaches to the same scenery. The founder of Stuttgart's *Skybeach* copyrighted his concept, sold franchises and licensed the name to others. *Skybeach* and one other city beach chain specialise in parking garage rooftops, where site and management factors are highly standardised. These sites remain dependably vacant each summer and will never be developed; eight are owned by one department store chain. Other independent operators copied the *Skybeach* model in 16 other cities. City beach chains can also share brand names, advertising, websites, furnishings, suppliers, performers and capital. A franchise is a durable set of such relationships that new entrepreneurs can rent access to. These open spaces may be temporary and throwntogether from loose materials, but their locations and operations are often very durable; some have remained in operation for 17 years.

The form of city beaches, and their success or failure as open spaces, rests on the active input of all the actors described in this chapter, and the strength and durability of the emergent relationships between them that have been sketched out above. The community organisers of Vaihingen's beach highlight that the power that produces these spaces does not exist beforehand. It develops in the process of making them:

> We meet in advance and talk about everything. Support and responsibility are shared between the council, the community association, and organizers of individual events ... We talk [to applicants who propose events for the

site] about the conditions, so that they are actually responsible for this themselves ... The *Ordnungsamt* [Public Order Office] trust us with this.

(Gassner et al. 2011)

The power to act and to shape the formation of a city beach, whether for people or for unused sites, furniture, concepts, excitement or specific activities, comes from responsibilities that are dynamically created, assigned and transferred. Munich's *Kulturstrand* highlights the negotiated nature of these responsibilities, as each of its new host sites and neighbourhood contexts inspired new spatial forms, programs and operational constraints (David 2010). These negotiated processes also help to explain regional variations in the location, number and form of city beaches (Stevens 2011).

The short-term, dynamic, seemingly haphazard arrangements that constitute city beaches allow them to maintain a ready potential to empower. Their physical looseness allows a high level of control to actors who can modify and extend these settings and their uses, and even their locations – whether these actors be the wind, a new kind of sunbed, a child with a shovel, or a church congregation seeking an outdoor venue.

The great flexibility and variability among city beaches confirm the burgeoning recent literature demonstrating that innovations in public space are not just about new formal types (indeed, these landscapes are stereotypical), but often involve new kinds of actors, locations and timeframes, new funding and management approaches and programming (Franck and Stevens 2007, Lydon and Garcia 2015). As spaces that are temporary and negotiated, city beaches illustrate how diverse networks of agents and mechanisms can re-imagine, re-develop, and re-purpose previously underutilised waterfronts, and other urban spaces, to bring varied new benefits. As spaces that are temporary and negotiated, city beaches illustrate a potential future for public spaces that is highly contingent, participatory, and open to change.

References

Arlt, P. (n.d.) Aktionen + Temporäre Bauten. Online, available at: www.peterarlt.at/index.php?kat=1 (accessed 31 July 2012).

David, B. (2010) Manager of *Kulturstrand*. Munich: Personal interview.
Färber, A. (2014) Low-budget Berlin: Towards an understanding of low-budget urbanity as assemblage. *Journal of Regions, Economy and Society* 7: 119–36.
Franck, K. and Stevens, Q. (eds) (2007) *Loose space: Possibility and diversity in urban life*. New York: Routledge.
Gale, T. (2009) Urban beaches, virtual worlds and 'the end of tourism', *Mobilities* 4 (1): 119–38.
Gassner, S., Schmidt-Hitschler, U. and Hitschler, T. (2011) Organisers of *Strandleben*. Vaihingen an der Enz: Personal interview.
Hou, J. (ed) (2010) *Insurgent public space: Guerrilla urbanism and the remaking of contemporary cities*. New York: Routledge.
Lange, B. (2011) Professionalization in space: Social-spatial strategies of culturepreneurs in Berlin. *Entrepreneurship and Regional Development* 23 (3-4): 259–79.
Latour, B. (2005) *Reassembling the social. An introduction to actor-network theory*. Oxford: Oxford University Press.
Lydon, M. and Garcia A. (2015) *Tactical urbanism: Short-term action for long-term change*. Washington, D.C.: Island Press.
Marshall, R. (ed) (2001) *Waterfronts in post-industrial cities*. London: Spon.
Massey, D. (2005) *For space*. Los Angeles: Sage.
Mean, M., Johar, I. and Gale, T. (2008) *Bristol beach: An experiment in place-making*. London: DEMOS.
Müller, M., Schmid, J., Schönherr, U. and Weiss, F. (eds) (2015) *Null Euro Urbanismus: Ein Katalog von Good Practice Beispielen*. Hamburg: Null Euro Urbanismus Studien- und Rechercheprojekt. http://www.null-euro-urbanismus.de/?page_id=81 (Accessed 30 July 2018).
Polyak, L. (2016) Civic space: The reappropriation of vacant buildings in four European cities, unpublished PhD thesis, Central European University, Budapest. www.etd.ceu.edu/2017/polyak_levente.pdf (accessed 19 July 2018).
Richards, G. and Wilson, J. (2006) Developing creativity in tourist experiences: A solution to the serial reproduction of culture? *Tourism Management* 27: 1209–23.
Schulz, C. and Abele, M. (2011) Managers of *Strandbar Mitte* and *Oststrand*. Berlin: Personal interview.
SenStadt (Senatsverwaltung für Stadtentwicklung Berlin) (ed) (2007) *Urban pioneers: Temporary use and urban development in Berlin*. Berlin: Jovis.
Stevens, Q. (2009) Artificial waterfronts. *Urban Design International* 14 (1): 3–21.
Stevens, Q. (2011) Characterising Germany's artificial 'city beaches': Distribution, type and design, 3rd World Planning Schools Congress, Perth, 2011.

Stevens, Q. (2015). Sandpit urbanism, in B. Knudsen, D. Christensen and P. Blenker (eds), *Enterprising initiatives in the experience economy: Transforming social worlds*. New York: Routledge.

Stevens, Q. and Ambler, M. (2010) Europe's city beaches as post-Fordist placemaking. *Journal of Urban Design* 15 (4): 515–37.

Tonkiss, F. (2013) Austerity urbanism and the makeshift city. *City* 17 (3): 313–24.

Chapter Five
Creativity

Quentin Stevens

Creative Production
Consumption of Creativity
Creative Approaches to Urban Development
Creativity Unleashed: Governing Temporary Uses
Conclusion

This chapter examines how various definitions and applications of the concept of 'creativity' have been developed and deployed in the emergent theoretical, empirical and planning policy literature on 'temporary uses' of derelict urban spaces, in order to explore how these understandings of creativity and temporary use are influencing the purposes and methods of planning itself. The chapter explores how this thinking links short-term uses of sites, disinvested urban real estate, the long-term vitality of urban districts, and creative work practices.

Temporary land uses have always existed in cities, ranging from circuses and squatting to materials storage and surface car parks. But until recently, such uses were not generally harnessed for the long-term transformation of disinvested urban districts. They were epiphenomena that were never seen as part of urban development planning. Jane Jacobs (1961) did not write about temporary uses specifically. But what she noted was that old, neglected buildings provide affordable space for a range of creative businesses (including her own profession, journalism) until those businesses become more profitable and move on, or until the space itself is redeveloped:

> The floor of the building in which this book is being written is occupied also by … a firm of ecclesiastical decorators, … a music society, an accordionists' association, … a studio for watercolor lessons, and a maker of costume jewelry. Among the tenants who were here and gone shortly before I came in [was] … a Haitian dance troupe. There is no place for the

likes of us in new construction. And the last thing we need is new construction. What we need, and a lot of others need, is old construction in a lively district, which some among us can help make livelier.

(Jacobs 1961:206)

Jacobs emphasised that such innovative, artistic, economically marginal business activities are important to both the everyday liveability and the economic development potential of cities. She argued that large-scale, master-planned urban development is inimical to the very presence of innovative businesses in city districts, because 'for really new ideas of any kind ... there is no leeway for such chancy trial, error and experimentation in the high-overhead economy of new construction ... New ideas must use old buildings' (Jacobs 1961:188).

Jacobs's thesis on the relationship between disinvested properties, innovation enterprises, and incremental development has been complemented and extended in recent decades by a new focus on temporary uses. In the late 1990s, two European studies (Bürgin and Cabane 1999, Urban Catalyst 2001) initiated a new area of planning thinking and research by defining 'temporary use' in terms of economically marginal activities that temporarily occupy and transform abandoned urban sites, and examining the potential importance of these uses for bringing new economic and social activity, jobs, and investment to cities. Key geographic and economic contexts for this were the reunification of Germany, widespread property vacancy and squatting in the former East Germany, and industrial decline in the Ruhr region (Honeck 2017). The two studies appear to have introduced at least four new points of focus to planning thinking about temporary use. First, temporary re-use is now seen to be an important economic and planning strategy for the redevelopment of former industrialised areas; one which takes place before, alongside, or instead of large-scale, long-term masterplans, and which contributes to long-term physical and economic development outcomes. Second, actors from the 'creative industries' are now understood as playing an important role in undertaking these temporary reuses and transformations. Third, temporary uses of sites are acknowledged by city administrations as being important opportunities for attracting and nurturing creative industries. Fourth, planning policy, which has traditionally focused on long-term visions and permanent rules, has begun looking at ways to support and promote particular short-term uses as a mechanism for driving urban change.

To explore the discourse of temporary use and the arguments around creativity that favour and legitimate it, this chapter draws centrally on a qualitative, thematic content analysis of the earliest research and policy studies of temporary uses in Western European cities (see References). These publications were identified through exhaustive internet searching using the key term 'temporary use' and its German equivalents (*Zwischennutzung, Temporäre Nutzung, Vorläufige Nutzung*) (Honeck 2017), and snowball sampling of further material cited in the identified sources. The publications examine projects and policies in Germany and in several countries surrounding it (Switzerland, Austria, the Netherlands, Belgium); a region where economic conditions, governments and entrepreneurs fostered the earliest emergence of new temporary uses of under-utilised urban spaces. All translations from German-language sources are the author's own. The literature covers the period from Bürgin and Cabane's pioneering study (1999) up until 2012, when the first major survey and analysis was published of emergent temporary uses elsewhere, in the United Kingdom (Bishop and Williams 2012). The significance of this period and region is corroborated by the findings of a recent detailed bibliometric analysis by Chang (2021), who notes that after 2011, the volume and diversity of research on t/t urbanism grew rapidly, shifting from empirical studies of temporary uses on the ground toward more conceptual and political explorations of the dimensions, implications and potentials of Temporary and Tactical Urbanism. While the geographical and conceptual breadth of research into temporary uses and their relation to creativity has continued to expand (Chang 2021, Honeck 2017, Henneberry 2017), the sample drawn on here illustrates the initial concepts, projects and evaluations of temporary uses within the economic, political and cultural context of the German- and Dutch-speaking world, which have subsequently had a significant wider influence on theory and practice. These analytical insights are supplemented by further arguments and evidence drawn from more recent literature.

To ground the emergent theorisation of temporary use as a new area of planning thought and practice, this chapter uses a qualitative content analysis of the identified set of early policy and research studies to explore the five key themes set out in Table 5.1.

The definition of temporariness that frames t/t urbanism practice was touched upon in Chapter 1 and will be explored in more detail in Chapter 6. The aims and benefits of t/t urbanism were examined in Chapter 2. The constellations of actors and contexts that drive and shape practice were the focus of Chapter 4. This chapter's inductive content analysis of the aims, perceived benefits and critiques of temporary uses that were expressed in the corpus of early t/t literature led to the identification and analysis of two additional, more specific and critical themes that were raised there (Table 5.2).

TABLE 5.1 Key themes in temporary use literature

Theme	Key sources
The definition of temporariness	Blumner 2006, Böhme et al. 2006
The temporal, economic and institutional contexts for temporary uses	Urban Catalyst 2001, SenStadt 2007
How temporary uses interact with other more permanent uses	Urban Catalyst 2007, Schwarting and Overmeyer 2008
The aims and perceived benefits of temporary uses	SenStadt 2007, Brammer 2008
The various types of actors who drive temporary uses	SenStadt 2007, Jorg 2008

TABLE 5.2 Key critiques expressed in temporary use literature

Theme	Key sources
How the idea of creativity is relevant to the development of temporary uses	Ebert and Kunzmann 2007, Jorg 2008, Angst et al 2009, Colomb 2012a, 2012b
Relationships between temporary uses, creativity and neoliberal economics and theory	Kruse and Steglich 2006, Lange 2007, 2008, Colomb 2012a

These latter two themes form the focus of examination in this chapter. This chapter does not presuppose any authoritative definition of creativity (in German, *Kreativität*), or the purpose of creativity or innovation within urban economies and urban development (cf. Landry and Bianchini 1995, Florida 2002), Instead, it examines three distinct but interrelated contexts where the concept of creativity has been defined and deployed within the academic and policy discourse about temporary use and the management and redevelopment of abandoned and underutilised sites. These three contexts are creative production, consumption and governance. The chapter closes with an examination of how these conceptions of creativity mesh together in planning thought with broadly neoliberal approaches to urban development and urban governance.

Creative Production

Creative production is seen as an increasingly important component of urban economies (Florida 2002, Hall 1998). In relation to the planning and management of urban built fabric, policy and theory also see the creative industries to have a more specific role, as an economically productive way to use vacant, derelict urban spaces temporarily. This is understood as both convenient and strategic. Compared to other branches of industry, creative enterprises are typically small, low-capital and flexible about the spaces they occupy. They are seen as a branch of industry that is uniquely willing and able to start operating at short notice and relocate in a piecemeal fashion, and as able to rapidly adapt their work practices to a wide variety and quality of existing sites, structures and infrastructures when they become available, without major capital investment (Becker 2010). Today's creative actors are frequently portrayed as 'footloose' or 'nomadic'; their production activities are not often fixed to physical and representational attributes of particular sites (MA18 2003, Urban Unlimited 2004, Dienel and Schophaus 2005). However, policy on temporary use typically prioritises the development of new creative activities, rather than relocating existing creative activities from elsewhere that may not engage creatively with the new site. Temporary use is portrayed, for example, as 'an attractive "first step" for numerous start-up ventures in the creative economy' (SenStadt 2007: 101). A major study of temporary uses in Switzerland highlights that the percentage of creative workers engaged in temporary businesses in Zurich's former rail yards was four times the national average, and almost half the companies on the site had been founded there (Angst et al. 2009).

Strategically, it is believed that creative actors such as artists and architects are particularly well suited to utilising disinvested, vacant spaces temporarily. They are able to perceive distinctive aesthetic, historic, and functional characteristics within disinvested, vacant spaces, and efficiently activate these potentials, and thereby add high symbolic, social and economic value to those sites (SenStadt 2007, BMVBS/BBR 2008). They are 'pioneers', 'truffle pigs' who unearth valuable, latent opportunities for the benefit of other investors who follow them (SenStadt 2007, Lange 2007b, Figure 5.1). Creative producers have 'a feel for unconventional and creative solutions', including experimental uses of sites (Bürgin 2010: 8).

An early summary by Kloos et al. (2007) finds that the existing planning policy literature on temporary uses embraces both this pragmatic view of the creative industries' capacities to make use of brownfields, as well as a more idealistic view of creative activities as having a positive influence on the wider development of local economy and urban form. More than just providing rent returns on devalorised properties, as would temporary warehousing activities or car parking, creative workers add significant symbolic and social capital to these disinvested sites, thereby accelerating their

FIGURE 5.1 Photomontage emphasising the role of 'Creative Nomads' (artists and musicians) in temporary activation of unused urban sites, from Urban Pioneers: Temporary Use and Urban Development in Berlin, the 'manual' based on the experiences of Berlin's Department of Urban Development (SenStadt 2007: 68–69).
Source: Urban Catalyst.

recuperation into the wider property market (Becker 2010, Smith 1996, Zukin 1982). While there may be real, direct economic dividends in increased cultural production, policies often intend artistic and cultural permissiveness in such brownfield areas to be only temporary and transitional (Andres and Grésillon 2013). In exchange for low rents, many creative workers invest a lot of their labour and expertise in modifying these spaces and bringing the public's attention to them (Bishop and Williams 2012). Because artistic projects often pursue goals beyond the purely economic, they will also often be driven forward even in the absence of profits (Becker 2010).

Bürgin (2010: 107) strikes a rare note of caution, pointing out that 'impetuous' creativity in temporary use can be disadvantageous for later users, if it brings adverse changes, damage or excessive wear to the building stock. Creative users may be wilful and unrealistic, making it difficult for landlords to manage properties and transfer them to new long-term tenants. Urban Catalyst (2001: 86) notes that creative workers at the end of their temporary tenancy of Berlin's Haus des Lehrers were 'stubborn, explosive and radical', and fought against relocation.

Inspiration in the creative use of vacant properties runs both ways. Original, creative activity is believed to be stimulated by vacated urban sites: their location, architecture and former uses; the mixtures of new actors that are accommodated within the given configuration such sites; the dense communication networks and collaborations that often arise among these actors; and the new and temporary nature of site occupation. These conditions inspire new artists as well as established ones (Angst et al. 2009, Bürgin 2010, Bürgin and Cabane 1999). The large scale, openness, and specialised infrastructure of many former industrial sites, which can present impediments to their recuperation for other long-term uses, is often attractive for the production and display of creative works, whether plastic arts, performance, media, or architecture (Bürgin 2010, Bishop and Williams 2012). Jacobs (1961) argued that the lower rents of older, disinvested buildings enable creative, risky experimentation, but the low rents in themselves do not actually encourage this. Low rents can also attract and support marginal businesses that are not creative.

Consumption of Creativity

A second component of creativity is the interesting consumption opportunities that new, temporary uses of urban spaces are believed to offer to residents and visitors. Different economic uses for derelict urban spaces are not necessarily in themselves novel activities or directly useful and interesting to the wider public; an architecture studio in a former factory is still a private architecture studio. Whereas creative production emphasises the tenants' practices, the emphasis here is on innovations in the products of creativity, and in particular consumers' experiences in and of the temporarily transformed urban spaces themselves.

Creative temporary uses are valued because they enhance the general cultural diversity and vitality of urban areas, by adding to the range of open space, social, cultural and commercial amenities (Bürgin 2010), and enabling new combinations of such activities, as well as providing them in new and interesting locations where existing urban form, property values, government regulations and private management policies had previously precluded them. Under conditions of fiscal austerity following the latest global financial crisis, creative uses also have an ameliorative role. Their flexible labour and their limited financial resources are being drawn upon to compensate for deficiencies in publicly funded delivery of social and cultural amenities (Ferreri 2015, Deslandes 2013, Tonkiss 2013, Urban Catalyst 2001).

Temporary uses of urban sites are seen to be more experimental than permanent projects that require larger budgets and face larger risks. They can cater to smaller and more specialised audiences. Unconventional and controversial uses are more likely to be tolerated if they are only occupying marginal spaces that were previously out of use, and only of relatively short duration (Bishop and Williams 2012, Havemann and Schild 2007).

Temporary uses of industrial brownfields and other derelict land often centre on the physical redevelopment of those spaces for public access and use. Many temporary uses are publicly accessible art or landscaping projects which have no intrinsic commercial function, although they may serve as attractions that stimulate spontaneous spending or long-term investment in their surroundings. This includes the provision of new kinds of informal, accessible spaces where the public can act, perform and interact: temporary places for relaxation, participative sports and games, commemoration, and protest (Bishop and Williams 2012, Haydn and Temel 2006). Among 43 pioneering temporary uses showcased in a government-sponsored study of Berlin (SenStadt 2007), 30 were novel open spaces for public leisure use: community gardens, accessible open spaces for people and animals; sports areas; and artificial beaches. Such consumption-oriented spaces and activities are, in contrast to creative *industries*, inherently unproductive, and therefore of relatively little direct importance to the mainstream economy. Their transcendence of the means-end rationality which governs long-term land-use planning underscores their inherent worth and meaningfulness to culture. Temporary gardening is one nominally productive activity that falls within this class of creative reuse and engagement with urban brownfields (Becker 2010, SenStadt 2007), but it is a very slow form of productivity that falls well short of the demands of urban property prices.

Creative public uses of formerly vacant sites often engage with and enrich the particularity of space and local identity. Artistic engagement with a vacant site sometimes engages directly and critically with the dynamics of the site's development, seeking to explore, comment on and shape those wider processes (Till 2011). For example, intensive, varied temporary uses of Berlin's Palast der Republik prior to its demolition sought to critique and experiment with the history and future of the building and of the East German society that produced it, to encourage a broad political, cultural and practical re-evaluation of its legacy

(Urban Catalyst 2007, Colomb 2007). Creative temporary uses are argued to be 'identity-giving' (*identitätsstiftend*) (Krauzick 2007). In all these respects, the creativity of temporary uses is primarily seen in terms of its benefits to social development, rather than property development. Temporarily unused spaces provide physical and temporal windows of opportunity for public appropriation of real estate for alternative cultural needs that are not met by the open market. These temporary uses might not in themselves be profitable. The aim is often instead for the city and its citizens to benefit from privately financed investments and services that enhance the general quality of life.

Some innovative temporary consumption spaces indirectly serve aims for economic and property development. Berlin's government has increasingly utilised entertainment- and leisure-oriented temporary uses as a form of city marketing, presenting such projects as 'new playgrounds for artists, creatives, young travellers and tourists, thus shifting the focus (away) from the iconic sites of inner city redevelopment such as Potsdamer Platz' (Colomb 2012a: 243). Such offerings attract creative workers who seek a high degree of quality, variety and novelty in urban leisure offerings (Jorg 2008). A report commissioned from Munich's city department of employment and business puts this clearly:

> Quality of life and a climate of openness and diversity are key criteria for the attractiveness of a location for highly skilled and creative workers ... varied lifestyles create an inspiring and stimulating environment for creative working people ... Arts and Culture are of particular importance for the quality of life of creative knowledge workers. Because the highly skilled especially demand art and culture in their spare time, a comprehensive cultural offering in the city presents highly creative people with a source of inspiration for their own creative production ... Whether high culture in opera, theatre and museums or the cultural scene in bars, in temporarily used army barracks, old factory buildings and brownfield sites, or temporary events in the summer such as Corso Leopold, the Streetlife Festival, and the 'beach' on the Cornelius Bridge of the Isar River [see Figure 5.2] - these are all appealing pastimes for creative knowledge workers. In addition, they help highly creative people with ideas for new products and services that are economically viable and that set new trends.
> (RAW München 2007: 22)

FIGURE 5.2 A concert in 2017 by Yalta Club on Kulturstrand, Munich, a temporary beach on the central Museum Island frequently used for performances and events.

Source: Sebastian Dürst.

Similarly, in Berlin pioneering temporary use projects:

> personify unusual but attractive urban lifestyles and hence cater to a demand that traditional urban structures fail to meet … The broad range of temporary use projects in Berlin has become a PR and economic factor for the city … a catalyst for the relocation of international companies (and) an attraction for tourists.
>
> (SenStadt 2007:41)

In contrast to the theorisations of creative productivity outlined in the first section of this chapter, which emphasise tangible material benefits through increased economic activity and reinvestment in the built environment, creative consumption activities on disinvested urban sites are believed to enrich the general quality of urban life, in both the short and long term. The example of sport and leisure activities illustrates that citizens can have a participatory role in such re-activations of spaces.

Creative Approaches to Urban Development

A third distinct aspect of creativity in the theorisation of temporary use, which links directly to urban planning practice, was already introduced in Chapter 2. Innovation within urban development practices is one of the five key values underpinning t/t urbanism. It is argued that governments, planners, property owners and temporary users all need to be more creative (here meaning innovative) in the rules, processes and investments they use to shape current activity on urban sites and future property development. This conforms to the broader historical case argued by Hall (1998), that in addition to cultural, intellectual, and artistic creativity, cities also thrive and develop through the technical and organisational creativity of city managers, particularly in terms of their engagements with local entrepreneurs (Jorg 2008; Figure 5.3). In the context of temporary uses, urban planning is not merely a supportive conduit for creativity, but its target:

> Here a fundamental distinction must be made ... The first thing that can be observed is the creativity and innovation *within* temporary uses. This means that within temporary uses, innovative things may arise. Secondly, temporary uses can contribute to *innovative urban planning*. This occurs particularly through the experimental nature that temporary uses often exhibit, which through the resultant urban development can demonstrate alternative solutions for various problems.
>
> (Waldis 2009, emphasis added)

This latter conception of creativity as innovative planning centres on an expanded decision-making role for the users (i.e., tenants) of urban spaces, vis-à-vis their owners and regulators (Haydn and Temel 2006). In line with broader neoliberal thinking, this discourse rejects long-range, top-down strategic approaches to urban development in favour of freeing up and encouraging individual entrepreneurial initiative and capital. Creative governance generally means less regulation. Nevertheless, Honeck (2017) notes that innovation in Germany included developing new ways of combining top-down formal planning processes with avant-garde actors and approaches, and that temporary uses and creative industries were introduced and nurtured even in prosperous cities which had little vacancy or dereliction. Becker (2010: 27) suggests that creative uses of space are hard to plan because they thrive on spontaneity and unexpected conditions and relations and argues for 'the removal of bureaucratic hurdles, the relaxation of public safety regulations, and the use of

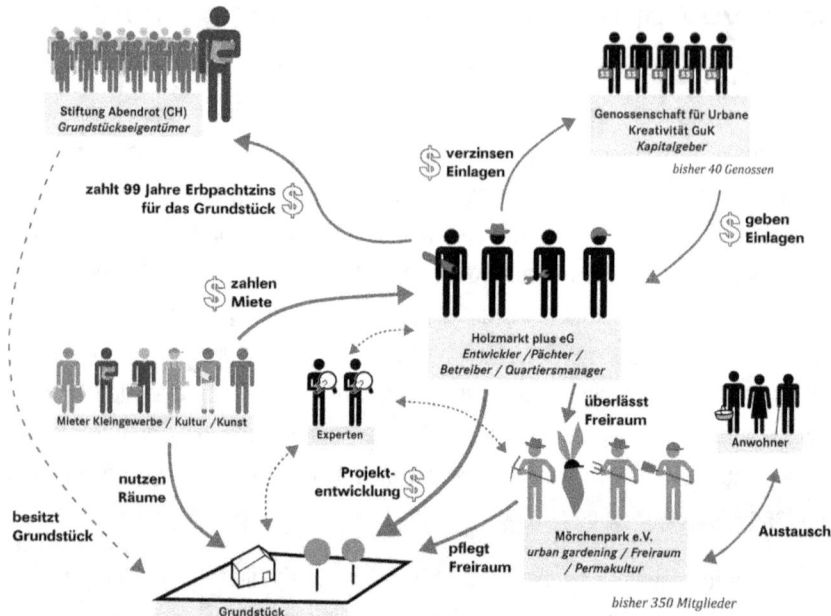

FIGURE 5.3 Conceptual diagram of the relationships among the various actors that are creatively assembled to enable temporary use of a site. From left to right, and top to bottom: the trust that owns the site; a mutual fund that provides investment capital; the user cooperative *Holzmarkt plus eG* that developed and managed the site; tenants from small business, arts and culture; experts with ideas; local residents; and a community gardening association that maintains the open spaces.

Source: Urban Catalyst. https://www.urbancatalyst.de/en/projects/holzmarkt-berlin-en.html

administrative discretion' – that is, liberalisation. Temporary users of sites are celebrated as 'pioneers' who lead and demand the attenuation or renegotiation of official planning strategies and controls and lease terms, and the opening up of both urban spaces and planning processes to a diversity of visions and inputs (SenStadt 2007, Groth and Corijn 2005). Although these uses frequently end up instrumentalised by municipal policy, or at least aligned to it, in theory and in policy these actors' approaches to the use and development of vacant sites are often represented as tactical: creative and somewhat resistant to conventional strategies and regulations (Mould 2014, Novy and Colomb 2013). Some analysts go so far as to portray creativity as a general characteristic of temporary uses (Dransfeld and Lehmann 2008).

With temporary uses, creative agents are able to demonstrate 'not only the possibility, but the necessity to overrule conventions, guidelines and red tape and conquer the murky terrain of legal and social obligations' (Kreuzer 2001: 19). Rules and relationships are creatively negotiated across a broad scope of conditions including lease duration, uses, rent levels, guarantees, insurances, and utility costs. The public sector and site owners provide many kinds of direct and indirect financial and professional advice to attract and enable new users. New kinds of leases and permits are developed to suit tenant needs and capabilities (SenStadt 2007). Creativity is employed by whichever actor is taking the initiative to encourage temporary use in a given location, according to three different scenarios: property owner seeks user, user seeks property owner, or urban developer seeks property owner and user (BMVBS/BBR 2008).

Creativity on the part of property owners involves flexibility in how they seek to meet their short- and long-term financial goals. This means 'engaging in "creative" (sic) reactivation of brownfields and underused sites beyond the typical economic recovery patterns of property' (Kloos et al. 2007: 6), and creativity in finding appropriate sets of tenants for large sites and buildings (Bürgin 2010). 'Creative rental concepts' may include short-term or even provisional leases, low rents supplemented by business profit-sharing, and cost-only rents to entice key artistic and cultural attractions to a location, to enhance the marketability of other properties (Rosic and Froessler 2009). Such innovations require that landlords become more exposed to short-term market risks. The flexibility, creativity and spontaneity of actors from the creative industries often clash with the expectations and existing approaches of property owners and managers, requiring openness to dialogue (Bürgin 2010). On the positive side, temporary creative uses allow landlords to test out and demonstrate the feasibility of new uses, which also helps market sites to potential long-term users (Becker 2010). Creativity is also applied to the place marketing process itself: temporary uses of derelict areas provide new techniques and new imagery to attract new groups of consumers and producers (Colomb 2012a).

These various kinds of creativity in land marketing, planning and management processes may or may not involve tenants from the creative industries. One analysis, of the redevelopment of a former slaughterhouse for 'research-oriented, innovative companies, creative business and cultural institutions' (Schwarting and Overmeyer 2008: 62), uses the German term *kreatives Gewerbe* (creative business) rather than the usual sectoral term *Kreativwirtschaft* (creative economy) and notes that less financially successful artists can no longer afford the rents at this site. A major

German government guide to temporary uses is careful to differentiate between the roles of 'creative industries' and innovative 'entrepreneurs', and uses the expression 'artistic-creative temporary uses' to clarify one case where both aspects are brought into play (BMVBS/BBR 2008: 92). These two aspects overlap most clearly in the environmental design professions (architecture, landscape architecture, urban design, interior design), whose core creative competency is the redevelopment of built form. These businesses are often strongly represented in the temporary use profiles of brownfield sites (Bürgin and Cabane 1999). These actors are often forming small, new firms to pursue new kinds of projects, clients and funding. They can readily imagine, enhance, and capitalise on both the productive usefulness of individual properties, for their own business, and on the wider spatial and symbolic potential of the surrounding brownfield area and the redevelopment processes going on within it, when selling their services to other temporary and long-term users (Lange 2008).

The dual aims of creatively utilising brownfield sites and facilitating the creative industries have also given rise to a new category of non-governmental, entrepreneurial mediating organisations whose role is as a conduit of information and negotiation between actors who need affordable space, the potentials of vacant buildings, and planning policies that regulate the development and use of those sites (Oswalt 2002, Kruse and Steglich 2006, Brammer 2008, BMVBS/BBR 2008, Angst et al 2009). These organisations include 'Urban Residue', 'Golfstromen' and 'Urban Resort' in Amsterdam, 'SpareSpace' in Groningen, 'Precare' in Brussels (Jorg 2008), 'k.e.i.m.' in Basle, and 'Coopolis' and 'Stattbau' in Berlin (SenStadt 2007, Blumner 2006).

For government planners, temporary uses of urban spaces by the creative industries can support the development of innovative planning strategies and policies in three distinct ways: as stimulus, delivery mechanism, or goal. As an inspiration or need for planning, temporary uses 'can stimulate the creative process of urban design' (Bornmann et al 2008: 18), by suggesting new combinations of uses and end-user groups and demonstrating alternative physical development potentials. Temporary uses also inspire a rethinking of planning processes through a creative understanding of how development happens, particularly in terms of the engagement of a wide variety of actors in decision-making and risk-sharing (Schwarting and Overmeyer 2008). Because creative use projects on brownfield sites are often interdisciplinary, they require interdisciplinary action and policies from local governments (Becker 2010). The complexity of creative temporary uses tends to necessitate the development of innovative forms of supervision, mediation or 'brokering' between and among government agencies, property owners and site users, and to inspire raised levels of citizen engagement in the planning and execution of projects (BMVBS/BBR 2008, BBR 2004).

The temporary use literature sees creative temporary uses as a conceptual inspiration for planning. The literature also sees planning's harnessing of temporary uses as a practical tool through which it can shape and test longer-term options for planning processes, regulations and physical development. Creative uses' typical attributes - small scale, low capital investment, flexibility and orientation toward rapid, high-visibility outcomes — mean that they provide a relatively cheap, low-risk, constrained, but also extendable way of bringing innovations into urban planning. They present opportunities for cities to try out new policies and management approaches for urban development. Such 'laboratories' or 'test phases' develop the competence of various actors, including the government itself, and build trust between them (Becker 2010, Bürgin 2010, Waldis 2009). In addition to being 'truffle pigs' for later investors (Lange 2007b: 136), artists are thus also guinea pigs for planners.

The two drivers of planning innovation outlined above can be applied in pursuit of many different planning goals, and the promotion of many kinds of land use, whether temporary or long-lasting. Although existing literature seldom identifies tools and policies that are focused on facilitating temporary creative industry tenancies specifically, suitable instruments appear to include giving creative users advice, financial support, preferential access to sites and providing detailed databases of available sites (SenStadt 2007, Böhme et al 2006). Oft-mentioned is the desirability of user- and goal-oriented 'one-stop-shops' (Schwarting and Overmeyer 2008) where potential temporary users — many of whom have little experience with the world of urban development and its regulation — can get advice and acquit the many necessary permissions; or of interdepartmental working groups to facilitate local government approvals for temporary projects (Schlegelmilch 2009). As mentioned above, new non-governmental mediators have also sprung into existence to occupy this interface, often with a normative orientation toward encouraging fledgling uses.

Healey (2004) notes that creative approaches to governance can help to foster a more creative society. But many analysts doubt the capacity of formal, 'top-down' planning and its tools to be creative and proactively supportive of creative temporary uses. Groth and Corijn (2005:521) note that the creative temporary uses of urban wastelands contrast with the lack of imagination and creativity shown by long-range, large-scale planning that has allowed such wastelands to arise in the first place: 'creative environments do not spring into being as a result of top-down measures ... they occur in the temporary lack of planning'. Similarly, Larsen et al (2011:88) suggest 'a possible alternative to the conscious design for creativity[:] ... sometimes creative practices emerge in the spaces that only wait for future development ... sometimes the temporarily empty spaces make room for surprising innovations that otherwise would not emerge'.

Bishop and Williams (2012) note that creative uses are difficult to create 'top-down' because these uses are themselves intrinsically 'bottom up'; the most important prerequisites are cheap rents, flexible spaces, and freedom from constraints. In keeping with Jacobs' (1961) theorisation of the role of old buildings in ensuring city diversity, it is the absence of commercial attention to urban spaces that allows new, creative actors, who have different, risky ideas and who are not purely motivated by profit, to inhabit and operate in run-down parts of the city, and thereby contribute to the processes of re-imagining, re-using and re-developing these areas. Becker (2010) suggests that the spontaneous, unplanned, short-term uniqueness of temporary creative uses is at odds with planning's general focus on fixed long-term visions. He argues that the emphasis needs to be on processual aspects: local governments showing openness to experiment; setting a clear basic framework of roles that creative actors can play, to provide clarity and certainty to their efforts; and 'creative support', rather than control, through new, flexible 'instruments of liberation and toleration' (Becker 2010: 81).

Hall's (1998) emphasis on the importance of exchanges between cultural, intellectual, artistic and managerial creativity highlights that innovations in the practices of the various actors are connected: their interactions stimulate their creativity. But these interactions are not necessarily smooth and cooperative. In the case of Zurich's railyards, creative temporary use was apparently inspired dialectically, through opposition to the interests of planners, government and the property industry: 'the erstwhile forbidden nature of the former industrial zones and the illegal appropriation of many factories was part of the subculture that established itself [there] against speculation, discrimination and exploitation and in favour of alternative culture' (Angst et al. 2009:32). The way that the temporary users engaged with regulation and order in this case also lent itself to creativity and difference within the outcomes. Colomb (2012b) points to fundamental tensions between the increasing profitability and marketability of successful temporary leisure uses of urban sites, government policies that rigidly prescribe the desirable range of creative temporary uses, and the great wealth of informal, experimental, often unconventional practices, not all of which can achieve political or economic traction.

Creativity Unleashed: Governing Temporary Uses

This closing section examines what implications the contemporary emphasis on creativity in the production, consumption and planning of temporary uses is seen to have for the role and form of planning in shaping urban redevelopment and local economic activity. In broad terms, the temporary use literature suggests the desirability of liberalisation of both economic activity and strategic decision-making, by encouraging the participation of a wider range of small-scale private investors, producers, and consumers. More diverse inputs and less regulations imply the introduction of new ideas and approaches.

The emphasis within recent analyses of temporary uses in European cities such as Berlin, on the key role of pioneering, artistic individuals who revitalise urban spaces and define new leisure lifestyles for highly mobile urban residents, has ample parallels to earlier waves of gentrification that have been documented in post-industrial New York and London (Colomb 2012a, Zukin 1982, Hamnett 2003, Pratt 2009). Creative actors are portrayed within the context of a 'new frontier' that demands self-sufficiency, initiative, and independent action (Ferreri 2015, Smith 1996). Both artists and the unused spaces they discover and transform are seen as among 'the few remaining pools of untapped resources' that define this particular frontier (Colomb 2012a: 244). Successful exploitation of such opportunities rests on governments allowing and encouraging mobile, creative minds to rush to these new goldfields of symbolic capital. Temporary artistic uses of urban space fit well with neoliberal demands:

> informal, spontaneous [temporary uses] ... whose primary characteristic is the use of available urban, programmatic, economic open spaces ... also have other features that make them perfectly compatible with the neo-liberal economy, from shifting risk to individuals to accelerating the use of space.
> (Pogoreutz 2006:79)

> Persons engaged in the cultural sector and temporary users coincide with the current principle of short, fast utilisation cycles ... the frameworks of both temporary use and subculture activities demand the same characteristics as contemporary entrepreneurial thinking: flexibility, cost-consciousness, environmental friendliness, efficiency, innovation, contemporary thinking, connectedness and liberality.
>
> (Erismann 2011:23)

Temporary artistic uses of derelict urban sites can be seen as a case of post-Fordist production: exploiting the niche of these amortised property investments; accelerating their recommodification; optimising their economic potential by enhancing their variegation and cultivating new consumer groups; distributed networking of production; and minimal capital outlays on construction and infrastructure, focusing instead on 'mediatisation' of the product, which gives urban space the status of a service or an event (Ioannides and Debbage 1997, Gale 2009), or a piece of software that users can 'populate and repurpose' (Bishop and Williams 2012:188). This process of renewing exchange value is best achieved if there is a reduction of structural rigidities in the property and labour markets and in land use regulations (Haydn and Temel 2006, Tonkiss 2013). Urban Catalyst (2001) note that in parallel to economic forces and technological development, two other significant causes of long-term vacancy of urban sites are the political and bureaucratic inertia of the planning system and misjudgement of the demand for particular uses. Economic liberalisation is thus seen to lie at the core of the phenomenon of creative temporary uses. This liberalisation also brings about the more rapid and widespread availability of sites for temporary occupation, by accelerating the amortisation of existing investments in land (Oswalt 2002, MA18 2003). The dynamics and diversity of disinvested urban spaces stimulate artistic creativity, which in turn serves consumers' rapacious desire for novel products (Bishop and Williams 2012).

The creative governance approaches that the literature identifies as appropriate for entrepreneurial temporary uses cover a spectrum of levels of agency, from permissiveness through facilitation to direct participation. 'Creative' planning for temporary uses often appears to mean less planning, allowing more flexibility in land use, construction, and risk management. One proposed strategy is increased toleration (in German, *Geduld*) of temporary projects, even when they have no formal planning permission. Such a stance implies that a creative re-use is recognised as being somehow beneficial, even when it falls outside the framework of the local government's and landlord's understandings of their own objectives and interests, or when it is technically illegal (SenStadt 2007, Ebert and Kunzmann 2007, Dransfeld and Lehmann 2008). Such judgments depend on careful distinctions and calibrations between short-term and long-term benefits and negative impacts, and the availability of alternative mechanisms to measure and control these. Prevention of temporary uses that are undoubtedly undesirable is acknowledged as an important tool in ensuring that sites remain available for other potential temporary uses that might offer more benefits (SenStadt 2007). Cases have been documented where tolerated uses later receive sanction, and even eventually permanent permission (BMVBS/BBR 2008). But a strategy of tolerance brings into question the relevance, predictability and consistency of the entire planning process. The question also arises as to if or how the potential benefits and impacts that a discovered temporary use has on its site and surroundings might be assessed, and by whom, if not through standard planning approvals.

Policies and studies identify a range of creative technical instruments that can be deployed to govern temporary uses, include specification of temporary uses for particular locations within local development, land-use and redevelopment plans, and permits for so-called 'flying buildings' which, once approved, can be relocated repeatedly, with time restrictions on any given site. Several other tools remain rather new and untested in the German context: uses that are permitted 'as of right' without the need for inspections and permits, the granting of time-limited and conditional planning permissions, and the revocation of existing permissions when a building is demolished or a longstanding use ceases, as a way of opening up spaces for other short-term use options (SenStadt 2007). Many of these tools illustrate planning and its instruments themselves becoming more temporary, focused on fine-tuning of current, localised performance outcomes instead of defining general long-term certainties. Such creative approaches are potentially complex, resource-intensive, disruptive and imperfect, but as Healey (2004: 98) notes, 'risky, experimental governance requires some redundancy (short-term inefficiencies) and learns from failure as well as success'. As noted earlier, the understood justification for operational risks and potential failures is the potential capacity of creative uses to increase land value, enhance local quality of life, and reform planning approaches themselves. As also already noted, the limited temporal and spatial scope of these experiments also constrains their risks.

The literature identifies a range of proactive roles that governments can play, which include supporting, commissioning, financing, partnering, and marketing temporary uses. The creative potential of planning to facilitate temporary use includes 'financial and creative enthusiasm for investment' (Kruse and Steglich 2006: 17). This suggests a characteristically neoliberal coupling of subsidies and deregulation. Planning's encouragement of temporary uses of urban spaces by creative actors fits the wider neoliberal shift from stable government-led urban service provision and regulation to flexible, facilitative governance, and increasing reliance upon entrepreneurial efforts and short-term, footloose private investments (Blumner 2006, Groth and Corijn 2005). In a time of reduced public spending, the vision of artists as 'entrepreneurial self-starters' and 'role models for a neoliberal society' is not without its problems (Lange 2007b: 142). These actors carry significant costs and risks; relatively few reap great rewards from success, and successful exploitation of an urban area forces out unsuccessful artists who cannot afford increasing rents. Ebert and Kunzmann (2007) suggest that policy may seek to improve the sustainability of certain clusters of creative industries in the face of gentrification, through careful policy choices such as controlling uses and rents, with particular attention to whether, which, and over what time frame such precincts might maintain a role in nurturing new, experimental practices and enterprises.

The academic and policy literature identifies a wide scope of roles and modes through which the public sector can shape temporary use projects so as to provide public benefits and minimise negative impacts; this extends well beyond traditional adversarial regulation. Governance of temporary uses is in numerous cases also enacted cooperatively by the public sector as one of many actors within a complex network. The public sector is also often landlord, manager, funder, guarantor, and/or provider of goods, services, staff and expertise for temporary uses, and therefore contractual agreements provide significant scope for steering or hindering the development and operation of those activities in the public interest. Creative planning does not inevitably mean not planning. Dransfeld and Lehmann (2008: 72) suggest that creative production should not go unregulated. To prevent temporary creative uses from unexpectedly becoming permanent and displacing envisaged long-term uses, they argue that governments and landlords should develop 'creative shackles': contractual agreements between landlords, users and other stakeholders to consensually define targeted scopes and timeframes for temporary uses. Rather than just holding out carrots or sticks, planning can thus act creatively to govern temporary uses by wearing different hats, negotiating complex relationships, and developing new frameworks. This area of practice illustrates Healey's argument that governance is not incompatible with creativity:

> too much risk and uncertainty may inhibit creative responses ... This implies that governance processes which seek to encourage creativity and innovation ... need to perform a delicate 'trick' of taking risks themselves in order to lessen the risks and uncertainties for others ... Over-management ... destroys more capacity than it builds.
>
> (Healey 2004:91)

Conclusion

Recent calls to support creativity through planning also often advocate more creativity in planning, which typically means more permissive approaches that tolerate more varied land-use activities and that help to identify and support a wider range of goals for a greater range of actors. The kinds of urban development actors and interests identified in this chapter were often undervalued or excluded by earlier planning practices. The key traits of creativity and temporariness point toward groups of actors – artists, ethnic minorities, young people – who typically have neither the political nor economic power to see their interests prevail in ordinary property markets or through standard urban development practices (Ferreri 2015).

The discourse of creativity tends to suggest an emphasis on use rather than on built form, even when the practices in question also often involve creative reinterpretation and transformation of the urban fabric. The focus of attention has moved away from pre-defined physical visions, and toward the processes and impacts of urban development. One line of thinking about the role of creative temporary uses in urban planning suggests that such practices are not merely a new and powerful mechanism for urban development, but that creative, artistic practice can be a new way to stimulate public engagement and critical reflection on urban development and economic activity, by experimenting with alternative ways of understanding and using urban space (Mould 2014, Novy and Colomb 2013, Tonkiss 2013, Till 2011).

Calls to introduce new forms of planning to control new and untested temporary land uses are today greatly exceeded by demands for more permissive and experimental planning tools that free up the unrealised potential of creative actors. The emergence and spread of temporary use thinking in the German-speaking world appear to not only reflect the decline of former urban industrial areas (which is less prevalent in Austria and Switzerland than in Germany) but also to respond to the particular rigidities of German-style planning systems (Honeck 2017). Andres and Golubchikov (2016) draw on case studies in Francophone Switzerland and Russia to note that not all cities have, or seek to nurture, short-term or long-term clusters of creative industries in abandoned areas. Different cities experience quite different alignments and trajectories of economics, industry, culture, spaces and governance. Creative, temporary uses of spaces can thus have varied relationships to government policy and to longer-term gentrification, industrial activity and property development outcomes.

The core conceptual connection that has been drawn between temporary use and creative industries would appear to be twofold: artistic people are good at adapting how they work to new spaces that lack tenants, and they are good at enhancing those spaces. But even when viewed positively, conceptually conjoining creative enterprise and temporary tenancy implies that creativity remains economically precarious and expendable (Tonkiss 2013, Mould 2014). If the ultimate goal for many creative workers is long-term employment, that should also be the goal of public policy. In this context, policy tools such as 'creative shackles' can potentially benefit these ostensibly precious creative workers by clarifying how particular temporary use arrangements align to their own long-term visions and needs.

References

Andres, L. and Golubchikov, O. (2016) The limits to artist-led regeneration: Creative Brownfields in the cities of high culture. *International Journal of Urban and Regional Research* 40 (4): 757–75.

Andres, L. and Grésillon, B. (2013) Cultural brownfields in European cities: A new mainstream object for cultural and urban policies. *International Journal of Cultural Policy* 19 (1): 40–62.

Angst, M., Klaus, P., Michaelis, T., Müller, R. and Wolff, R. (2009) *Zone*imaginaire: Zwischennutzungen in Industriearealen*, Zürich: Vdf Hochschulverlag.

BBR (Bundesamt für Bauwesen und Raumordnung) (2004) *Zwischennutzung und neue Freiflächen –städtische Lebensräume der Zukunft*, Berlin: H. Heenemann.

Becker, C. (2010) Kreativwirtschaft als Chance der Brachflächenreaktivierung, in F. Dosch and S. Glöckner (eds), *Neue Zugänge zum Flächenrecycling (Informationen zur Raumplanung 1/2010)*, Bonn: Bundesamt für Bauwesen und Raumordnung, pp. 71–82.

Bengs, C., Hentilä, H. and Nagy, D. (2002). *Urban catalysts: Strategies for temporary uses – Potential for development of urban residual areas in European metropolises*, Espoo: Centre for Urban and Regional Studies Helsinki University of Technology.

Bishop, P. and Williams, L. (2012) *The temporary city*, New York: Routledge.

Blumner, N. (2006) *Planning for the unplanned: Tools and techniques for interim use in Germany and the United States*, Berlin: Deutsches Institut für Urbanistik.

BMVBS/BBR (Bundesministerium für Verkehr, Bau und Stadtentwicklung and Bundesamt für Bauwesen und Raumordnung) (eds) (2008) *Zwischennutzungen und Nischen im Städtebau als Beitrag für eine nachhaltige Stadtentwicklung*, Bonn: BBR.

Böhme, C., Henckel, D. and Besecke, A. (2006) *Brachflächen in der Flächenkreislaufwirtschaft*, Berlin: Bundesamt für Bauwesen und Raumordnung.

Bornmann, F., Erbelding, D. and Froessler D. (2008) *Zwischennutzungen: Temporäre Nutzungen als Instrument der Stadtentwicklung*, Düsseldorf: Innovationsagentur Stadtumbau NRW.

Brammer, M. (2008) Zwischennutzung in Berlin Neukölln: Kreativwirtschaft als Motor in einem sozial benachteiligten Binnenquartier. *Standort – Zeitschrift für Angewandte Geographie*, 32: 71–77.

Bürgin, M. (2010) *Leitfaden Zwischennutzung*, [online] available at: http://www.zwischennutzung.areale.ch/images/pdf_D/varianten/pdf_alle_bsp_d.pdf (accessed 22 August 2017).

Bürgin, M. and Cabane, P. (1999) Akupunktur für Basel: Zwischennutzung als Standortentwicklung auf dem Areal des DB-Güterbahnhofs in Basel, [online] available at: http://www.areal.org/areal_alt/download/zn_mb.pdf (accessed 11 April 2012).

Chang, R. (2021) How do scholars communicate the 'temporary turn' in urban studies? A socio-semiotic framework. *Urban Planning* 6 (1): 133–45.

Colomb, C. (2007) Requiem for a lost Palast. Revanchist urban planning and burdened landscapes of the German Democratic Republic in the new Berlin. *Planning Perspectives* 22 (3): 283–323.

Colomb, C. (2012a) *Staging the New Berlin: Place marketing and the politics of urban re-invention Post-1989*, London: Routledge.

Colomb, C. (2012b) Pushing the urban frontier: Temporary uses of space, city marketing, and the creative city discourse in 2000s Berlin. *Journal of Urban Affairs* 34 (2): 131–52.

Deslandes, A. (2013) Exemplary amateurism: Thoughts on DIY urbanism. *Cultural Studies Review* 19 (1): 216–27.

Dienel, H. and Schophaus, M. (2005) Urban wastelands and the development of youth cultures in Berlin since 1945, with comparative perspectives on Amsterdam and Naples, in A. Schildt and D. Siegfried (eds), *European cities, youth and the public sphere in the twentieth century*, Aldershot: Ashgate, pp. 119–33.

Dransfeld, E. and Lehmann, D. (2008) *Temporäre Nutzungen als Bestandteil des modernen Baulandmanagements*, Dortmund: Forum Baulandmanagement NRW.

Ebert, R. and Kunzmann, K. (2007) Kulturwirtschaft, kreative Räume und Stadtentwicklung in Berlin. *DisP - The Planning Review* 43 (171): 64–79.

Erismann, E. (2011) *Temporary use during Kleinhüningen's harbour renewal process: A case study of characteristics, opportunities and tools for successful implementation*, unpublished masters thesis, University of Applied Sciences Northwestern Switzerland.

Ferreri, M. (2015) The seductions of temporary urbanism. *Ephemera: Theory and Politics in Organization*, 15 (1): 181–191.

Florida, R. (2002) *The rise of the creative class and how it is transforming work, leisure, community and everyday life*, New York: Basic Books.

Gale, T. (2009) Urban beaches, virtual worlds and the end of tourism. *Mobilities* 4 (1): 119–38.

Groth, J. and Corijn, E. (2005) Reclaiming urbanity: Indeterminate spaces, informal actors and urban agenda setting. *Urban Studies* 42 (3): 503–26.

Hall, P. (1998) *Cities in civilization: Culture, innovation, and urban order*, London: Weidenfeld and Nicolson.

Hamnett, C. (2003) Gentrification and the middle-class remaking of inner London, 1961 -2001. *Urban Studies* 40 (12): 2401–426.

Havemann, A. and Schild, W. (2007) You can use my tights or: The phenomenon of temporary solutions. *Landscape Research* 32 (1): 45–55.

Haydn, F. and Temel, R. (eds) (2006) *Temporary urban spaces: Concepts for the use of city spaces*, Basel: Birkhäuser.

Healey, P. (2004) Creativity and urban governance. *Policy Studies* 25 (2): 87–102.

Henneberry, J. (ed) (2017) *Transience and permanence in urban development*, Hoboken, NJ: Wiley Blackwell.

Honeck, T. (2017) From squatters to creatives: An innovation perspective on temporary use in planning. *Planning Theory and Practice* 18 (2): 268–87.

Ioannides, D. and Debbage, K. (1997) Post-Fordism and flexibility: The travel industry polyglot. *Tourism Management* 18 (4): 229–41.

Jacobs, J. (1961) *The death and life of great American cities*, New York: Random House.

Jorg, J. (2008) *Make use: A comparison between temporary-use strategies of intermediary organizations with the goal of using vacant buildings as workplaces for social and creative entrepreneurs*, unpublished masters thesis, POLIS MA in European Urban Cultures, Amsterdam/Brussels.

Klanten, R. and Hübner, M. (eds) (2010) *Urban interventions: Personal projects in public spaces*, Berlin: Gestalten.

Kloos, M., Knüvener, T. and Wachten, K. (2007) *Freiräume auf Zeit: Neue Konzepte für Grünflächen in Stadterneuerungsgebieten*, Aachen: Internationales Institut für Gartenkunst und Landschaftskultur Schloss Dyck.

Krauzick, M. (2007) *Zwischennutzung als Initiator einer neuen Berliner Identität?*, Berlin: Universitätsverlag der TU Berlin.

Kreuzer, S. (2001) Temporäre Freiräume: Szenarischer Replik zum Vortrag des Soziologen Peter Arlt. *Zolltexte* 38: 18–19.

Kruse, S. and Steglich, A. (2006) *Temporäre Nutzungen: Stadtgestalt zwischen Selbstorganisation und Steuerung*, Lüneburg: Fakultät III – Umwelt und Technik, Universität Lüneburg.

Landry, C. and Bianchini, F. (1995) *The creative city*, London: Demos.

Lange, B. (2007a) *Die Räume der Kreativszenen. Culturepreneurs und ihre Orte in Berlin*, Bielefeld: Transcript.

Lange, B. (2007b) Entrepreneurial temporary use: An incubator for the creative economy, in SenStadt (ed), *Urban pioneers: Temporary use and urban development in Berlin*, Berlin: Jovis, pp. 135–42.

Lange, B. (2008) Accessing markets in creative industries: Professionalization and social-spatial strategies of culturepreneurs in Berlin. *Creative Industries Journal* 1 (2): 115–35.

Larsen, J. L., Elle, M., Hoffmann, B. and Munthe-Kaas, P. (2011) Urbanising facilities management: The challenges in a creative age. *Facilities* 29 (1-2): 80–92.

MA18 (Magistratsabteilung 18 Stadtentwicklung und Stadtplanung, Stadt Wien) (2003) *Urban catalyst: Strategien für temporäre Nutzungen – Entwicklungspotentiale für urbane Residualflächen in europäischen Metropolen; Amsterdam –Berlin –Helsinki –Neapel –Wien*, Vienna: City of Vienna.

Mould, O. (2014) Tactical urbanism: The new vernacular of the creative city. *Geography Compass* 8 (8): 529–39.

Novy, J. and Colomb, C. (2013) Struggling for the right to the (creative) city in Berlin and Hamburg: New urban social movements, new 'spaces of hope'?. *International Journal of Urban and Regional Research* 37 (5): 1816–38.

Oswalt, P. (2002) Die Stadt stimulieren: Standortentwicklung mit kapitalschwachen Akteuren und temporären Programmen. *Werk, Bauen, Wohnen* 6: 44–49.

Pogoreutz, M. (2006) Urban Intelligence, in F. Haydn and R. Temel (eds) *Temporary urban spaces: Concepts for the use of city spaces*, Basel: Birkhäuser, pp. 75–80.

Pratt, A. C. (2009) Urban regeneration: From the arts feel good factor to the cultural economy: A case study of Hoxton, London. *Urban Studies* 46 (5–6): 1041–61.

RAW München (Referat für Arbeit und Wirtschaft, Landeshauptstadt München) (2007) *München – Standortfaktor Kreativität*, Munich: Referat für Arbeit und Wirtschaft.

Rosic, N. and Froessler, D. (2009) *Leerstandsmanagement: Konzeptpapier zur Durchführung eines Leerstandsmanagements in Steinheim*, Düsseldorf: Innovationsagentur Stadtumbau NRW.

Schlegelmilch, F. (2009) Zwischennutzen – leichter gesagt als getan. *Informationen zur Raumentwicklung* 7: 493–502.

Schwarting, H. and Overmeyer, K. (2008) *Suboptimale Nutzungen lieben lernen: Eine Schlüsselstrategie der integrierten Stadtentwicklung*, Wiesbaden: Hessisches Ministerium für Wirtschaft, Verkehr und Landesentwicklung.

SenStadt (Senatsverwaltung für Stadtentwicklung Berlin) (ed) (2007) *Urban pioneers: Temporary use and urban development in Berlin*, Berlin: Jovis.

Smith, N. (1996) *The new urban frontier: Gentrification and the Revanchist city*, New York: Routledge.

Till, K. (2011) Interim use at a former death strip? Art, politics and urbanism at Skulpturenpark Berlin Zentrum, in M. Silberman (ed), *After the wall: Berlin in Germany and Europe*, New York: Palgrave Macmillan, pp. 99–122.

Tonkiss, F. (2013) Austerity urbanism and the makeshift city. *City* 17 (3): 313–24.

Urban Catalyst (2001) *Analysis report Berlin study draft*, Berlin: Technische Universität Berlin.

Urban Catalyst (Philipp Oswalt, Philipp Misselwitz, Klaus Overmeyer) (2007) Patterns of the Unplanned, in K. Franck and Q. Stevens (eds), *Loose space: Possibility and diversity in urban life*, Abingdon, UK: Routledge, pp. 271–88.

Urban Unlimited (eds) (2004) *The shadow city, freezones in Brussels and Rotterdam*, Rotterdam: Urban Unlimited.

Waldis, S. (2009) *Zwischennutzung urbaner Brachflächen und Nachhaltigkeit: Theoretisches Konzept zur Verbindung von Zwischennutzungen und Nachhaltigkeit*, Unpublished masters thesis, University of Basel.

Willinger, S. (2005) Leerstand als Möglichkeitsraum. Urbanistische Strategien zur Revitalisierung in den Innenstädten. *Informationen zur Raumentwicklung, 6*: 397–407.

Zukin, S. (1982) *Loft living: Culture and capital in urban change*, Baltimore: Johns Hopkins University Press.

Chapter Six
Temporality

Quentin Stevens

Temporary Exemptions
Maintaining the Myth of Transience
Temporariness as Opportunity
Durable but Mutable
Assembling New Actors
Temporary Uses Seen in Two Temporal Perspectives
The Benefits of the Temporary
Conclusion

A key question underlying many of the themes explored in this book is if, and how, temporary urbanism is really any different from regular urbanism. This chapter examines what is special about temporariness as a concept and a productive force within current urban planning and design practice.

Cities rise and cities fall, as do skyscrapers, freeways, and open space designs. All urban spaces are more-or-less impermanent assemblages of materials, people, technologies and concepts. All of them can be, and eventually are, disassembled. Nothing lasts forever. Time is always a factor in the city's development, whether people consider time in terms of temporariness, 'design life', planned obsolescence, amortisation, land banking, or long-term visions; and time is always limited. Jacobs et al. (2012: 128) suggest that rather than reifying the built environment as a fixed reality, we should consider even the largest and ostensibly most permanent built forms as a series of 'building events' which are 'always being "made" or "unmade", always doing the work of holding together or pulling apart', and which in all cases eventually come to an end. From this perspective, the ontology of built form is flattened, even in a temporal sense. Built form is itself constantly changed. The city's physical changes also influence a myriad of other decisions and actions.

What is distinctive about the current trend of 'temporary' uses and 'temporary' physical interventions in urban spaces is that they are consciously conceived and presented as being very temporary. Recognition and constant reinforcement of their very limited duration are crucial to their coming-to-be, what they are, and how they work. This chapter uses Assemblage Thinking and Actor-Network Theory to explore the contemporary idea and practice of temporary use. The chapter emphasises that time is not just a passive backdrop against which the city is built. Time is an actant: its properties materially influence other actants that it comes into contact with. Its speed, its texture and its durations all influence other actors in the city, shaping what they want and what they do. Temporariness is an actor with specific aims, needs and effects, which define specific kinds of 'building events'.

One major strand of recent research into temporary uses has focused on how influential they are in cities' development, pointing to their long-term impacts, as catalysts for lasting changes to spaces and to their planning, development and management processes (Oswalt et al. 2013; Lydon and Garcia 2015). That focuses on temporariness creating something permanent. This chapter seeks to overcome such a valorisation of duration. It explores how, within short-term urban design projects, temporariness creates, extends and stabilises specific networks of making and care, and relationships to other actors and forces, without necessarily fixing these for a long time. The chapter explores how the labelling of particular transformations and uses of urban spaces as 'temporary' can be a means of making them immutable, by durably aligning and associating these urban design projects with a network of other actors, forces and interests, assembling a set of relationships that support, stabilise, defend and rely on it. Before, during, and after the existence of a temporary use, people, regulations and materials are won over to its benefits. Its temporariness helps it to resist challenges.

This view may initially seem paradoxical. Temporary uses and tactical actions are typically presented and reified as ways of loosening up urban spaces and urban development processes. They are argued to help in ending droughts of capital flow, sidestepping burdensome regulations, overcoming bureaucratic inertia, and breaking existing legal deadlocks. They seem to be oriented toward change, and counteracting other urban practices and policies that are seen as rigid, slow and outdated (Lydon and Garcia 2015). But like any urban design initiative, temporary uses gain power and develop 'traction' by becoming aligned with a range of agents and forces that support them. These actors can include concrete and bolts, but also land titles, planning ordinances, market demand and ideas.

Temporary use projects create new relationships among actors that allow resources to flow in new ways for a certain period of time. There are other examples of new assemblages of actors which have changed how built environments are produced and maintained, most of which are long-term. For example, BOOT (build, own, operate and transfer) projects, and leaseback contracts for public assets such as infrastructure, shift the allocations of investment, management, risk and benefit among institutional actors such as governments and pension funds, restructuring the traditional relationships between the ownership and use of 'public' infrastructure. These contracts provide desired long-term certainty for built form, use and flows of resources (Walker et al. 2000). Temporary uses, in contrast, provide a desired certainty that arrangements are *not* fixed over the long term. This enables the involvement of new actors who, for varied reasons, only want to, or only can, make shorter-term commitments. In the case of temporary uses, short-term use of commonplace materials such as shipping containers, forklift pallets and potted plants makes it possible for the owners of these materials to rent them cheaply (or to freely loan them), because they can still be recovered, re-rented or sold afterwards with a similar form and value. They are not consumed; nor are they bound into durable assemblages such as concrete or ecosystems. In many cases, neighbours of temporary uses tolerate them (and thereby help authorise them) precisely because they are temporary, and thus their external impacts are finite, allowing neighbours to arrange their own actions and spaces to manage those impacts. This contrasts with permanent redesigns or uses of an urban site, which often develop strong, durable opposition.

The limited duration of temporary uses also allows alignment to other actors that do desire more long-term relationships, providing them with better control or flexibility over when they finalise their own land-use plans, funding arrangements, and construction activities, and better matching these to fluctuating market needs. For example, temporary uses on vacant industrial properties can cover site holding costs and attract future customers and potential investors during the long years of redevelopment (Oswalt et al. 2013). Madanipour (2017) highlights that temporary uses can be deployed to manage supply and demand for urban space, smoothing the market. In such cases, they are aligned within a long-term trajectory of reinvestment.

Madanipour also points out that time itself is a social construction, an instrument that society created and can use. His analysis emphasises that society expands the resource of time by increasing its speed and multiplication, to increase production. Giedion (1948) shows how the desire to use time efficiently has shaped new assemblages of spaces and human activities through mechanisation, dictating the organisation and coordination of the actions of individuals, groups, machines and spaces, initially in factory assembly lines, and subsequently on farms and in the home kitchen. Traffic lights, transport planning, spatial programming, 'office hours' and 'hot desking' all illustrate ways that ideas about the correct and limited time necessary for various human activities shape the production, form and use of urban space. While cities and city life are not entirely mechanised, an aversion to allowing spaces, capital and labour to lie idle guides the arrangement and duration of all manner of actors and activities. But time can also be partitioned to protect it from such forces. Temporary uses also show how the fragmentation of time can create distinctive opportunities for social and material arrangements other than those delivered by the conventional urban property market.

Temporary Exemptions

Society constructs and manages time to suit its needs. But seen from the opposite perspective, specific time frames navigate their way through social arrangements, forming more-durable or less-durable relationships. For example, structures and uses of urban spaces which only exist for short periods of time are typically exempted from the dreaded 'red tape': assessment against requirements for health and safety, structural integrity, durability, accessibility, intensity (including waste management and noise limits), and from other controls on quality, including visual aesthetics. Temporary uses can thus also avoid all of the investments in risk management that necessarily go along with these requirements. If a temporary use looks bad, does not work, or fails economically, it does not matter much, because it will be gone soon enough. Making a spatial event 'temporary' may even allow it, and the other actors that constitute it, to be exempted from established political responsibilities (for example, to follow decision-making processes that are accountable, transparent and fair) and from economic commitments on rent, utilities, salaries and taxes.

Temporary use, as a legitimating basis for government approval or toleration of urban construction and land uses, often operates within – indeed, creates – a state of exemption which can be likened to Agamben's (2005) state of exception, the suspending of normal laws. Agamben argues that the state of exception, which was meant to be a provisional arrangement, has in fact been normalised as a way of governing. Similarly, local governments, along with a range of other human actors, have enabled 'temporary use' to become a normal paradigm for governing urban space, for planning. As argued in Chapter 2 and evidenced in Chapter 3, rather than focussing on fostering long-term investments and certainty, formal planning processes worldwide have begun to support short-term innovation and transformation. The acute but changing demands of combatting the COVID-19 pandemic have increased the exercise and extent of emergency powers, and accelerated this shift to short-term, reactive planning.

Just as with the state of emergency, support for temporary uses has been constituted by planners, economists, realtors and others as a political necessity, as something required by contemporary economic and social conditions, which renders traditional planning processes and instruments useless and invalid (Oswalt et al. 2013). As Haid (2017) notes in a study of informal food vending practices in Berlin's parks, it is the powerful actors of the state who have chosen to enable these new short-term flexibilities, to 'neoliberalise' planning. They have done this to enable and empower informal actors to help meet the government's strategic objectives in times of reduced tax revenues (to provide amenities and jobs for residents, prevent urban land lying fallow and declining in value and attracting more serious crime). In addition, the state enables new ways of policing and controlling activities (outside existing frameworks) that might otherwise become 'too successful': activities that might lead to negative impacts, actors gathering too much power around themselves, or a loss of government control. Beyes (2009) and Färber (2014) similarly document entrepreneurial reorganisations of urban land uses and governance processes in Berlin and Hamburg which enable – indeed, require – rapid change. As it proceeds, this temporalised, flexible, precarious governance of urban space disassembles the existing relationships that have traditionally been used to 'fix' the city: land, labour, capital, knowledge and power. Temporary use creates new relationships among actors that allow resources to flow in new ways for a certain period of time. In a broader sense, it also disassembles existing understandings of urban land uses and of city development as being permanent. Defining urban actions as temporary is a conscious governance strategy of de-linking certain urban spaces and certain material and behavioural conditions from the strictures that have conventionally been imposed by the long-term assemblage of the planned, managed city. This is a necessary step for them to subsequently be enrolled into other realms of practice.

As Chapter 2 noted, whether temporary uses are intended to catalyse definite long-term plans or to stimulate innovation, they seem well-adapted to neoliberal urban development, with its uneven, boom-bust cycles of creative destruction, its loosening of regulations and its public support for private entrepreneurship (Tonkiss 2013). Temporary urbanism is often deployed top-down by governments to achieve strategic outcomes. But it can be seen as a neoliberal outsourcing of government functions to potentially less-representative, less-accountable organisations. The emphasis on short-term, do-it-yourself planning may signal a long-term retreat of the state from producing and managing public spaces. Temporary, experimental, entrepreneurial initiatives are not always transparent, accountable or socially equitable. They may be new forms of uneven development that facilitates some citizens' interests better than others.

Maintaining the Myth of Transience

The contours of a broad, socially constructed ontology of transience in urban development are sketched out by Schwarzer (1994), who presents this in diametrical contrast to historic preservation. Historic preservation, Schwarzer notes, defines and enacts a 'myth of permanence' in the built environment, by choosing to exempt certain built forms from the economic threat of demolition, the ravages of time, and from ongoing accretions and modifications. As a form of recorded history, preservation of certain aspects of the built environment can reinforce the allegiance of individuals and spaces to a particular definition of nationhood, and thus reproduce power relations, and actively resist change. Schwarzer counterpoints this to an antagonistic myth of transience, which valorises dynamism, newness, progress, and the mobility of settlement across the landscape (in his case, westward expansion in Nineteenth-Century America). He notes that 'the vast majority of American built environments are unplanned, haphazard places that grow rapidly and are often as quickly abandoned when times change' (Schwarzer 1994: 6). He connects this to Americans' historically specific 'ideological desires to escape from potentially burdensome ties to either the natural environment or the social community', because 'permanently occupied structures ... represent a tradition of European building relating to feudal social organization and deep-seated public commitments' (Schwarzer 1994: 7). He thus presents the transience of much American (and also, more broadly, Modernist) urban development as an embodiment of individual freedom. While the quest for a mythical permanent order has tended to dominate Western metaphysics, it has its ontological opposite in this Nietzschean philosophy of creative becoming, where everything must be assembled anew. Schwarzer argues, like Jacobs et al. (2012), that historic preservation 'overlooks ... the continual renewal of both buildings and cities, the successive waves of alterations and inhabitants ... the fragmentary and rapidly changing history of the built environment in the modern city' and 'overemphasize[s] the permanence of built culture' (Schwarzer 1994: 8). Traditional urban planning policies have the same tendency to reify and protect existing built form, for example by setting out long-range visions and by limiting changes in built form and land use.

Schwarzer highlights that the actors necessary to preserve built form (values, laws, people, spaces, materials, time frames) must assemble, and that the same is true for the transient spaces of the frontier, which are produced, held open, and when desired, locked down or emptied again, by the strategic alignments of some actors and the suppression or elimination of others. Planning practices, instruments, people and spaces are enrolled in enabling temporary urbanism, just as they are in preserving existing urban form. Dovey and King (2011) note that informal urbanism often has an ambiguous status, between temporary and permanent. Sometimes tenure over space is socially assembled through informal, unofficial equivalents of official rent and title, or through political agreements. These alliances are tactically manipulated to maintain flows of money and political power.

Temporariness as Opportunity

Beauregard's examination of 'Temporalities' in urban planning considers how various forms and conceptions of time that are deployed by various actors 'deeply influence how planning is done' (Beauregard 2015: 152). For example, planners, politicians and financiers choose specific time horizons that influence what urban plans might seek to achieve, and how. But Beauregard's ontology of time is not as flat and open as it could be. He suggests, following Latour (1988), that time is the passage from one moment to the next, that it is defined by moments. Yet he remains wedded to an idea of time as unfolding into the future, of progress; to an idea of planning as changing the long-term future to create a desired, presumably more fixed world, and of time as a teleological unfolding from current causes to future effects. But the rise of temporary uses shows that not all plans and projects are meant to, or able to, change the city permanently. Temporary uses reveal a quite radical notion for urban planning: that there is a time that continues to unfold after the plan, after the project.

In this context, the limited duration of the temporary use, a defined slice of time, has a specific role in gathering other actors around it. Madanipour (2017) identifies three key ways that temporariness in itself creates distinctive economic advantages that encourage and shape short-term transformations and uses of urban spaces. First, the novelty of these uses attracts attention, and often free media coverage. Second, temporary interventions and uses distinguish a site from more permanent competitors offering similar services and can attract new customer groups. Third, brevity is a type of market scarcity that stimulates consumption demand. This is particularly important in economic downturns when consumption slows. A fourth way that temporariness creates opportunities for using urban spaces is implied by Madanipour's observation that public authorities will say yes to unusual proposals and temporarily suspend normal rules and requirements because the use helps them in 'maintaining a degree of tax revenues and the appearance of vibrancy on the streets' (Madanipour 2017: 52). It helps them to maintain flows of people, money and services during temporary economic downturns and vacancies. These same principles essentially hold true for non-commercial temporary interventions, in terms of generating community interest and patronage.

Durable but Mutable

Chapter 4 examined one temporary use: artificial 'city beaches' placed on vacant urban sites. These illustrate a range of ways that short-term transformations of urban spaces, and the assemblages of actors that gather together around them, become durable, and have wider and longer-term impacts on urban space and how it is used and managed (Stevens 2011). Some temporary uses repeat across time, for example by reappearing in the same location each summer or winter. The artificial beach *Paris Plage* was originally conceived and developed as a six-week one-off event, constrained in duration by the summer closure of a section of riverside freeway. Now, the beach's sand is scraped up at the end of each summer and carried away by barge to a storage depot upstream on the Seine and is then brought back and reassembled the following summer. This project thus aligns itself to available transport and storage facilities, and to the calendar cycle, alternating with the seasonal traffic on the riverside freeway (Stevens and Ambler 2010). City beaches also illustrate the spatial translation of a temporary use. They are designed from loose and collapsible elements that can be moved intact from one site to another or replicated across multiple sites.

Chapter 4 showed how the success of short-term city beaches has also led to other wider impacts, by reshaping local government regulations for such uses, working relationships (between the projects' operators, funders, landowners, regulators and consumers), contractual arrangements (for example, with beverage suppliers and music performers) and decision-making processes (Stevens 2011, 2015). These durable shifts have, in turn, shaped other temporary uses, and even permanent ones. For example, a temporary beach in Amsterdam, *Blijburg aan Zee*, was so popular that it forced the city's development corporation to alter the masterplan for the future housing area where it had been introduced as a temporary promotional attraction (Stevens and Ambler 2010). Local residents rallied to help it persist. It displaced other forms of open space that were originally intended to supplant it. The temporary use enmeshed itself with, and transformed, the longer-term form and use of its site and the surrounding district, becoming aligned to other permanent uses and their networks. The artificial beach has in itself become a durable idea, a prototype, even if each use or site is of limited duration.

A second example is the temporary 'parklet', which began as a guerrilla intervention in 2005 in San Francisco by occupying a kerbside car parking space for just two hours and installing a temporary park with grass, potted trees and a bench (Thorpe 2020). Longer-lasting parklets were then installed by cafés starting in 2010. These fit long-term local government strategies to traffic-calm local shopping streets and encourage public socialising. The first parklet in Perth, Australia, was inspired by a successful short-term street festival initiated by a local community organisation that united residents and retailers. The festival stimulated the organisation's engagement with the local government. One young group member, a planning graduate, subsequently joined the council staff and, with the community group's guidance, led the creation of a temporary parklet to demonstrate the potential for a street-side open space and to gather user feedback to refine the concept. That parklet subsequently became a permanent public park that closed part of the street. This sequence of short-term parklet interventions creating social relationships that drove longer-term organisational and spatial changes has been repeated in several other Australian cities. Another Perth parklet, by a different community organisation in a different local government area, was initially supported by the adjacent business, a bookshop, but removed after several months at their request because the parklet's timber pergola obscured their shopfront. The two Perth examples highlight temporary interventions' unique advantage for diverse stakeholders: they disrupt the status quo, but flexibly; allowing rapid testing, refinement, or reversal.

Over recent decades, temporary uses have become a robust, recognised and valued category of land use, one which has both been aligned to, and helped to develop, theories, a related literature, and a set of protagonists and supporters. In all these ways, ostensibly ephemeral land uses can increase their durability by developing alignments to other actors.

Assembling New Actors

Temporary open space projects often attract human actors and develop relationships that build these actors' capacities, opportunities and durability. 'Temporary use' is a concept that has enabled a new range of human actors to engage in 'informalised' urban development and space management processes and to be aligned with resources that were previously restricted to professionally accredited architects and landscape architects. The rise of temporary use has provided a means for a new range of actors – artists, community activists, sociologists, social workers, place makers, place managers and other local custodians of places – to become involved in production, decision-making and management processes for the built environment. This has provided them with new skills and helped develop new relationships and communication between actors that build capacities, trust, opportunities and durability (Lydon and Garcia 2015). It has improved their access to the large, ongoing capital works budgets and grants that were traditionally only available for longer-term, carefully deliberated investments in city building, often without their having to meet existing standards and requirements. Temporary uses are cheaper and show quick impacts, especially visually. This endears them to politicians who are motivated by affecting rapid shifts in the opinions of voters and other stakeholders such as business owners and property investors.

Chapter 5 noted how the recent wave of temporary uses has especially drawn in workers from the various creative industries. They are typically able to start operating at short notice, to quickly identify and respond to the distinctive aesthetic, historical and functional opportunities of sites when they become available, and rapidly add to sites' symbolic, social and economic value. The new and temporary nature of these opportunities to transform sites is believed to help stimulate creative solutions (SenStadt 2007). The impermanence and precarity of these projects have co-evolved alongside the growth of freelance creative workers or 'culturepreneurs' (Lange 2007) who create them: actors who have to divide their work arrangements flexibly between projects, teams and cities. In Berlin, and in many other centres of temporary use, the careers of the individual creative industry workers who produce and consume these temporary spaces have dissolved into a collective of flexibly compartmentalised times and tasks, just as the cities' urban spaces have been subdivided and shared spatially and temporally (Färber 2014). Planning policies often specifically intend that artistic permissiveness on vacant sites should only be temporary and transitional (Andres and Grésillon 2013).

These actors have been able to make themselves into 'obligatory passage points' (Callon 1986) for newly defined 'lighter, quicker, cheaper' urban development processes (PPS 2018) that substitute for, and compete with, the old slow ones: community participation rather than consultation; hands-on making and donations rather than construction and procurement contracts; short-term agreements rather than durable laws; evoking qualitative dynamic atmosphere instead of meeting quantitative standards for quality, durability, sustainability and social inclusion. These actors provide the organisational skills and contacts to quickly bring these assets together for maximum impact, and to disperse them quickly again when no longer needed – often within mere hours if they occupy a floodplain, or weeks if a vacant site finds a buyer.

The short-term arrangements that temporary uses create are able to gather other actors around them and gain power in part because they undermine the power and connections of the existing city and the mythology of its permanence and value. Schwarzer (1994) characterises the transient, open city of the American West in terms of its freedom from the rigid, burdensome, hierarchical and corrupt social and physical constraints of the traditional European city. Today's temporary urbanism is similarly post-structural and non-deterministic; it is a performative critique that enacts and demonstrates the breaking of existing rules, roles and relationships in urbanism, opening up new possibilities and freeing up resources and actors to forge new and flexible alliances (Madanipour 2017). Madanipour suggests that these new alignments of actors define *kairos*, time that is experienced and managed as moments of opportunity, of becoming, which is in contrast to *chronos*, the sense of time as continually, regularly unfolding.

Beauregard's (2015) Actor-Network analysis of the temporalities of planning highlights different time frames within which city plans can be developed and carried out, and the different time horizons for which plans are developed. Both of these temporalities influence the nature of what is being planned and which actors are involved. Beauregard notes that city development is uneven across time. But he remains wedded to the idea that 'time-defining moments must be irreversible. It has to be impossible for the things that have been gathered to be returned to their original states' (Beauregard 2015: 159). He assumes a teleological view of planning in which 'action is path dependent, where once government activities are … in place, non-government actors react with compatible investments and actions that reinforce them', because diverging from this would 'abandon the benefits … that actors enjoy by being so entangled' (Beauregard 2015: 160). Beauregard's perspective privileges the forward motion of time. Like Madanipour, he acknowledges that society and planning modulate time's speed and constancy, but ignores the ways that the nature of time, including its segmentation, may influence how cities are planned, how they change, and who is involved.

Beauregard also presumes actors consistently work together over time toward common, predetermined goals, although temporary uses are, in many cases, times of experimentation, where the actors involved and their networks of action are intentionally not stable and enduring but are instead developed and tested. Dovey (2010, 2013) notes that the character of some places is defined by this dynamic quality of mixing and becoming. Temporary urbanism similarly establishes times when new place identities can be established. In this context, Madanipour (2017) emphasises that every use of public space is temporary. The public realm is defined by a lack of fixity, the absence of permanent occupation and control by any one actor. Madanipour qualifies this by noting that all uses of public space are conditioned by power. But power itself, and the agreements and institutions that wield it, are also constantly being produced or undermined by various actors, including time. When 'landlords and regulators aren't equipped to handle temporary uses' and planners 'apply licensing burdens, lease agreements, and review processes that are unsuitable for projects that may only last four weeks', temporary uses have a tactical role in testing new pathways that circumvent or replace these actors and processes (Madanipour 2017: 165 citing Fidler 2011; Lydon and Garcia 2015). The time frame helps to determine what other relationships will prevail. In the conclusion of his study of the role of time and temporary urbanism in cities, Madanipour notes that time can be seen as relational, circumstantial, defined in terms of the relationships between events. He argues that time is socially produced, and thus it can be changed. But time can also be seen as relational in terms of the relationships that it establishes with other actors in the city. Temporary uses can also change actors' perceptions of, and relation to, time itself.

Temporary Uses Seen in Two Temporal Perspectives

Madanipour's distinction between *chronos* and *kairos* reflects a general split in the literature on temporary urbanism between two broad understandings of temporary uses, which we outlined in Chapter 1. The logic of c*hronos* focuses on time-limited 'interim' uses that occupy a space only until a higher and better durable use comes along, thereby maintaining the city's regularity and progress by filling 'lost time', whereas *kairos* links to 'tactical' urbanism, which tries to bring about long-term shifts in urban development and management processes for urban spaces (Bishop and Williams 2012, Lydon and Garcia 2015).

Oswalt et al. (2013) provide a more nuanced framework that identifies eight different types of dynamic relationships between the 'temporary' and 'long-term' uses of a site (Figure 6.1). In three of these types, the temporary use does not last. In the first, *Stand-in*, a site is only available for a limited time, and this fixed window of time is one of the factors that produces the new site condition. This fixed window influences the other actors and their roles: financing, people, materials and so on are all engaged in the project on the basis of the restricted time frame. It shapes their expectations, their availability and their actions. These factors also condition the maximum time that a stand-in use can operate. In the second type, *Displacement*, the relationships that enable the activity already exist. For some reason, the usual site of an activity temporarily becomes unavailable, for example during renovation or

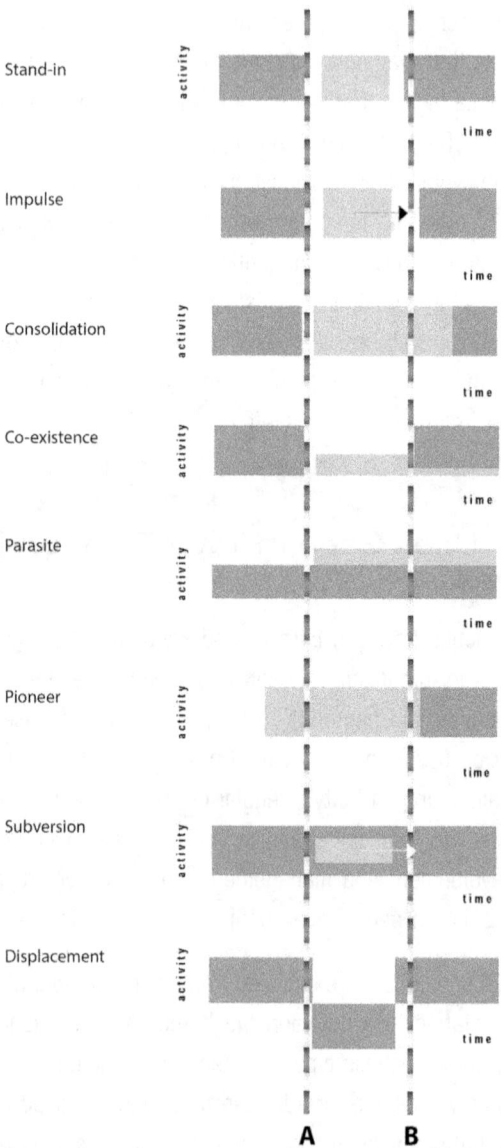

FIGURE 6.1 Eight ways that time frames temporary uses. A typology of potential relationships between permanent uses of urban spaces (dark shading) and temporary uses (light shading) over time (running left to right), as developed by Studio Urban Catalyst. The dashed lines demarcate the temporary period between A, when a permanent use or disuse of space stops or leaves the site, and B, a future point in time when that use will resume. Moments A and B may be known or undefined. This interim time allows new uses to emerge, develop, and combine with pre-existing uses. The know-ability of A and B and the duration between them affect the actors that engage in the temporary use and the prospects and form of its continuation.

Source: Image based on Bengs et al. 2002: 35–36.

expansion of its permanent home. The time away from the original site threatens these relationships, which actors thus try to preserve during this break. Once that period ends, the institutionalised activity returns to the space that suited it best. In a third model, *Subversion*, the temporary use is intended to be time-limited; it is often very brief because its purpose is to quickly effect a change in existing social and land-use relationships. Such temporary uses should not endure; their role is to disrupt and transform long-term use. This parallels Lydon and Garcia's (2015) idea of tactical urbanism: the action is short-term, whether by choice or necessity. But the impact on a site, on the surrounding city, or on actors and their relationships, is intended to be long term.

Four of Oswalt et al.'s other models, *Pioneer*, *Consolidation*, *Coexistence* and *Impulse*, characterise different ways that a land-use originally intended to be temporary might become more durable, by establishing a new use successful enough to endure in its own right, to continue in synergy with future development, or to carry over into the planned long-term development of a site. In all such cases, relationships evolve, including the relationship between site, use and the duration of physical forms. These four types emphasise the catalytic role of temporary use, to intensify urban activity in response to economic stagnation and vacant space. They reflect the neoliberal economic consensus that urban planning's key aim is economic growth, without necessarily questioning why inner-city spaces have lain underutilised. In this context, temporary urbanism can be highly strategic, aligned to the staging of long-term, large-scale physical and economic development plans.

The Benefits of the Temporary

The power of temporary use to influence and align to other actors comes largely from the capacity of that temporariness to enhance one or more of the five key benefits that are typically attributed to temporary urbanism, as outlined in Chapter 2: enhancing urban intensity, resilience, community engagement, innovation, or place identity. These prospective benefits help to determine which actors become engaged in supporting a temporary use, and thus help determine its viability.

The two benefits which most often align to temporary use projects are their capacity to increase urban intensity and resilience. Sharing space in time increases its utilisation. Short-term uses that fill underutilised spaces in underutilised times increase outcomes, by combining available time and space with the maximal inputs of a wide range of other actors, both producers and consumers. Allocating (dividing up) time among a variety of activities so that a space can be used most efficiently contrasts with the idea of planning and designing urban development around single, fixed land uses (organising uses spatially, rather than temporally), which leaves much space lying idle much of the time. Temporary uses are part of a broad shift of attention in planning to the programming of space, complementing the optimisation of physical design. Just-in-time production and the gig and sharing economies are examples of making production relationships more flexible and reorganising them in time so that time is not wasted and resources do not sit idle. The resilience of a city is also increased when a wider range of users and contents can be combined with a wider range of spaces. Dividing up time makes this possible. Land uses that occupy spaces and gather together various actors for a limited time increase the city's capacity to rapidly and flexibly adapt to unforeseen changes and to other localised, time-limited opportunities (Lydon and Garcia 2015, Greco 2012). These post-Fordist flexibilities are particularly well-suited to times of economic uncertainty (Stevens and Ambler 2010, Tonkiss 2013).

Short time frames are particularly important for making spaces available for urban activities and social groups that are small, marginal, or in conflict with dominant and conventional urban land uses, and which are thus rarely allocated scarce urban space on a permanent basis. These include informal recreation, nature, art, casual socialising, and activities that benefit minority groups (SenStadt 2007). This links to a third common perceived benefit of temporary urbanism, increasing community engagement. Not everyone who can contribute to the enlivening of urban spaces can commit to it as a full-time, permanent career. Urban space projects that are only short-term enable the participation of a wide range of new actors who have not previously been involved in developing and managing urban spaces, who bring new ideas, skills, networks, and resources. This especially includes lay citizens (Finn 2014, Lydon and Garcia 2015). Much learning and creativity are condensed within the short time frames of temporary projects.

In terms of innovation, the short-term nature of temporary urbanism lowers the cost barrier to entry that is presented by the long-term tenure arrangements for most urban spaces. Time limits also reduce the negative impacts and risks for other actors, especially those, such as neighbours, who might feel they have little to gain from allowing new and experimental uses. Short-term arrangements encourage – even necessitate – rapid innovation, as well as testing and iteration, in contrast to long-term planning which commits resources to a particular fixed vision of the future, even though the future is likely to develop quite differently. This includes experimentation around actors and their relationships, experimentation with design solutions, and designing for flexibility. Parklets, for example, have provided opportunities for designers to experiment and demonstrate innovation in a short-term, low-cost way. They provide a rapid user-testing feedback loop that helps designers learn. One local landscape practice in Perth, SeeDesign, drew on their first experiences designing parklets to develop a pair of modular parklets, with elements that could be rearranged, recombined and redeployed to suit different size and shape sites, or to suit changing weather and the interests of hosts and users. The parklet's impermanent form allowed it to better serve a wider range of needs.

The fifth potential benefit of temporary urbanism is its contribution to place identity and urban character. This may seem contradictory, as place identity is often understood as being stable and grounded in continuity with the past. How can fleeting changes and experiences transform character? But as suggested above, temporary urbanism's intensification and diversification of urban spaces' forms and uses, and the informality, creativity, dynamism, and broadening of community engagement within its procedures, transform the overall meaning and value of urban spaces and precincts for different users, even when changes are only temporary. As Madanipour (2017) notes, the transience of uses can heighten novelty and interest, add distinction by providing contrast to a city's enduring character, and create scarcity value. The continued enthusiasm of cities for hosting major international events such as the Olympic Games and the Football World Cup is testament to the continued belief that temporary activations of the city have a major, enduring impact on many actors' perceptions of, and relationships with, a city's character and its spaces (Gold and Gold 2017).

Local governments and landowners sometimes temporarily make spaces available and temporarily suspend rules in city districts that have a strong, fixed character. In such circumstances, temporariness is a necessary instrument to enable action and innovation. For example, the temporary city beaches and pop-up stores in the historic centres of European cities such as Berlin and Paris leverage their proximity and their physical and experiential contrast to heritage-listed museums and long-standing institutions (Stevens and Ambler 2010). Tourists enjoy these temporary and shifting contrasts. In Oswalt et al.'s (2013) terms, these temporary uses are generally *Parasites*, dependent on the 'real', 'permanent' local character, or *Stand-Ins* that only occupy spaces during a time when they are underutilised. As Schwarzer (1994) notes, examples of temporary urbanism such as those mentioned above may also illustrate Oswalt et al.'s (2013) characterisation of *Subversion*. With their different aesthetics, activities and people, temporary uses often challenge the grounding and fixing of local urban identity in a single authorised history and its preservation through built form. As we argued in Chapter 2, in situations where heritage controls limit or prevent permanent changes to built form, temporariness is a key that facilitates otherwise-inadmissible interventions that can both challenge local identity and enrich it by presenting new experiences and understandings of place.

In other cases, the very character of an urban place derives from its dynamism, its shifting mixture of forms, uses and users, and its openness to change (Dovey 2010). The art critic Karl Scheffler (1910) thus defined Berlin as an ungrounded, colonial frontier city in Europe's East, 'damned forever to become, never to be'. Cities continually change, under the influence of economic, political, demographic and technological forces. Land uses that are temporary can provide the innovation and resilience to develop responses to these changes, while still allowing future changes, instead of locking down character. Temporary interventions can engage new actors – new producers and users, new technologies and sources of investment – which align them to the identity of a place in ways that permanent, built form perhaps cannot. This is another way of looking at what the Chicago School characterised as the 'Zone of Transition', the ring of neighbourhoods around the city centre which were constantly being transformed by new waves of in-migration, by the physical expansion and intensification of the city centre, and changes in land-use patterns (Park et al. 1925). In such neighbourhoods, temporariness is permanent.

Conclusion

Temporary urbanism is defined by short time frames of planning, constructing and financing changes in urban space, and short-term reorganisation of actors. But such changes involve new fixities and can become permanent and have wider effects. Tactical forms of temporary urbanism aim to inform and re-shape broader urban planning approaches. Temporary urbanism is also deployed top-down by governments and corporations to achieve strategic outcomes. These dynamics highlight that all urban spaces are more-or-less impermanent assemblages of materials, people, technologies and concepts, which are constantly being deployed and adjusted to meet changing resources and needs, and to define new relationships. With that in mind, analysis of urban design processes should not seek to draw strict boundaries between the temporary, the tactical, and the ostensibly permanent, but explore the dynamic relationships between them, and in particular the role of time itself as one of the complex assemblages of factors and actors that shape these processes.

References

Agamben, G. (2005) *State of exception*, Chicago: University of Chicago Press.
Andres, L. and Grésillon, B. (2013) Cultural brownfields in European cities: A new mainstream object for cultural and urban policies. *International Journal of Cultural Policy* 19 (1): 40–62.
Beauregard, R. (2015) Temporalities, in *Planning matter: Acting with things*, Chicago: University of Chicago Press, pp. 151–71.
Bengs, C., Hentilä, H. and Nagy, D. (2002) *Urban catalysts: Strategies for temporary uses – Potential for development of urban residual areas in European metropolises*, Espoo: Centre for Urban and Regional Studies, Helsinki University of Technology.
Beyes, T. (2009) Spaces of intensity – Urban entrepreneurship as redistribution of the sensible, in D. Hjorth and C. Steyaert (eds) *The politics and aesthetics of entrepreneurship*, Cheltenham, UK: Edward Elgar, pp. 92–112.
Bishop, P. and Williams, L. (2012) *The temporary city*. New York: Routledge.
Callon, M. (1986) Elements of a sociology of translation: Domestication of the scallops and the fishermen of St Brieuc Bay, in J. Law (ed) *Power, action and belief: A new sociology of knowledge?* London: Routledge, pp. 196–233.
Dovey, K. (2010) *Becoming places*. London: Routledge.
Dovey, K. (2013) Planning and place identity, in G. Young, et al. (eds), *The Ashgate research companion to planning and culture*, London: Ashgate.
Dovey, K. and King, R. (2011) Forms of informality: Morphology and visibility of informal settlements. *Built Environment* 37 (1): 11–29.
Färber, A. (2014) Low-budget Berlin: Towards an understanding of low-budget urbanity as assemblage. *Journal of Regions, Economy and Society* 7: 119–36.
Fidler, E. (2011) Temporary uses can enliven city neighborhoods, Greater Greater Washington. http://greatergreaterwashington.org/post/12674/temporary-uses-can-enliven-city-neighborhoods/ Accessed 28 July 2020.
Finn, D. (2014) DIY urbanism: Implications for cities. *Journal of Urbanism* 7 (4): 381–98.

Giedion, S. (1948) *Mechanization takes command: A contribution to anonymous history*. New York: Oxford University Press.

Gold, J. and Gold, M. (eds) (2017) *Olympic cities: City agendas, planning and the world's games, 1896–2020*. New York: Routledge.

Greco, J. (2012) From pop-up to permanent. *Planning* 78 (9): 15–16.

Haid, C. (2017) The Janus face of urban governance: State, informality and ambiguity in Berlin, *Current Sociology Monograph* 65 (2): 289–301.

Jacobs, J. M., Cairns, S. and Strebel, I. (2012) Doing building work: Methods at the interface of geography and architecture, *Geographical Research* 50 (2): 126–40.

Lange, B. (2007) *Die Räume der Kreativszenen. Culturepreneurs und ihre Orte in Berlin*. Bielefeld: Transcript.

Latour, B. (1988) *The pasteurization of France*. Cambridge, MA: Harvard University Press.

Lydon, M. and Garcia, A. (2015) *Tactical urbanism: Short-term action for long-term change*. Washington, D.C.: Island Press.

Madanipour, A. (2017) *Cities in time: Temporary urbanism and the future of the city*, London: Bloomsbury.

Oswalt, P., Overmeyer, K. and Misselwitz, P. (2013) *Urban catalyst: The power of temporary use*. Berlin: DOM publishers.

Park, R., Burgess, E. and McKenzie, R. (1925) *The city*. Chicago: University of Chicago Press.

PPS (Project for Public Spaces) (2018) The lighter, quicker, cheaper transformation of public spaces. https://www.pps.org/article/lighter-quicker-cheaper (accessed 28 July 2020).

Scheffler, K. (1910/2015) *Berlin: ein Stadtschicksal (Berlin: Psychogramme of a City)*, F. Illies (ed), Berlin: Suhrkamp Verlag.

Schwarzer, M. (1994) Myths of permanence and transience in the discourse on historic preservation in the United States. *Journal of Architectural Education* 48 (1): 2–11.

SenStadt (Senatsverwaltung für Stadtentwicklung Berlin) (ed.) (2007) *Urban pioneers: Temporary use and urban development in Berlin*, Berlin: Jovis.

Stevens, Q. (2011) Characterising Germany's artificial 'city beaches': Distribution, type and design 3rd World Planning Schools Congress, Perth.

Stevens, Q. (2015) Sandpit urbanism, in B. Knudsen, D. Christensen and P. Blenker (eds), *Enterprising initiatives in the experience economy: Transforming social worlds*, New York: Routledge.

Stevens, Q. and Ambler, M. (2010) Europe's city beaches as post-Fordist placemaking. *Journal of Urban Design* 15: 515–37.

Thorpe, A. (2020) *Owning the street: The everyday life of property*, Cambridge: MIT Press.

Tonkiss, F. (2013) Austerity urbanism and the makeshift city, *City* 17 (3): 313–24.

Walker, D., Hampson, K. and Peters, R. (2000) *Relationship-based procurement strategies for the 21st century*, Canberra: Ausinfo.

Chapter Seven
Capacities

Kim Dovey

Assemblage and Resilience Thinking
Analyzing and Mapping Capacities
Spaces of Possibility
Expanding Capacities

Practices of temporary and tactical (t/t) urbanism rely on the capacity to adapt public spaces. But what does 'capacity' mean? What are the conditions of possibility that make public space amenable to the adaptations of temporary and tactical transformation? This chapter investigates this concept of 'capacity' in both its theoretical and practical dimensions. This work is based in assemblage thinking, wherein capacities are understood as real, even when not currently actualised or manifested. I argue that capacities can be mapped as a means to develop more adaptive and agile practices of urban design and planning, where the pursuit of fixed future outcomes is replaced by a more comprehensive understanding of the city as a space of possibility. Such an approach expands the prospects of designing public space for undesignated futures, planning for the unplanned.

'Capacity' is, like 'place', a term that is relatively uncomplicated in everyday life yet becomes problematic under interrogation. The concept can be understood in at least three main ways as 'extension', 'intensity' and 'power'. First, capacity is the maximum amount that something can contain – the 'capacity crowd' is the one that fills an available space. In this sense, capacity is embodied in the material property of a room, park, street or sidewalk, defined in terms of extension and the limits to density. This definition can be linked to the ways t/t urbanism can identify and exploit the underutilisation of public space. Second, capacity is also the maximum amount of something that can be produced when a machine or person is working at 'full capacity' or maximum intensity. t/t urbanism brings greater intensity to public life – a greater production or flow of ideas and interactions within the same volume of space. Finally, capacity is about the power to achieve a desired end – the root of the word 'power' is the Latin *potere* – 'to be able'. t/t urbanism embodies the individual or collective power to transform public space, to exercise the right to the city (Lefebvre 1996). While there is often a tendency to identify power with hierarchy (power *over* others), power as capacity (power *to*) has long been seen as the primary form of power (Isaac 1992, Dovey 2008).

In practice, these definitions overlap and the waters are muddied; notice how capacity is first defined as material spatial conditions but then slips into social conditions and relations between them. Capacities for t/t urbanism in urban public space are found in a complex mix of capacities to contain the full extent of public life, morphological capacities to produce public life, and the agencies and desires to appropriate public space. The forms and spatial relations of the material city are always already the result of centuries of practices of power and desire. Capacities are embodied in the streets and neighbourhoods that we have, the cards we have been dealt, but they are also embodied in the desires to change it.

A capacity is not simply a property of the material world like the greenness, flatness or softness of grass – this is to objectify what is a relational concept. Capacities are opportunities, possibilities, affordances, assemblages. The challenge here is to activate new ways of thinking. The concept of 'capacity' is a useful tool for thinking in this context partly because it is also common language in the development industry where the capacity of a potential development site lies in a cluster of relations between site extent and morphology, urban context and prevailing governance controls that enable and constrain possibilities for development and profit. Capacities are not singular but multiple – the same morphological conditions and properties can be adapted to many different outcomes.

Capacity thinking is an approach that deals with the cities, neighbourhoods and streets that we have; not with utopian ideals that we might hope to impose. Urban morphology has great inertia. Plans and regulations can be changed if political conditions allow; buildings can be demolished and replaced within those frameworks if capital is available. Yet the morphology of street networks generally endures for centuries. Urban development can be stopped, controlled or enabled, but the infrastructure for development is a very long-term investment. The capital costs and political difficulties of pressing reset on the urban fabric are too high. This is where temporary and tactical urbanism comes into play by enlarging the capacity for change.

A capacity is a possibility that is real but not (yet) actual. Capacities may be designed or not – a rock may become a seat or a stage in different contexts and in relation to different desires of different agents. Capacities of people differ by age, gender, size, ability, ethnicity and social class. Capacities will differ with urban context – what is possible on a sidewalk or street will differ according to whether it is lined with housing or shops. They will differ by times of day, week and season. Capacity is not simply utility, like the capacity of a restaurant or a briefcase, it is about spaces of 'possibility' and 'becoming'.

Capacity thinking enables us to move beyond the limitations of 'rational' planning oriented toward concrete goals, to engage with possibilities where the predictability required of an effective 'master plan' is not available. The challenge is to design and build public space as a living laboratory where experimentation is the norm; where different approaches are tested and adapted in response to how they work. Capacity thinking heralds an era where t/t urbanism becomes a mainstream approach to urban planning because it is a key mode of planning for the unplanned.

Assemblage and Resilience Thinking

t/t urbanism requires that we think differently about the city, about the complexity and dynamics of interrelations between its populations and materialities. Capacity thinking is relational thinking – thinking about assemblages rather than things-in-themselves. I have long been trying to develop what is loosely called assemblage thinking in urban design (Dovey 2010, 2016, Dovey et al. 2018) based on the work of Deleuze and Guattari (1987). Assemblage thinking is relational thinking – don't look for things, look for the connections between things and between people and things. Look for the flows of desire – the attractions, alliances, symbioses and synergies between entities. Don't reduce the city to origins or causes, rather ask how it works and how it is changing. Don't look only at actual or designated functions of public space but at the many kinds of potential co-functioning. Try to understand the city in terms of verbs rather than nouns – walking, cycling, driving and parking as well as eating, talking, playing, planting, sitting, thinking, building and designing. Define the lines of movement rather than establishing points of order. Look at how the city is produced before deciding how it is to be regulated. Assemblage thinking is multiscalar thinking where the large scale does not subsume, and is not more important than, the small scale; where power is practiced bottom-up, top-down and laterally. This is a world where differences are primary, and where identities emerge from fields of difference.

Assemblage thinking is not easy to understand and is scarcely a developed theory, but one does not necessarily need theory to practice assemblage thinking. It is the method that Jacobs (1961) used to crack open our understanding of what it is that makes cities tick. It is a way of understanding issues such as place, informality, density and walkability (Dovey 2010, 2012, Dovey and Pafka 2020). Many seminal thinkers in urban design theory – Jacobs, Sennett, Alexander, Koolhaas, Cerdá, Gehl, Lynch, Hillier, Sitte, Geddes – were relational thinkers of one kind or another, producing theory that emerged from detailed observation of the complexities of how cities work in everyday life, and much of this is observation, recognition and understanding of capacities. Capacity is not simply found, but emerges from the interrelations between people and things, and also from differences between people and differences between things.

Assemblage is a form of materialist thinking where the morphologies, materialities and spatialities of urban public space really matter. It is a way of understanding the agency of the material world without descending into physical determinism – the idea that built form determines anything. It is a way of understanding the power of discourse and representation without descending into textual determinism – the idea that there is 'nothing outside the text'. It enables understanding morphogenesis and the emergence of place without descending into formularised 'placemaking' (Dovey 2020). Assemblage thinking is an approach to both research and practice that understands capacity as real, even when not currently actualised or manifested. From such a view, urban public space is a 'space of possibility' (DeLanda 2006, 2011).

Assemblage thinking involves an inversion of common understandings of the relations between identity and difference. Deleuze (1968) wants to replace any notion of the 'thing-in-itself' with the concept of 'difference-in-itself' – differences precede identities that emerge from the world as a 'field of differences'. This concept of a 'field of differences' is important for assemblage thinking as a framework for understanding patterns that emerge within a given field without a reduction to essentialised elements or types. Thus, typical t/t projects such as guerrilla gardening, yarn bombing or parklets are interconnected practices that emerge from within this field.

I have argued elsewhere that the concept of place might be usefully defined as a 'complex adaptive assemblage' - a concept that marries the fields of resilience thinking and assemblage thinking (Dovey 2012). Resilience thinking, based on the science of complex adaptive systems, is largely derived from ecological systems (Holling and Gunderson 2002). It is focused on the adaptive capacities of complex systems to adapt to forces for change. A simple definition of resilience is: "the capacity to undergo some change without crossing a threshold to a different system regime – a system with a different identity" (Walker and Salt 2006: 32). The idea of a 'complex adaptive assemblage' brings Deleuzian social theory into the picture and also cuts across the prevailing notion that resilience is necessarily positive – a hangover from the study of natural systems. Dysfunctional and inequitable urban neighbourhoods are often locked into particular forms of place identity and are deeply resilient to regime change.

The concept of capacity in the context of temporary/tactical urbanism has many parallels with the capacities of complex systems to adapt in a resilient manner where change at an incremental scale builds resilience against regime change. It is part of the very definition of a temporary change that the more permanent regime will remain in place. However, the capacities for change embodied in t/t urbanism also work in the opposite direction – part of the very definition of tactical urbanism is 'short-term action for long-term change' (Lydon and Garcia 2015). Permanent regime change is the strategy, and the temporary tactics are designed to chip away at the resilience of a dysfunctional assemblage, often due to car dependency, lack of walkability, privatisation, low density or mono-functionality.

Resilience thinking invokes the key concept of a resilience cycle which moves through phases of expansion, consolidation, collapse and re-organisation before expanding again (Holling and Gunderson). These cycles occur at multiple inter-connected scales where the larger system is termed *panarchy*, to evoke the concept of an all-embracing interconnected system that is neither anarchy nor hierarchy, where the sense of order and control is emergent. My use of the word assemblage rather than system here is to assert that there is nothing systematic about how such change takes place, to bridge between the science and the social theory, and to incorporate the expressive and discursive dimensions as well as the materialities of urban design (Dovey 2016: 263–71). Within resilience thinking, one key form of adaptation is known as 'revolt' – where an event or change at one scale cuts across the prevailing order at the larger scale, and the larger scale learns, adapts and 'remembers' accordingly. The best example from t/t urbanism is perhaps the parklet movement as a revolt against the car-dependent city, leading in turn to the more organised, formalised and regulated versions that become parts of the planning system rather than forms of revolt.

Another important concept from resilience thinking is the focus on 'key slow variables' – significant factors that change slowly until they reach a turning point where the larger assemblage adapts by slipping into a new regime. While resilience thinking is generally focused on stopping regime change, t/t urbanism often has regime change as a goal. In many streets, car traffic is a key slow variable that has increased historically to largely eradicate vital pedestrian life – t/t urbanism can be a way of reversing an historic regime change, chipping away incrementally until the assemblage slips into a new regime.

Analyzing and Mapping Capacities

While the city's capacities for temporary and tactical transformation are not simply material properties, one way to engage with capacities in the real world is through mapping. Both research projects and teaching about forms of t/t urbanism can provide insight in this regard. The first project I will discuss was entitled 'what is urban character?', where it emerged that graffiti and street art (however defined) were salient issues in the minds of those who were defending certain neighbourhoods on the basis of 'urban character'. These practices were a form of tactical and temporary intervention in urban spaces that were seen by some to threaten existing character and by others as a means of creating character. The inner-city neighbourhoods of Melbourne that we were studying have a good deal of graffiti, ranging from saturation tagging of back lanes to much-celebrated urban street art that had become a tourist attraction. Our primary questions were not about the content or legality of graffiti but its role in the construction of place identity – the 'place of graffiti' (Dovey et al. 2012). Through interviews, we discovered that most residents are an ambivalent audience – appreciating street art but opposing tagging, without clearly defining the difference. We also mapped the prevalence of graffiti, and these maps reveal how the capacity for this form of t/t urbanism is mediated by street and lane networks of the inner-city (Figure 7.1). Capacities for graffiti and street art are

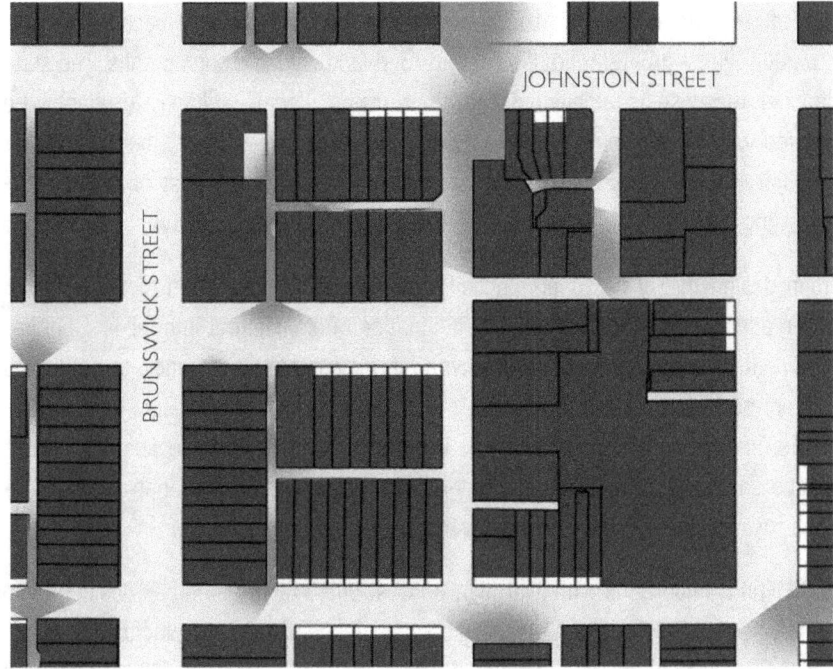

FIGURE 7.1 Graffiti mapping – Fitzroy, Melbourne.
Source: Kim Dovey and Simon Wollan.

generated by smooth blank walls that are publicly visible but are not identified with the occupants of the building. This means the side or rear of a building or fence constructed on a boundary – primarily laneways. The need for smoothness, blankness, visibility and anonymity reveals one way in which capacities are inherently multi-modal and multi-scalar. The street art scene in Melbourne could not have emerged without the particular urban design ideologies, technologies, industrial functions and speculative practices that prevailed in the 19th century to produce this urban morphology. Graffiti needs density because it is building density that produces blank walls on public-fronting property boundaries and streetlife density that produces an audience. We argued that capacities for graffiti are often found in the ambiguous territories between categories. The surfaces need to be visible in order for the work to gain an audience, yet the practice of painting graffiti is illegal. Practitioners can be arrested and the work will be erased if it is seen to contaminate the formal order of the authorised city. It is often the spaces between major streets and minor lanes that hold the most capacity – the laneway walls that are visible from the streets, backspace that is visible from frontspace. While graffiti remains a form of revolt (and much of it is seen as 'revolting'), it has also become a major attraction with a proliferation of street art tours and wedding photographs. The state planning response is ambiguous: graffiti remains illegal, building occupants are assisted with graffiti removal, but a blind eye is also turned. Thus, the capacity for temporary street art is maintained. Attempts to preserve the best of street art – converting temporary to permanent – can only reduce this capacity.

Urban design theory has generally followed Jacobs' (1961) notion of the value of 'active edges' and a more general condemnation of blank street interfaces. Gehl has long identified small-grain frontages with high levels of transparency, sociality and frequent building entries as a primary form of urban design quality (Gehl et al., 2006). This is fundamentally correct, but it is not the end of the story, because as Jacobs also noted it is the marginalised, undervalued spaces of the city that create capacities for marginalised activities (Stevens and Dovey 2004).

In 2019 (in collaboration with Matthijs van Oostrum), I taught an urban design studio at the University of Melbourne focused on capacities for temporary/tactical urbanism in inner-city Melbourne. We proceeded from an initial literature review to analyze a broad range of existing t/t projects, to mapping such projects in the city, to mapping capacities and then designing new projects. The first task was to find and present a broad range of everyday cases of t/t urbanism from different cities across the globe. This was partly a way of defining loose distinctions – between temporary/tactical, temporary/permanent, tactics/strategies and between projects/events.

These projects were then subjected to what we called a what/how/when/where/why analysis (Figure 7.2). The 'what' question exposed the form of intervention – what material forms were being introduced? The question of 'how' the intervention took place covered processes such as attaching, constructing and so on. The 'when' question invoked the ways in which different projects were geared to the daily, weekly and seasonal rhythms of the city. 'Where' produced a typology of spatial contexts. Finally, the 'why' question involved an interrogation of desires and activities.

Figure 7.2 shows that any particular t/t/ project can be mapped against this table, which can be augmented as necessary to produce an assemblage of interconnected places, practices, times and materials. This form of analysis reveals a 'field of differences' of t/t practices and the scope of public imagination. While certain patterns

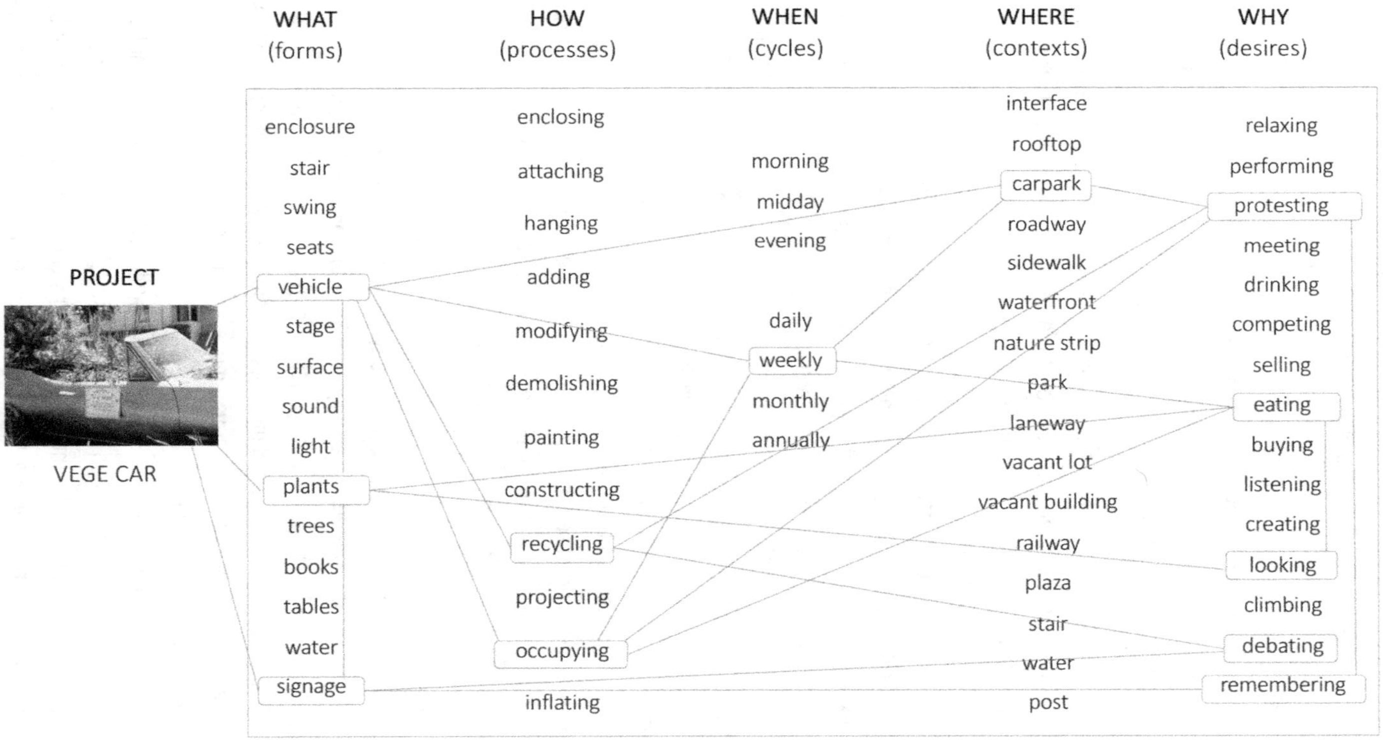

FIGURE 7.2 A field of differences for t/t urbanist projects.
Source: Kim Dovey.

emerge for different forms, processes, rhythms, contexts and desires, the complexity and range of differences resist any reduction to project types. Any such typology is likely to be reduced to a coherent set of somewhat formularised stereotypes such as parklets, chair bombing, pop-ups and so on. Assemblage thinking involves a prioritisation of differences over identities, it sees differences as productive forces and identities as emergent outcomes, and it embodies an imperative to understand the field of differences without reduction to essential types.

As part of this analysis of existing t/t urbanism projects, students were asked to produce a single diagram to encapsulate each design. In assemblage thinking the diagram is also called an 'abstract machine' – an abstract image that reveals a set of relations between forces, flows and things that produces an outcome. A diagram is abstract because it is about general conditions rather than particulars, and it is machinic in that it embodies a capacity to produce something. The diagram is neither a map of existing conditions nor a design or plan for what might be built, yet it mediates actual and possible worlds. Drawing diagrams that were more than a mimetic representation of the particular design proved to be the most daunting of tasks. Yet the requirement to produce a diagram raised interesting discussions. On the one hand, a diagram can narrow down thinking, when used as a formula for reproducing a particular solution. I am reminded here of the work of Alexander whose 'pattern language' included a diagram with each pattern – work that was at once seminal yet widely reduced to formulae (Alexander et al 1977). The most simple and abstract diagrams are the most potent because they have a larger scope of application and cannot be applied without creating a new design.

We then undertook to explore both the actualities and capacities of t/t urbanism across about eight square kilometres of inner-city Melbourne. The urban morphology includes a patchwork of nineteenth-century grids overlaid with expressways, tramways and railways, with street widths ranging from a 100m-wide freeway to a plethora of 3m-wide back laneways. Functions include main-street shopping strips, sporting fields, a cemetery and university campus as well as mixed residential and industrial zones. Densities range from single-story row-housing to high-rise commercial and public housing estates. Each student was allocated a square kilometre to map, but the territories overlapped so that most of the city was mapped by at least two students. The task was to walk the territory extensively at different times of day and week, and to identify locations with a capacity for better or more intensive utilisation through t/t adaptation, whether public or privately owned. This was not a map of capacity for permanent development, which would be mapped differently. We excluded two-dimensional spatial transformations (such as graffiti) from the mapping because they are too prolific and would have consumed too much attention. The mapping of actual t/t projects was one way of revealing capacities that was then extrapolated to identify unutilised capacities.

The capacity maps were initially presented individually and then overlaid with other students' mappings of the same territory through the same lens. Students were asked to reach agreement on what constituted capacity in the overlapped zones. Through a process of debate and discussion, we developed a typology of 6 capacity spaces – greenspace, carspace, pedestrian space, laneways, interfaces and vacant spaces. 'Greenspace' was largely parks, gardens, wild spaces and landscaped road and freeway verges. 'Carspace' included all spaces designed for and/or dominated by motorised vehicles, mostly comprised of roadways and parking. 'Pedestrian space' was a category of spaces designed for pedestrian use including sidewalks and plazas. 'Laneways' within this typology are primarily rear lanes originally designed for sewerage and services that have become an ambiguous and abject space that is generally car-free. 'Interfaces' was a category for semi-public spaces such as building setbacks and entry areas that mediate between public and private spaces. The final category of 'vacant' included unused plots or buildings, both publicly and privately owned.

The resulting montage (Figure 7.3) is problematic, not least since it cannot distinguish categories in black and white at this scale – every space that is not black was identified as embodying capacity for t/t urbanist projects. A typology is a lens through which we might better understand a field of differences. What appears on the map are not capacities but defined spaces in which capacity was identified. There could be 100 categories, but any map with more than seven categories will become an unreadable 'soup'. These are categories that mix materiality, function and context. Greenspace is primarily identified by materiality; carspace and pedestrian space are labelled by function but require hard pavements. Laneways and interfaces are defined by context and vacant space by a lack of function. There are ambiguities – when does a laneway become carspace, or a park become a plaza? An interface can be a park or a plaza.

Mapping is the means more than the end. The purpose is not so much to produce a fixed map locating capacities but to learn more about the dynamics of the various desires and forces at play and to debate the ways they are mediated. They include

FIGURE 7.3 Capacity mapping – Inner-city Melbourne.
Source: Student work curated by Kim Dovey.

the desires of political leaders to produce emblems of their power, to show what they have done for the community, and to gain political capital. They include the desires of capital to privatise and exploit public space for private gain. But most importantly, they include the desires of residents and citizens for a better quality public space. Much of the public space was designated underutilised because it was never designed to be utilised – empty strips of grass and concrete; wide roads and extensive parking areas designed for peak periods or flows; railway and freeway easements designed when noise, safety and pollution could not be managed. The student map is not consistently rigorous work; indeed it is hard to define what rigour means in mapping capacities. What is interesting is not the discrete categories that emerged so much as the number of seemingly discrete categories - too many to map without producing a map that looks like soup or reducing the categories to stereotypes. It was interesting to see that students identified capacities for temporary and tactical change that cover such extensive parts of this inner-city urban fabric, including neighbourhoods that local residents widely regard as fixed and finished.

A third piece of research that was revealing of capacities for temporary and tactical change was focused on architecture but also holds lessons for public space. In this project (conducted with Kenn Fisher), we analysed the ways secondary school architecture adapts as schools move away from the 'bells and cells' regime of hierarchical education toward pedagogies of self-organised learning (Dovey and Fisher 2014). Based on mapping and diagramming, we suggested that what is often generalised as the 'open plan' could be differentiated in terms of the production of 'streetspace' and 'commons'. 'Streetspace' is busy with passing traffic, a space of encounter and engagement but not one of discussion, collaboration or concentration. Streetspace is difficult to appropriate without disrupting flows. The 'commons' is also open and accessible, but a place to go 'to' more than 'through'; quieter and easier to appropriate, with a wider range of learning modes and a capacity to retreat, but without the continuous engagements of the streetspace. This distinction is clearly non-binary and ultimately non-measurable, although it can be mapped and diagrammed (Dovey and Fisher 2014). These categories of streetspace and commons are drawn from public space and suggest a similar field of differences, from carspace and sidewalks to the more protected green spaces, back lanes and the *terrain vague* of the city. Many of these new schools are deliberately designed for adaptation, with embodied capacities to adapt to changing desires and modes of learning. While there is no clear analogy between schools and public space, it is notable that progressive education regards learning as something that happens everywhere and all the time; t/t urbanism involves the same kind of thinking. As in schools, there are different capacities in public space depending on how it is engaged with the intensities of urban life streetspace and the intensities of urban commoning that can be an antidote. In this regard, we are soon to experience an important transformation – as electric cars remove the roar and smell of traffic from streetspace, this new soundscape and smellscape will change the relations of streetspace to commons and enlarge the capacities for engagement and learning in public space.

Spaces of Possibility

I now want to return now to assemblage thinking and the idea that capacity thinking is based in an ontology of becoming rather than a fixed sense of being or identity. As an ontological concept, capacity can be traced to Kant, who called it the 'conditions of possibility' in a general and transcendental sense – in this sense, 'space' is the condition of possibility for the material world. This is not a cause-effect relation; buildings or streets are not caused by 'space' but they cannot exist without it. Foucault's concept of the 'episteme' is the 'condition of possibility' for particular forms of knowledge. The same phrase can be used to better understand 'conditions of possibility' for profit or political change. In the work of Deleuze, this idea becomes part of an immanent or 'flat' ontology where conditions of possibility lie in differences, where there is no such thing as a 'thing-in-itself', where identities emerge from 'spaces of possibility'.

In this sense, capacity thinking is non-linear thinking that seeks to understand the ways outcomes emerge from interactions between parts, and that can't be reduced to cause-effect relations. It is important not to confuse capacities with properties embodied in the material world. As DeLanda (2011) points out, a knife has both the property of 'sharpness' and a capacity to cut. These are ontologically different because the property of sharpness is an actual material condition while the capacity is a form of potential or possibility that requires an entity with a related property (cuttability) and an event (cutting) in order to become actualised. A grass surface has a property of softness and capacities for sitting or digging, but the capacity is not actualised without another entity with a capacity and desire to sit or dig. DeLanda also distinguishes capacities from 'tendencies', such as the tendency to melt or burn at a certain temperature, or the tendency of a structure to collapse, or land to slide, at a certain tipping point. Tendencies are predictable while capacities are produced by unpredictable relations with other entities. While tendencies are inherent and limited, capacities can expand with the multiplicity of capacities of other entities to interact with. A key part of assemblage thinking is to learn to see capacities as real even when not actualised, to see the urban design potential in shaping material relations to generate new capacities.

If we return to the what/how/when/where/why analysis, we can see that the 'what' and 'how' of t/t urbanism are primarily focused on the ways in which materials with different properties, tendencies and capacities are brought together in public space; the 'when' and 'where' is focused on how capacities are enabled by temporal and spatial contexts; and the 'why' involves the desires of different populations to exploit these possibilities. For DeLanda the 'space of possibility' is structured by the sets of capacities and tendencies of the material world. The structure of the space of possibility is the diagram of the assemblage; it constrains the range of possibility.

Diagrams do not transcend the assemblage, but are immanent to material conditions and flows of desire. The various mappings produced in Figures 7.1–7.3 can be understood as tactics for opening new ways of thinking about harnessing the capacities of everyday spaces through t/t projects.

The concept of capacity as a space of possibility has strong affinities with the concept of 'affordance' introduced long ago as part of Gibson's ecological psychology (Gibson 1979). This is a very productive concept that has become somewhat limited in its applications to the design of public space. In its original form, affordance was defined in terms of the possibilities for action that are 'afforded' to an organism by certain material properties of an environment. However, affordance theory has long struggled with the lack of a relational ontology – as discussed here within the frame of assemblage thinking (Stevens et al. forthcoming). An affordance is a material condition connected to a desire; what is afforded is a flow of desire. We have shown in this book that t/t urbanism represents a particular set of temporal, spatial, material, economic and ideational patterns among these many flows.

Expanding Capacities

The goal of this chapter has been to open questions and to suggest ways of thinking about, mapping and designing capacities. In the end, capacities are too complex to be conclusively defined because they emerge within the relations between multiple clusters of factors. Spatial and morphological factors include land slope, the width of streets, lanes or sidewalks, the length of blocks, the density of buildings and populations, and the mixing of functions. These exist in relation to flows of pedestrians, goods, cars, cyclists, trams, trains and buses, together with the speeds and volumes of traffic. Capacities change in relation to daily, weekly and seasonal rhythms of activity. They change in relation to regimes of discourse and the production of identity. Forms of agency and governance range from self-organisation to state regulation – these occur within a context of public safety, flows of revenue and prevailing politics and law. The task is not to select which of these we might identify capacity with, but to discover which interrelations between them might generate new capacities. Capacities are not fixed and closed, but open and dynamic.

Capacity thinking entails a fundamental change to the ways we conceive of urban planning and design at every scale from sidewalk to metropolis. We have seen throughout this book, and in the broader literature of which it is a part, that t/t urbanism expands capacities in a number of ways – new spaces, new agents, new uses and new users, involving a gamut of practices from guerrilla action to state-initiated policy. However, most of this involves taking advantage of existing capacities, with permanence and strategy as the context within which the temporary and tactical takes place. Within this conception, t/t urbanism fills the gaps in space and time produced by the failures of strategic planning and market-based capitalism. The broader challenge is to integrate capacity thinking with the strategic design and planning practices that shape the city in a more permanent manner.

For designers, the challenge is not only designing t/t projects as outcomes, but designing a city with an enhanced capacity for change, shaping urban public spaces in a manner that enables multiple outcomes. Capacity thinking needs to permeate the broad assemblage of urban planners, architects, developers, urban designers and landscape architects – where it needs to displace any lingering notion of a fixed or permanent city. The design of every public/private interface, sidewalk, street, neighbourhood and district of the city needs to be considered in relation to what might come next – without any fixed master plan. This does not mean there is no planning, only that there is no master. Strategic planning means long-term thinking, but long-term does not mean fixed or final outcomes. The challenge for urban design and planning is not one of imposing a final solution, but of finding, releasing and designing for capacity. This means integrating capacity thinking at different scales without privileging the larger scale. It means integrating the permanent with the temporary, and the strategic with the tactical, without privileging the permanent and strategic. t/t urbanism does not replace the larger, more strategic and permanent urban transformations, but augments them and stimulates them – expanding the overall capacity for change. The number and extent of small, incremental, tactical projects means that they are at least as important as major projects in the transformation of cities (Adams et al. 2018).

To end where this chapter began, 'capacity', like 'place', is a deceptively simple everyday term that turns out to be highly complex. Capacity thinking involves a focus on capacities for the transformation of place, at every scale from sidewalk to city. But here we also encounter a dilemma – t/t urbanism can do harm as well as good. We live in a world where transformational change is imperative, but change is also ontologically unsettling. Good public space forms a stable setting wherein everyday life 'takes place'. A stable sense of place stabilises our lives in a world of change. At the same time, the temporary and tactical are part of what comprises the sense of home in public space - the informal order of self-organised placemaking geared to a common social life. Through its incrementalism and reversibility, t/t urbanism is a way of generating transformational change without generating ontological insecurity. Perhaps this capacity is the most enduring and strategic aspect of t/t urbanism.

References

Adams, R., Dovey, K. and Jones, R. (2018) Melbourne futures, in Dovey, K., Adams, R. and Jones, R. (eds), *Urban choreography*, Melbourne: Melbourne UP.

Alexander, C., Ishikawa, S. and Silverstein, M. (1977) *A pattern language*. New York: Oxford University Press.

DeLanda, M. (2006) *A new philosophy of society*, London: Continuum.

DeLanda, M. (2011) *Philosophy and simulation*, New York: Continuum.

Deleuze, G. (1968) *Difference and repetition*, New York, Columbia U.P.

Deleuze, G. and Guattari, F. (1987) *A thousand plateaus*, London: Athlone.

Dovey, K. (2008) *Framing places* (2nd ed), London: Routledge.

Dovey, K. (2010) *Becoming places,* London: Routledge.

Dovey, K. (2012) Informal settlement and complex adaptive assemblage. *International Development Planning Review* 34 (3): 371–90.

Dovey, K. (2016) *Urban design thinking: A conceptual toolkit*, London: Bloomsbury.

Dovey, K. (2020) Place as assemblage, in T. Edensor, U. Kothari and A. Kaladides (eds), *The Routledge handbook of place*, London: Routledge, pp. 21–31.

Dovey, K. and Pafka, E. (2014) The urban density assemblage. *Urban Design International* 19 (1): 66–76.

Dovey, K. and Pafka, E. (2020) What is walkability: The urban DMA. *Urban Studies* 57 (1): 93–108.

Dovey, K., Pafka, E. and Ristic, M. (eds) (2018) *Mapping urbanities*, New York: Routledge.

Dovey, K. and Fisher, K. (2014) Designing for adaptation: The school as socio-spatial assemblage. *Journal of Architecture* 19 (10): 43–63.

Dovey, K., Wollan, S. and Woodcock, I. (2012) Placing graffiti. *Journal of Urban Design* 17 (1): 21–41.

Gehl, J., Johansen, L., & Reigstad, S. (2006) Close encounters with buildings. *Urban Design International*, 11, 29–47.

Gibson, J. J. (1979) *The ecological approach to visual perception*, Boston: Houghton Mifflin.

Holling, C. and Gunderson, L. (2002) Resilience and adaptive cycles, in L. Gunderson and C. Holling (eds), *Panarchy*, Washington, D.C.: Island Press. pp. 25–62.

Isaac, J. (1992) Beyond the three faces of power, in T. Wartenberg (ed), *Rethinking power*, Albany: SUNY Press, pp. 32–55.

Jacobs, J. (1961) *The death and life of great American cities*, New York: Vintage.

Lefebvre, H. (1996) *Writings on cities* (transl. E. Kofman and E. Lebas) Oxford: Blackwell.

Lydon, M. and Garcia, A. (2015) *Tactical Urbanism*. Washington, D.C.: Island Press.

Stevens, Q. and Dovey, K. (2004) Appropriating the spectacle: Play and politics in a leisure landscape. *Journal of Urban Design* 9 (3): 351–65.

Stevens, Q., Daly, J. and Dovey, K. (forthcoming) Designing for possibility in public space: Affordance, assemblage and ANT.

Walker, B. and Salt, D. (2006) *Resilience thinking*, Washington, D.C.: Island Press.

Chapter Eight
Futures

Quentin Stevens and Kim Dovey

Urban Intensity
Community Engagement
Innovation
Resilience
Place Identity
Conclusion

In this concluding chapter, we draw together the various threads of analysis we have introduced throughout the book and speculate on the future of t/t urbanism. The COVID-19 pandemic has opened up many opportunities for t/t urbanism and demonstrated the need for more agile, adaptive and resilient forms of public space. A great deal of public space in many cities has been re-claimed from car space for more productive, creative and convivial uses. Cities around the world have recognised the opportunity to mitigate the loss of public life during the pandemic by repurposing street space for people — but what comes next? Are the tactical transformations of cities during COVID-19 a temporary change before a return to car-dependent cities driven by real-estate markets within idealised masterplans, or are they a harbinger of a more agile urban realm? Perhaps a long-term legacy will be the realisation that unpredictable disruption will become the new normal. Perhaps the temporary and the tactical might emerge from the margins of the urban imagination to become the mainstay of a more agile urban planning and design.

This chapter is structured by a return to each of the five key matters of concern identified in Chapter 2: urban intensity, community engagement, innovation, resilience and place identity. Here, we want to expand on them to reflect more broadly on what we have learnt over the past few decades, with a focus on three key questions. First is the question of how this field is defined — the definitions, differences and interrelations between tactical and temporary urbanism. How useful

DOI: 10.4324/9781003284390-9

and sustainable is it to define a field of research and practice as a set of relations? Second is the question around public interests and the outcomes of t/t urbanism in terms of social equity and spatial justice. How to best understand the tensions between t/t urbanism as guerrilla urbanism and as neoliberal urbanism? Third, we reflect on the circumstances and outcomes of the COVID-19 pandemic – what comes next for public space?

Urban Intensity

In Chapter 2, we defined t/t urbanism's potential to increase urban intensiy, in terms of both the volume and the variety of uses and users of urban spaces. For more than a decade, t/t urbanism practices have explored how underused urban spaces could be used more efficiently, sustainably and equitably. In terms of community engagement, discussed further below, tactical urbanism had focused on transforming spaces to better meet the underserved needs of certain social groups. Temporary urbanism, by contrast, focused on quickly responding to and facilitating *variations* in urban intensity – not just increases. New, intense uses may pop up and pop down.

In Chapter 4, we highlighted a range of interconnected factors that drive temporary variations in the intensity of land development and use over different time frames: changes in weather, seasons and climate; economic cycles and cycles of growth and decline in specific industry sectors; the consequent movements of people and capital between these sectors; development or decline in the organising capacity of local governments, entrepreneurs and citizens; political shifts such as the fall of Communism; large-scale events that bring short-term flows of people and resources; and the stimulus of new ideas, models and programs for urban space use.

The COVID-19 pandemic has changed attitudes and needs regarding the intensity of urban space use. It has brought major shifts both in the use of existing urban spaces (due to reductions in travel, commuting, tourism, office work, shopping and group leisure activities) and in the amount and spatial and temporal patterns of people's physical exercise and social interactions. Governments, businesses and citizens have used t/t urbanism approaches to rapidly retrofit urban streets to take advantage of the temporarily reduced intensity of city traffic, to serve rapidly increasing needs for outdoor walking, cycling and dining, and to provide the increased amount of space that such activities now require due to physical distancing requirements. Pedestrian activity has intensified in some locations, but it has also needed to expand spatially because proximity and spatial intensity pose a health risk (Mehta 2020). Established t/t urbanism tactics such as temporary bicycle lanes, parklets and markets on parking lots have been deployed to quickly rebalance the allocation of urban space from cars to pedestrians and cyclists. Residents are using their local commercial and residential streets, parks and empty spaces more intensively (Daly et al. 2020). In some cases, these changes may be a temporary, one-off adaptation to maximise the use of available urban space. In other cases, such as Barcelona and the authors' home city of Melbourne, these shifts have dovetailed with ongoing, pre-pandemic urban planning strategies to remove or slow vehicular traffic in urban streets to enable more intensive pedestrian and cycling use of local street space (Dovey et al. 2021).

In yet other cases, temporary and tactical interventions introduced in response to the COVID-19 pandemic have presented entirely new possibilities for urban intensification. Even in ostensibly low-density, car-dependent neighbourhoods, people have begun walking more and shopping and socialising locally. Parklets are thriving in some outer-suburban shopping mall carparks. As people seek to avoid the dangerously intense shared interiors of public transport, many have begun commuting long distances by bicycle on new temporary cycle lanes. Some suburban golf courses closed by pandemic restrictions have been invaded by local residents with limited open space options for their permitted daily close-to-home exercise. A low-spatial-intensity sport has yielded to a different, rapidly increasing recreational demand.

The discussion of temporality in Chapter 6 drew on Madanipour's (2017) use of the ancient Greek concepts of *kairos* and *chronos*, a distinction between time experienced as moments of opportunity for radical change, and the sense of time as continual, regular progress toward a better future. Tactical urbanism relates mostly to *kairos*, the lived time and timeliness of urban intensity, while also becoming part of a strategy for long-term change. Temporary urbanism, by contrast, is more geared to *chronos*, with interim uses as a way to fill 'lost time' with short-term intensities that are intended to remain subordinated to long-term plans.

Chapter 6 also drew on Urban Catalyst's analysis of eight different modes through which temporary uses relate to the pre-established and ongoing uses of a site (Oswalt et al. 2013, Figure 8.1). We can interpret these different modes of t/t urbanism here in

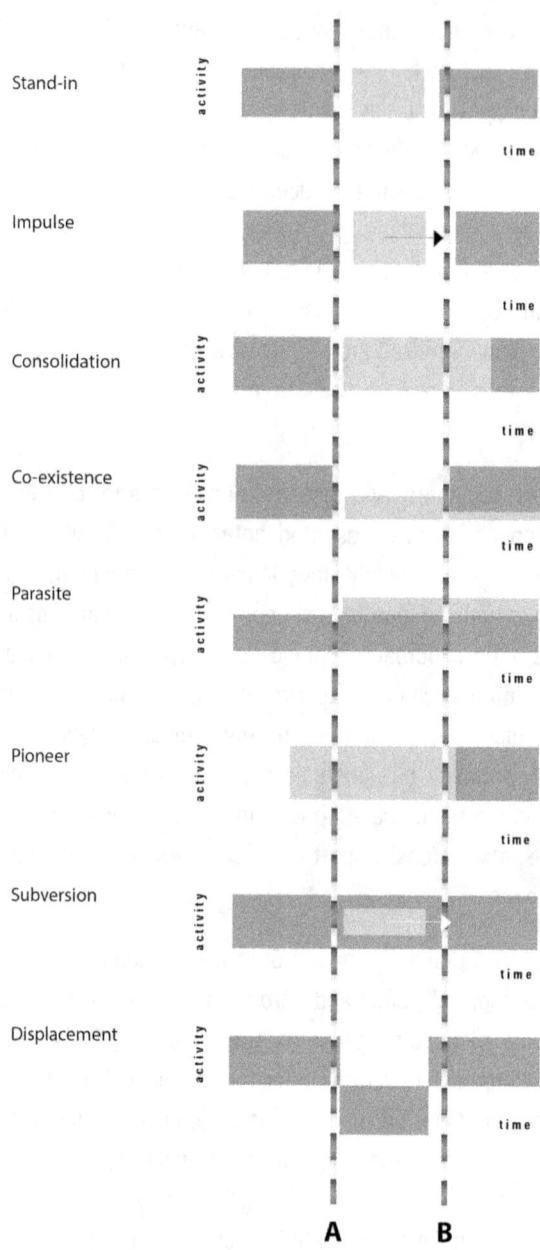

FIGURE 8.1 Eight ways that time frames temporary uses.
Source: Image based on Bengs et al. 2002, pp. 35–36.

terms of whether the new spaces, uses and actors have potential to bring extra intensity to the city or are merely filling a gap and lost intensity. This can help us to understand better whether the various changes in urban spaces and activities in response to the COVID-19 pandemic might be transformational, or are just filling an interval before a return to 'normal' city life. Four of these modes of temporary use (*Consolidation, Coexistence, Parasite* and *Pioneer*) might lead to long-term intensification by adding extra functions and users to a site. These kinds of temporary interventions establish new uses that transform, replace or share space with an earlier one. The other four modes (*Stand-In, Impulse, Subversion* and *Displacement*) change the use of a site temporarily without intensifying or modifying its long-term use – the original use persists or returns at its usual intensity.

Both public- and private-sector property managers often create or attract temporary uses such as pop-up parks or shops as part of longer-term redevelopment plans, to activate spaces, intensify their image and attract both consumers and property investors. These t/t projects meet a market demand for novelty and difference, creating an impression of intensity and change. As discussed in Chapter 5, artists are sometimes drawn to underused spaces and intensify their use and their image; they may not want their intense engagement with a place to be temporary, but their intensification of the character and value of a place is just an interim step in the planned intensification of property value. One expert interviewed in Chapter 3 went so far as to suggest that the most interesting temporary urbanism projects are always aligned with the gentrification of inner-city areas. Other experts noted that sometimes property developers actually use temporary urbanism projects to compensate for a loss of amenity and character in inner-city areas that residents see as overdeveloped – too much intensity.

The timing and duration of temporary interventions also reflect particular time frames and time pressures linked to key human actors and flows of resources in longer-term economic and property development cycles. Cities experience times of intense interest in temporary and tactical interventions, which may precede, coincide with, or counterbalance longer-term stability and large-scale, durable urban construction. Chapter 4 highlighted the intense excitement around temporary city beaches in Germany in 2006, linked to the country's hosting of the Football World Cup and an especially warm summer. Chapter 6 noted that emergency conditions and emergency powers, including the COVID-19 pandemic, can intensify both the pressures and the opportunities to tactically reshape urban spaces. The t/t experts we interviewed in Chapter 3 noted that sometimes property developers created temporary community infrastructure to help them secure development approvals and funding, and local politicians implemented them to secure their re-election. Sometimes these interventions are of low quality and durability, and occur instead of high quality, well-designed, durable public realm improvements, rather than being in addition to them. In such cases, temporary uses create temporary intensity, but may actually diminish longer-term prospects. Short-term action can lead to short-changing of communities in the long term.

The concept of 'intensity' has an important place in assemblage thinking, where it is defined in opposition to 'extension'. Unlike volumes, spaces or things, intensities are indivisible - like temperatures, atmospheres or sense of place. Urban intensities are linked to the material densities of people and spaces, but are characteristics of human experience and social encounter. Cities combine varying intensities of activity, flows and traffic, but also intensities of sound, colour and form, of sunlight, shade and darkness, even of solitude and anonymity, of being lost in a crowd. Urban intensity is a key matter of concern for t/t urbanism not because it is always a positive thing, but indeed because it is often contested.

The COVID-19 pandemic has shifted the intensities of urban open space use, due to changes in commuting, housing choices, shopping, exercise and socialising; it has changed the physical distances between people when they interact, and where they congregate. In Melbourne, long pandemic lock-downs restricted movement to within 5 km of home, bringing new intensities to suburban environments. The pandemic has stimulated a move away from cities, seeking more private space and more cohesive local communities. During the twentieth century, cities were fundamentally re-shaped by car-dependency and the three primary urban types invented to augment it – the shopping mall, the low-density suburb and the corporate office tower. We are now in the midst of a fundamental re-think of these urban types, each of which has long been under attack as mono-functional and anti-urban; islands of monotony that undermine real urban intensity. Investors and policymakers are questioning the degree to which downtown office towers might become obsolete. It remains to be seen whether this re-gearing of the intensities of urban life will have a similar impact to the post-war suburbanisation of cities in the Global North. Temporary and tactical urbanism offer opportunities to test new kinds of urban intensity.

Community Engagement

There are many ways that t/t urbanism potentially strengthens community engagement in shaping and managing urban spaces. The incremental scale of t/t projects means they can be closer and more hands-on and adaptable to individual and community needs than large-scale, centralised, slowly delivered projects. The label 'Do-It-Yourself' urbanism invokes the idea of individual or community-based action, rather than passive consumption of urban space as a finished project. In Chapter 4, we noted that even visitors to already-built t/t projects are 'prosumers' who actively perform the spaces' possibilities. t/t projects often involve actors who are new to urban development and who bring new ideas and skills. In Chapters 4 and 5, we highlighted the key involvement of artists and the important roles of hospitality and event management businesses. The COVID-19 pandemic has brought restrictions on social contact and density that have decimated both hospitality and the arts, forcing them to pivot to greater use of outdoor public spaces and more flexible, low-cost physical infrastructure, such as laneway closures and parklets. In Chapter 3, our interviewees noted the diverse scope of skilled professionals who help make t/t projects happen. This reflects a broader integration of urban planning, urban design and governance. Unlike the events staged for consumption in the private plazas of the shopping mall, t/t urbanism embodies a concern for 'building community' by knitting together places with networks of local people and a wide range of smaller-scale, often person-centred arts practices, such as visual arts, sculpture, performance, storytelling and live music.

One of t/t urbanism's greatest innovations for urban design practice is its ways of assembling different actors. This is particularly the case with tactical urbanism in the United States, which emphasises decentralised approaches and overcoming rigidly structured procedures for communication, decision-making and acting (Lydon and Garcia 2015). Community engagement is increased through the development of new networks and the sharing of skills and knowledge. This often involves new intermediary actors who facilitate contacts, exchanges and partnerships.

In Chapter 4, we emphasised that from an Actor-Network perspective, 'engagement' should not be confined to human actors. t/t projects often sell themselves, by injecting new, unpredictable and unusual forms, values and opportunities. People are drawn into engagement with t/t projects by the agency of available sites, appealing and comfortable furnishings, creative energy and excitement, powerful ideas and examples; they can also become engaged by the lure of profit or be driven by financial necessity.

We showed in Chapter 3 that local governments and urban design consultants are aware of these potentials, and are increasingly deploying them strategically, using t/t urbanist approaches as part of larger, longer-term projects and programs that meet broad community needs. The public sector also uses t/t projects to engage the public and businesses, in debate, strategic planning and larger-scale spatial development projects. 'Short-term action for long-term change' (Lydon and Garcia 2015) has become as much a mantra for governments as it has for guerrilla groups.

Despite the frequent attention in t/t urbanism literature to 'communities', new actors and new, less-hierarchical relationships, the state clearly retains a significant and multifaceted role in most kinds of t/t practices, which covers the gamut of initiating, designing, curating and tolerating projects. The state remains engaged because guerrilla gardeners are not professional landscape architects, and 'pop-up' projects are often driven by desires for profit or marketing rather than lasting public benefit. The amateurism of t/t urbanism and its 'lighter, quicker, cheaper' approaches can produce projects that are problematic or unsafe. The state has a responsibility to act on behalf of both individual and collective interests to protect and improve the quality, equity, liveability, usefulness, safety, and resilience of public space.

The state's role also includes protecting public space from private expropriation. The state creates and endows an urban commons, as we discussed in Chapter 7. It also mediates competition over the limited resource of urban space. Yet by creating capacity in public space, it also inevitably opens up capacity for profit – for private actors to extract and privatise the extra value that is created. Neoliberal urban governance sees profit as a virtue, focusing on private investment and management, deregulation and small government. We suggest that t/t urbanism cannot be reduced to a by-product of profit-seeking or neoliberal austerity, nor to some idealised version of grassroots democracy and the right to the city. It must be understood through both lenses, and as embodying their contradictions. Neoliberalism brings an emphasis on individual responsibility and enterprise. Market-based policies and self-regulated control of t/t projects can limit accountability, access and fairness. The ideas of 'amateur' or 'pop-up' urbanism are increasingly being instrumentalised by commercial interests and by powerful community groups to control urban spaces and sometimes dis-engage other human actors (Deslandes 2013, Douglas 2018).

We noted at the end of Chapter 4 that the power of any actors, human or otherwise, to act and to shape t/t urbanism comes from responsibilities that are dynamically created, negotiated, assigned and transferred. These projects also involve complex constellations of personal and collective aspirations, obligations and risks. Our discussion in Chapters 4–6 raises questions about choice and control. Who wants a given t/t project to be temporary and/or unofficial, and who seeks to give it greater permanence, legitimacy and power? Both temporary and tactical urbanism illustrate challenges for the state in fulfilling its mandate to protect and provide for the public good. State agencies are often slow, bureaucratic and prone to over-regulation. In its engagement with t/t urbanism, the state takes on a set of paradoxical obligations: to plan for the unplanned, to design for the undesignated.

The spatial distancing imperatives of the COVID-19 pandemic have paradoxically both increased and decreased community engagement in the ways public space is designed and managed. On the one hand, we find increased public acceptance of centralised government control and spending, based on a temporary emergency. However, this has also stimulated opposition to government curbs on freedom of action, movement and enterprise in urban space, some concern that such controls may not be temporary, and new community claims on spaces close to home. After extended lock-downs, major shifts toward working from home and living locally, and significant interruption to patterns of social interaction, cities need to rethink how citizens can best participate in shaping, managing and activating urban spaces. If the pandemic state of emergency becomes the harbinger for a more deeply entrenched surveillance state, then forms of community engagement will become formalised and formularised, and t/t urbanism will be largely restricted to informal, clandestine guerrilla projects.

Innovation

We noted in Chapter 2 that t/t urbanism can encourage experimentation and greatly accelerate innovation in urban space design and management because it involves techniques that are small scale, low cost, easily adjustable, moveable and reversible, and thus low risk. These benefits have come to the fore during the COVID-19 pandemic, when open space needs, risks and restrictions have been ill-understood and are frequently changing based on a continuing stream of epidemiological and economic data. Governments, businesses and residents have had to rapidly change their spatial practices, using limited resources and with little certainty about future needs and constraints. Cities' responses to the pandemic have demonstrated that people can rapidly adjust where and how they use urban space, drastically reducing use of motor vehicles, increasing active transport, shopping and socialising more locally and outdoors, and more intensively using low-density urban spaces such as vacant lots, golf courses and wide streets. During the pandemic, we have also seen that the fixities and conventions of the built environment can be rapidly overcome if governments are willing. Traffic can be redirected and street space quickly reshaped for other uses.

Innovations in urban design often emerge slowly. During the pandemic, governments have used the already-existing tactical urbanism playbook to quickly create new forms of public space by drawing on a palette of low-cost, widely available and flexible materials, objects, structures and construction techniques. We noted in Chapters 2 and 5 that t/t urbanism's contribution to innovation has mostly been about processes and actors rather than novel physical forms. Innovation can mean finding a new use for an already-developed urban form, such as the parklet does within the framework of the parking space. Innovation can also mean changing the framework – during the pandemic we have seen greatly increased political, administrative and financial investment to enable hospitality businesses to claim carspace for open-air, socially distanced seating.

While the pandemic has driven higher acceptance of temporary and tactical changes in urban space, t/t urbanism can also increase community and commercial acceptance of innovations. This is because it increases stakeholders' active engagement in shaping changes, and allows people to see and evaluate how changes can look and work before those changes are made more permanent – seeing is believing. The practitioners we interviewed in Chapter 3 noted the role of guerrilla urbanism in raising awareness about new design possibilities and changing mindsets about the processes, outcomes and impacts of urban design. The interviewees also identified several potential drawbacks of t/t innovations: while they may be lighter, quicker and cheaper, they don't always deliver high quality, durable infrastructure; nor do they necessarily enhance environmental resilience and social justice. The innovation may lie in merely finding creative ways of circumventing existing controls, undermining longer-term urban design strategies and public interests. Are these ephemeral transformations of public space introducing a rapid cycle of consumable, disposable fashion into the staid world of urban design, as Devlin's (2017) critique suggests? In the early days of t/t urbanism, the temporary greening of carspace, the spread of community gardens and avant-garde artistic experiments illustrated its potential to realise a better world by transforming neglected urban spaces. But t/t urbanism has subsequently developed in other directions.

A key question lies in the degree to which t/t urbanism's innovations are socially transformative, or whether they only prosper when they align with a neoliberal program based on individual, profit-seeking entrepreneurship and, accordingly, the needs and desires of privileged social groups. We observed in Chapter 5 the tendency to exploit the creativity of artists and cultural producers to re-value brownfield real estate. The chief innovation is in better managing the time frame and economic returns of the slow points in the property cycle, not in different ways of living in cities.

With the onset of the COVID-19 pandemic, government-supported t/t urbanism has focused on spatial innovations that narrowly support immediate economic and health issues. Parklets have neatly addressed an increase in hospitality-industry demand for outdoor space by taking advantage of the sharp decrease in demand for inner-city car parking. One kind of temporary private appropriation of public space (car parking) has been traded for another (dining). This innovative spatial format is predicated on the prospect of an easy, complete reversion to car parking. However, if seeing is believing, then once belief takes root, change becomes more difficult to reverse. This example illustrates the tension between temporary urbanism and tactical urbanism that forms a key thread of this book. Is it really temporary – just a cheap, quick and innovative way to adapt during a state of emergency, to essentially maintain business-as-usual, shaped by the conventional actors, rules and formats? Or is this a tactic within an innovative longer-term strategy to transform a wider assemblage of interests, objects and practices, producing new and better futures? Are parklets just a *Stand-In,* or are they a *Pioneer* or *Subversion,* a catalyst for a different city (Figure 8.1)?

The complex and novel relationships and interactions that define t/t urbanism projects mean that their impacts often exceed pre-defined desires, needs, expectations and roles. In addition to helping maintain revenues, parklets have transformed urban atmosphere and sense of place, increasing foot traffic and social encounters, and making streets safer at night. The proliferation of parklets in neighbourhoods where many restaurants and bars front onto walkable streets has created new dynamics. In one street in Melbourne, an alliance of businesses and residents, who have come to value the changed character of the street, have campaigned to retain parklets when the municipality has sought to reclaim them for car-parking revenue. We are seeing a renegotiation of intersecting public interests in vehicle access, safety, vitality and social atmosphere. While the dependence on private cars will not vanish overnight, t/t urbanism has the potential to innovate in response to further changes in urban traffic. The innovation of autonomous vehicles brings particular new opportunities because it partially detaches the vehicle from the destination; reducing demand for adjacent parking but increasing demand for drop-off and pick-up space.

The key innovation of parklets was not the expansion of sidewalk dining, but that they tactically subverted an existing system for temporarily allocating street space (Lydon and Garcia 2015). The conformity to the 2 m × 6 m spatial increment of the parking bay is crucial to the capacity for adaptation, resilience and creativity. This increment was not newly designed; the innovation was in rethinking urban design at this spatial and temporal scale. While the original parklets were defiantly public, hospitality parklets have re-privatised this space. Yet some cities have deployed parklets during the pandemic to advance larger-scale, longer-term plans to transform formerly vehicular streets into shared spaces (Stevens et al. forthcoming). t/t urbanism is incremental urbanism. Transforming the city in 12 m² segments has demonstrated that we can re-imagine and re-assemble the street for a diversity of uses and contingencies. This raises the question of what other uses and designs might be possible. In this regard, one of the key questions for the future of public space is the future of cycling. In many cities, cycling is the most efficient form of urban transport for most urban trips in the 1–10 km range. A safe cycle lane is 2 m wide and aligned with the kerb, just like car parking spaces. In most streets, there is competition between pedestrians, cars and cyclists for the primary use of public space. However, cycle lanes cannot be implemented effectively in small increments because they are necessarily continuous lanes and not discrete bays. The best prospect for expanding cycle lanes lies in the temporary rather than the tactical: if we build safe but temporary cycle lanes, people will get out of their cars and onto their bikes. If cycle lanes are used, they will be defended and upgraded; if not then that space becomes available again. Innovation in t/t urbanism requires an experimental approach, using the city as a laboratory. This is an addition to, rather than an alternative to, more traditional urban design and planning. Innovative t/t means thinking both short- and long-term (*kairos* and *chronos*) at multiple scales; integrating tactics with strategies and temporary with durable changes.

t/t urbanism shows the benefit to cities of encouraging a diversity of experiments from which we learn and adapt. The COVID-19 pandemic has presented a crucial opportunity for such innovation. After the pandemic wanes, if we hope for something better than a return to car dependency and further privatisation of public space, the imperative is for more experimentation. Innovation will flow top-down, bottom-up and laterally. It will come from new actors with new skills who think and design in new ways.

Resilience

Resilience is a measure of how well a city can adapt to change while maintaining an overall identity and functionality. t/t urbanism first emerged from the need for cities to adapt to the economic collapse of industrial areas and a decline in public investment. More recently it has involved responses to climate change, urban intensification and an increase in community expectations. t/t urbanism represents a range of small, fast, short-term, localised, diversified and flexible practices that enable rapid and repeated adaptation of city spaces; it is not a new system that seeks to supplant an old one. These resilient qualities of t/t urbanism – already developed, trialled and shared for 20 years – have been particularly useful during the COVID-19 pandemic. They aligned well with the need to swiftly and cheaply adapt to shifts in spatial distancing and in broader patterns of travel, exercise and consumption.

While the development of t/t urbanism practice has had little connection to the emergence of resilience thinking within academic circles, there are many parallels. Resilience thinking, also known as complex adaptive systems theory, is an attempt to understand the dynamics of complex systems where the behaviour of the system depends on unpredictable interactions between parts (Gunderson and Holling 2002, Walker and Salt 2006). This is an attempt to engage with unpredictable outcomes when independent and interdependent entities interact in complex ways, where outcomes cannot be determined in advance but rather emerge from practices of adaptation and self-organisation. Over time a 'regime' with certain characteristics emerges and settles down. An urban settlement with a particular identity or character is a regime. As argued in Chapter 7, resilience is defined as a capacity to adapt and change without slipping into a new regime or identity. Resilience is not a static property, but a dynamic capacity to move between a range of adaptive states without crossing a threshold of no return. In this sense, t/t urbanism is a capacity to bring adaptive change without regime change. Resilience theory involves a focus on certain 'key slow variables' that have potential to push the system across a threshold into a new regime. In urban design terms, these variables include land value, economic vitality, parking revenue, cycling, gentrification, street width, car dependency, traffic speed, building and population density, social mix, governance, crime and public transport. As any of these variables changes, others adapt. A street is a very complex adaptive assemblage (Dovey 2012). Resilience thinking is multi-scalar: the 12 m^2 scale of the parklet is geared to the global production of vehicles; the face-to-face scale of viral transmission is geared to the global pandemic; the vacant lot produced by a local property market is geared to neoliberal capitalism. The resilience of the street or neighbourhood and its emergent properties can only be understood through a multi-scalar approach – change can be initiated, enabled or constrained at different scales. The accretion of t/t projects is itself a key slow variable that can escalate, stabilise or decline.

t/t urbanism practice has consciously optimised the application and adaptability of its models and ideas, harnessing the potential of ready-made, transportable materials and finished projects, and engaging a broad range of human actors by providing access to free online how-to manuals. Resilience is constructed through what we might call a 'learning assemblage' that expands from the street, neighbourhood or city to incorporate websites, hardware stores, social media, and books like the one you are now reading. t/t urbanism is an expanding reservoir of possibility that brings new resilience to cities, by sharing new ways of producing, managing and using urban space.

The twofold name t/t urbanism emphasises its two most distinctive contributions to resilience in urban design. The temporary is the idea that an urban space can be redesigned within and for a short time frame, and that urban design components – usually thought of as heavy, slow to arrange and expensive – can then be easily rearranged, packed away and/or reused in some other place or time. The tactical is the idea that small increments of adaptive change involving small and varied sets of resources are more agile than master planning. Assemblage thinking and Actor-Network Theory, a broader set of ideas that predate t/t urbanism, provide a helpful nomenclature and logic for these dimensions of resilience: t/t urbanism is mobile, mutable, and involves non-hierarchical relationships, whereby any actor or factor can adapt to others. As argued in Chapter 7, resilience can be understood as forms of capacity that emerge through these complex interrelations.

Resilience does not mean resisting change; it means managing change differently. In Chapter 6, we examined how different time frames of planning and action, and the ways that various actors value, manage and use time, have enabled the rapid, agile, adaptable kinds of spatial interventions that characterise t/t urbanism. We noted that transience represents freedom from the fixities of long-term spatial arrangements, investments and social relationships that traditionally characterise urban design, allowing urban space to be transformed and managed nimbly in response to changing contingencies. One of the unsettling impacts of the COVID-19 pandemic has been its restructuring of human experience of time, disrupting the conventional flows of city life – rush hour, lunch time, after-five get-togethers, weekends, holidays – and creating new ones. During lockdowns, there has been a surge in people running the internet query 'what day is it?'. In some cities, citizens have been allocated separate set times for their daily strolls and their shopping, to prevent crowding. The pandemic has provided an opportunity to experience and use time differently, to adjust how and where we move and spend time in the city. Public space has been reallocated for walking and cycling as key forms of exercise and local transport, for open-air schooling, dining, food markets and pop-up clinics. Urban spaces have been temporarily transformed to better support social interactions which were suddenly not possible in indoor spaces, with new lane markings, distancing circles, and seating arrangements (Mehta 2020). Everyone has been trying to identify and establish a 'new normal' for public life. However, the upheaval of the pandemic has also reminded us that cities will always face future shocks, including impacts of climate change, rising sea levels, migration, economic inequality, changing living arrangements and new technologies.

The idea that cities are permanent and fixed has always been a myth. Just as all buildings must die (Cairns and Jacobs 2014), so it is with the spaces between buildings. With the COVID-19 pandemic, policymakers and property investors have begun contemplating whether high-density, city-centre apartments and office buildings might be rendered obsolete, as both work and social life have shifted to the suburbs and beyond. Housing has been redesigned for working and learning from home; a shift that will never fully be reversed. Ongoing restructuring of cities is inevitable. Assemblage thinking focuses our attention on how new forms of cooperation and order can emerge in urban space and urban design practice to address such shifts. t/t urbanism casts a spotlight onto the different timeframes and the varied actors through which cities adjust.

While much discussion of t/t urbanism has emphasised how the arrangement of cities, citizens, spaces, materials and time can become more flexible and agile, we noted in Chapter 6 that t/t urbanism has also created new, durable assemblages. The 'pop-up' shopping mall Box Park (Bishop and Williams 2012) has never popped down. East Berlin's *Palast der Republik* hosted temporary uses for 16 years, after only serving its originally designed functions for 14 years (Oswalt et al. 2013). Parklets have become widespread, and in some cases permanent. Assemblage thinking also helps us to understand how the relationships that constitute t/t urbanism give its new ideas and projects staying power.

Place Identity

By its nature, t/t urbanism tends to transform place identity, shifting away from a relatively fixed, deep-rooted sense of place toward more open, multiple and dynamic identities. Temporary urban design projects challenge the idea that places and values are stable. Tactical urbanism questions and contests a single, authorised identity and seeks to change how places are made and managed, and by whom. t/t urbanism informs future development by engaging critically with the historical legacy of places and the powers that control them. Because t/t urbanism is transitory and partial, it enables the city to encompass both preservation and change, to embody the tensions between history and progress, singularity and multiplicity.

We noted in Chapter 2 that t/t urbanism's impacts on urban character and place identity are not always viewed positively. Such projects can serve new interests and groups, potentially disrupting the attachments to place of individuals or groups who are deeply invested in them and cannot easily move. Another key concern relates to design quality – t/t projects often lack the forethought and resources to create well-designed contributions to urban character and lack the authorisation and maintenance that extend their impact. While many t/t project types – the astroturfed parklet, the shop in a shipping container, the little free library – were innovative when first introduced, they have gradually developed a very generic global character.

The very extensive tactical transformations of many cities during the COVID-19 pandemic may go the way of the many temporary city beaches created in German cities, many of which were permanently removed once their sites were re-developed for longer-term tenants. Some beaches are re-assembled each summer to produce seasonal character without changing the city in any permanent way. Only in rare cases have they become permanent fixtures that transformed a city's overall image and function (Stevens 2011).

Early writings on t/t urbanism suggested that short-term urban design actions could be a catalyst for broad, long-term transformation of the character of urban neighbourhoods. These writings also documented provisional, 'pop-up' installations that in some cases have remained and become core elements of local urban character. Like other forms of urban design, t/t urbanism seeks to create better places both by harnessing what is special about a location and by giving form to new possibilities. Temporary urbanism is part of the character of all places. All urban spaces are, by their nature, shared spaces, which temporarily host different objects and functions for different lengths of time and at different intervals.

t/t urbanism emerged in its contemporary forms primarily in industrial brownfields and marginalised, disinvested cities and neighbourhoods. These places often had rich local place identity but a lack of financial resources to maintain spaces of commercial and social vitality. Temporary urbanism in Europe and the United Kingdom sought to explore new uses that could rejuvenate old places and harness their distinctive character. Tactical urbanism in the US sought to sustain the social and economic vitality of places and achieve a better fit between their legacy infrastructure and current needs. In these contexts, the key critique levelled at t/t urbanism's impact on place identity was that it is a form of place rebranding and marketing: capturing attention, attracting new clientele, enhancing private property values and driving out existing uses and users. As Douglas (2018) notes, ostensibly 'DIY' urbanism may not be local and inclusive; it often imprints the identity of wealthy, highly educated, white producers and consumers onto disinvested but character-filled places, effectively colonising these places, suppressing or amending their history and dis-placing difference.

Rather than reducing t/t urbanism to some form of gentrification, we suggest that this be understood as a paradox: t/t urbanism is a form of deep, participatory democracy that takes place under conditions of neoliberal capitalism.

Recent temporary transformations of street spaces in Melbourne, Australia, in response to the COVID-19 pandemic illustrate different ways that local urban character can be shaped by the interactions of economic forces, governance regimes, and people's individual preferences. Across metropolitan Melbourne, hundreds of parklets have been deployed for hospitality industry businesses through local government procurement processes. These mostly use generic forms, materials and colour schemes that differentiate one municipality from another but produce uniformity within each area. The rare municipalities that have allowed businesses to design individual parklets – the key creative clusters of Moreland and Yarra – have produced varied streetscape aesthetics that range from very shabby to highly creative. The City of Yarra's approach provides nothing more than distinctive pink and purple concrete bollards defining and protecting the parklet envelope. Some of these spaces are only furnished at night, while others are elaborately themed to produce distinctive atmosphere and brand identity. It is yet to be seen whether these temporary changes will propagate lasting shifts in local place identity. In San Francisco, the thousands of parklets that have become emblematic of that city's street life have recently been granted permanent status. Their character has emerged through a combination of regulations, support and funding from the Mayor's Office of Economic Development, changing economic and public health imperatives, and the predilections of individual businesses and their paying customers.

Conclusion

Temporary and tactical urbanism are now well-established practices used by governments, established businesses, fledgling entrepreneurs and non-professional citizens to (re)assemble and (re)activate under-utilised urban spaces. The COVID-19 pandemic has driven a major increase in interest in these responsive and adaptive policies and practices for creating and managing urban spaces. Modern urban planning developed in the nineteenth century largely in response to public health crises. Up until that time, each epidemic would kill a significant portion of the urban population due to overcrowding and poor sanitation. Urban design shifted then to prioritise the free movement of air, people, goods and information. We now face the next step in this shift, another moment to reimagine urban space and urban life to make cities more flexible and adaptive. How this plays out is an open question. While this chapter offers a few speculations, there can be no conclusion about the possible city.

Transforming public spaces has traditionally been a slow, bureaucratic, resource-intensive process. During the COVID-19 pandemic, governments have scaled-up, sanctioned and even systematised experimental, bottom-up forms of tactical urbanism such as parklets, guerrilla crosswalks and pop-up bike lanes. Both the Global Financial Crisis of 2007-08 and the pandemic have moved temporary and tactical urbanism from the margins of urban design practice to the mainstream. This shift has provided clear public benefits, but we warn against any conclusion that the temporary and tactical can be co-opted in service of the permanent and strategic. t/t urbanism may augment and enhance more traditional urban design and planning practices, but it remains in tension with them.

t/t urbanism is not a short-term fashion; indeed it can be understood as an integral aspect of all cities. Cities have always been a mix of the temporary and permanent, the tactical and strategic, the informal and formal. In the contemporary context, t/t urbanism can be usefully understood within the framework of urban informality that was originally developed to better understand cities of the Global South, where informal settlement, street vending and public transport are prevailing modes of producing, managing and using urban space. While definitions of informality are contested, it is well understood that all cities mix informal and formal practices in different ways – informal and formal are not binary categories. As with t/t urbanism, the concept of urban informality combines definitions of illegality and inferiority with incrementality, irregularity and insurgency (Dovey et al 2021). t/t urbanism is scarcely noticed in highly informalised cities of the Global South, where the temporary and tactical are very common ways of organising urban space. t/t urbanism requires a formal context in order to be identified; it is largely a movement framed in contrast to the over-formalised cities of the Global North. t/t urbanism is paradoxical, being at once a form of deep democracy and largely produced by neoliberal capitalism. There can be no resolution to the question of which of these is primary – t/t urbanism cannot be reduced to either. Like public space itself, the practices of t/t urbanism will remain a field of contested interests. A key challenge lies in keeping this field alive and contested. While t/t urbanism has become formalised in many cases, it is essentially a seed ground for new ideas about the future of public space. It is at the informal end of this spectrum – the spontaneous, self-organised, creative and guerrilla activities of citizens – where new ideas primarily emerge.

References

Bengs, C., Hentilä, H. and Nagy, D. (2002) *Urban catalysts: Strategies for temporary uses – Potential for development of urban residual areas in European metropolises*, Espoo: Centre for Urban and Regional Studies, Helsinki University of Technology.

Bishop, P. and Williams, L. (2012) *The temporary city*, New York: Routledge.

Cairns, S. and Jacobs, M. (2014) *Buildings must die: A perverse view of architecture*, Cambridge, MA: MIT Press.

Daly, J., Dovey, K. and Stevens, Q. (2020) We can't let coronavirus kill our cities. Here's how we can save urban life. *The Conversation*, 5 May.

Deslandes, A. (2013) Exemplary amateurism: Thoughts on DIY urbanism. *Cultural Studies Review* 19 (1): 216–27.

Devlin, R. (2017) Asking 'third world questions' of first world informality. *Planning Theory* 17 (4): 568–87.

Douglas, G. (2018) *The help-yourself city: Legitimacy and inequality in DIY urbanism*, London: Oxford University Press.

Dovey, K. (2012) Informal settlement and complex adaptive assemblage. *International Development Planning Review* 34 (3): 371–90.

Dovey, K., Morley, M. and Stevens, Q. (2021) What next for parklets? It doesn't have to be a permanent switch back to parking. *The Conversation*, 4 May.

Dovey, K., Shafique, T., van Oostrum, M. and Chatterjee, I. (2021) Informal settlement is not a euphemism for 'slum'. *International Development Planning Review* 43 (2): 139–50.

Gunderson, L. and Holling, C. (eds) (2002) *Panarchy: Understanding transformations in human and natural systems*, Washington, D.C.: Island Press.

Lydon, M. and Garcia, A. (2015) *Tactical urbanism: Short-term action for long-term change*, Washington, D.C.: Island Press.

Madanipour, A. (2017) *Cities in time: Temporary urbanism and the future of the city*, London: Bloomsbury.

Mehta, V. (2020) The new proxemics: COVID-19, social distancing, and sociable space. *Journal of Urban Design* 25 (6): 669–74.

Oswalt, P., Overmeyer, K. and Misselwitz, P. (2013) *Urban catalyst: The power of temporary use*. Berlin: DOM publishers.

Stevens, Q. (2011) Characterising Germany's artificial 'city beaches: Distribution, type and design', *3rd World Planning Schools Congress*, Perth.

Stevens, Q., Morley, M. and Dovey, K. (forthcoming) Mapping Melbourne's parklets: Understanding the capacities of urban street spaces.

Walker, B. and Salt, D. (2006) *Resilience Thinking*. Washington, DC: Island Press.

Bibliography

Adams, R., Dovey, K. and Jones, R. (2018) Melbourne futures, in: K. Dovey, R. Adams and R. Jones (eds) *Urban choreography*, Melbourne: Melbourne UP.

Agamben, G. (2005) *State of exception*. Chicago: University of Chicago Press.

Alexander, C., Ishikawa, S. and Silverstein, M. (1977) *A pattern language*, New York: Oxford University Press.

Andres, L. (2013) Differential Spaces, power hierarchy and collaborative planning: A critique of the role of temporary uses in shaping and making places. *Urban Studies* 50 (4): 759–75.

Andres, L. and Golubchikov, O. (2016) The limits to artist-led regeneration: Creative brownfields in the cities of high culture. *International Journal of Urban and Regional Research* 40 (4): 757–75

Andres, L. and Grésillon, B. (2013) Cultural brownfields in European cities: A new mainstream object for cultural and urban policies. *International Journal of Cultural Policy* 19 (1): 40–62.

Andres, L. and Zhang, Y. (eds) (2020) *Transforming cities through temporary urbanism: A comparative overview*, Cham, Switzerland: Springer.

Andres, L., Bakare, H., Bryson, J., Khaemba, W., Melgaço, L. and Mwaniki, G. (2021) Planning, temporary urbanism and citizen-led alternative-substitute place-making in the Global South. *Regional Studies* 55 (1): 29–39.

Angst, M., Klaus, P., Michaelis, T., Müller, R. and Wolff, R. (2009) *Zone*imaginaire: Zwischennutzungen in Industriearealen*, Zürich: Vdf Hochschulverlag.

Arefi, M. and C. Kickert (eds) (2019) *The Palgrave handbook of bottom-up urbanism*. Cham, Switzerland: Palgrave Macmillan.

Arlt, P. (n.d.) 'Aktionen + Temporäre Bauten'. Online, available at: www.peterarlt.at/index.php?kat=1 (accessed 31 July 2012).

Barron, P. (2014) Introduction, in P. Barron and M. Mariani (eds) *Terrain vague: Interstices at the edge of the pale*, New York: Routledge.

BBR (Bundesamt für Bauwesen und Raumordnung) (2004) *Zwischennutzung und neue Freiflächen - städtische Lebensräume der Zukunft*, Berlin: H. Heenemann.

Beauregard, R. (2015) Temporalities, in *Planning matter: Acting with things*, Chicago: University of Chicago Press, pp. 151–71.

Becker, C. (2010) Kreativwirtschaft als Chance der Brachflächenreaktivierung, in F. Dosch and S. Glöckner (eds) *Neue Zugänge zum Flächenrecycling (Informationen zur Raumplanung 1/2010)*, Bonn: Bundesamt für Bauwesen und Raumordnung, pp. 71–82.

Bela, J. (2015) User-generated urbanism and the right to the city. in J. Hou, et al. (eds), *Now urbanism: The future city is here*, New York: Routledge, pp. 149–64.

Bender, T. (2010) Reassembling the city, in I. Farias and T. Bender (eds), *Urban assemblages*, London: Routledge, pp. 303–23.

Bengs, C., Hentilä, H. and Nagy, D. (2002) *Urban catalysts: Strategies for temporary uses – Potential for development of urban residual areas in European metropolises*. Espoo: Centre for Urban and Regional Studies, Helsinki University of Technology.

Bermann, K. and Marinaro, I. C. (2014) 'We work it out': Roma settlements in Rome and the limits of do-it-yourself. *Journal of Urbanism* 7 (4): 399–413.

Beyes, T. (2009) Spaces of intensity – urban entrepreneurship as redistribution of the sensible, in D. Hjorth and C. Steyaert (eds) *The politics and aesthetics of entrepreneurship*, Cheltenham, UK: Edward Elgar, pp. 92–112.

Biddulph, M. (2011) Urban design, regeneration and the entrepreneurial city. *Progress in Planning* 76: 63–103.

Bishop, P. and Williams, L. (2012) *The Temporary City*, New York: Routledge.

Blumner, N. (2006) *Planning for the unplanned: Tools and techniques for interim use in Germany and the United States*, Berlin: Deutsches Institut für Urbanistik.

BMVBS/BBR (Bundesministerium für Verkehr, Bau und Stadtentwicklung and Bundesamt für Bauwesen und Raumordnung) (eds) (2008) *Zwischennutzungen und Nischen im Städtebau als Beitrag für eine nachhaltige Stadtentwicklung*, Bonn: BBR.

Böhme, C., Henckel, D. and Besecke, A. (2006) *Brachflächen in der Flächenkreislaufwirtschaft*, Berlin: Bundesamt für Bauwesen und Raumordnung.

Bornmann, F., Erbelding, D. and Froessler D. (2008) *Zwischennutzungen: Temporäre Nutzungen als Instrument der Stadtentwicklung*, Düsseldorf: Innovationsagentur Stadtumbau NRW.

Bragaglia, F. and Rossignolo, C. (2021) Temporary urbanism as a new policy strategy: A contemporary panacea or a trojan horse?. *International Planning Studies*, DOI: 10.1080/135 63475.2021.1882963

Brammer, M. (2008) Zwischennutzung in Berlin Neukölln: Kreativwirtschaft als Motor in einem sozial benachteiligten Binnenquartier. *Standort – Zeitschrift für Angewandte Geographie* 32: 71–77.

Brenner, N. (2015) Is "Tactical Urbanism" an Alternative to Neoliberal Urbanism?. *MoMA Post: Notes on Modern and Contemporary Art around the Globe*, viewed 7 April 2021, http://post.at.moma.org/content_items/587-is-tactical-urbanism-an-alternative-to-neoliberal-urbanism

Brenner, N., Madden, D. and Wachsmuth, D. (2011) Assemblage urbanism and the challenges of critical urban theory. *City* 15 (2): 225–40.

Brown, A. (ed) (2006) *Contested space: Street trading, public space and livelihoods in developing cities*, Rugby, ITDY.

Bürgin, M. (2010) *Leitfaden Zwischennutzung*, online, available at: http://www.zwischennutzung.areale.ch/images/pdf_D/varianten/pdf_alle_bsp_d.pdf (accessed 22 August 2017).

Bürgin, M. and Cabane, P. (1999) Akupunktur für Basel: Zwischennutzung als Standortentwicklung auf dem Areal des DB-Güterbahnhofs in Basel, online, available at: http://www.areal.org/areal_alt/download/zn_mb.pdf (accessed 11 April 2012).

Cairns, S. and Jacobs, M. (2014) *Buildings must die: A perverse view of architecture*, Cambridge, MA: MIT Press.

Callon, M. (1986) Elements of a sociology of translation: Domestication of the scallops and the fishermen of St Brieuc Bay, in J. Law (ed) *Power, Action And Belief: A new sociology of knowledge?* London: Routledge, pp. 196–233.

Carr, S. and Lynch, K. (1968) Where learning happens. *Daedalus* 97 (4): 1277–91.

Carr, S. and Lynch, K. (1981) Open space: Freedom and control, in L. Taylor (ed) *Urban open spaces*, New York: Rizzoli.

CDS and SPC (CoDesign Studio and Street Plans Collaborative (2014) *Tactical Urbanism Vol. 4: Australia and New Zealand*, viewed 12 June 2019, available at: http://tacticalurbanismguide.com/guides/tactical-urbanism-volume-4/

Chang, R. (2021) How do scholars communicate the 'temporary turn' in urban studies? A socio-semiotic framework. *Urban Planning* 6 (1): 133–45.

Christiaanse, K. (2013) Preface, in P. Oswalt, K. Overmeyer and P. Misselwitz (eds), *Urban catalyst: The power of temporary use*, Berlin: DOM Publishers, pp. 6–7.

Colomb, C. (2007) Requiem for a lost Palast. Revanchist urban planning and burdened landscapes of the German Democratic Republic in the new Berlin. *Planning Perspectives* 22 (3): 283–323.

Colomb, C. (2012) Pushing the urban frontier: Temporary uses of space, city marketing, and the creative city discourse in 2000s Berlin. *Journal of Urban Affairs* 34 (2): 131–52.

Colomb, C. (2012) *Staging the New Berlin: Place marketing and the politics of urban re-invention post-1989*, London: Routledge.

Daly, J., Dovey, K. and Stevens, Q. (2020) We can't let coronavirus kill our cities. Here's how we can save urban life. *The Conversation*, 5 May. Online, available at: https://theconversation.com/we-cant-let-coronavirus-kill-our-cities-heres-how-we-can-save-urban-life-137063

David, B. (2010) Manager of *Kulturstrand*, Munich. Personal interview.

de Certeau, M. (1984) *The practice of everyday life*, Berkeley: University of California Press.

DeLanda, M. (2006) *A new philosophy of society*, New York: Continuum.

DeLanda, M. (2011) *Philosophy and simulation*, New York: Continuum.

Deleuze, G. (1968) *Difference and repetition*, New York: Columbia University Press.

Deleuze, G. and Guattari, F. (1987) *A thousand plateaus*, London: Athlone Press.

Deslandes, A. (2013) Exemplary amateurism: Thoughts on DIY urbanism. *Cultural Studies Review* 19 (1): 216–27.

Devlin, R. (2017) Asking 'third world questions' of first world informality: Using southern theory to parse needs from desires in an analysis of informal urbanism of the global North. *Planning Theory* 17 (4): 568–87.

Dienel, H. and Schophaus, M. (2005) Urban wastelands and the development of youth cultures in Berlin since 1945, with comparative perspectives on Amsterdam and Naples, in A. Schildt and D. Siegfried (eds) *European cities, youth and the public sphere in the twentieth century*, Aldershot: Ashgate, pp. 119–33.

Dobson, S. and Jorgensen, A. (2014) Increasing the resilience and adaptive capacity of cities through entrepreneurial urbanism. *International Journal of Globalisation and Small Business* 6 (3/4): 149–62.

Dotson, T. (2016) Trial-and-error urbanism: Addressing obduracy, uncertainty and complexity in urban planning and design. *Journal of Urbanism* 9 (2): 148–65.

Douglas, G. (2014) Do-it-yourself urban design. *City and Community* 13 (1): 5–25.

Douglas, G. (2018) *The help-yourself city: Legitimacy and inequality in DIY urbanism*, London: Oxford University Press.

Dovey, K. (2008) *Framing places* (2nd ed.), London: Routledge.

Dovey, K. (2010) *Becoming places*, London: Routledge.

Dovey, K. (2012) Informal settlement and complex adaptive assemblage. *International Development Planning Review* 34 (3): 371–90.

Dovey, K. (2012) Uprooting critical urbanism. *City* 15 (3–4): 347–54.

Dovey, K. (2013) Planning and place identity, in G. Young, et al. (eds) *The Ashgate research companion to planning and culture*, London: Ashgate.

Dovey, K. (2016) *Urban design thinking: A conceptual toolkit*, London: Bloomsbury.

Dovey, K. (2020) Place as assemblage, in T. Edensor, U. Kothari and A. Kaladides (eds) *The Routledge handbook of place*, London: Routledge. pp. 21–31.

Dovey, K. and Fisher, K. (2014) Designing for adaptation: The school as socio-spatial assemblage. *Journal of Architecture* 19 (10): 43–63.

Dovey, K. and King, R. (2011) Forms of informality: Morphology and visibility of informal settlements. *Built Environment* 37 (1): 11–29.

Dovey, K. and Pafka, E. (2014) The urban density assemblage: Modelling multiple measures. *Urban Design International* 19 (1): 66–76.

Dovey, K. and Pafka, E. (2020) What is walkability?: The Urban DMA. *Urban Studies* 57 (1): 93–108.

Dovey, K., Morley, M. and Stevens, Q. (2021) What next for parklets? It doesn't have to be a permanent switch back to parking. *The Conversation*, 4 May. Online. Available at: https://theconversation.com/what-next-for-parklets-it-doesnt-have-to-be-a-permanent-switch-back-to-parking-159534.

Dovey, K., Pafka, E. and Ristic, M. (eds) (2018) *Mapping urbanities*, New York: Routledge.
Dovey, K., Shafique, T., van Oostrum, M. and Chatterjee, I. (2021) Informal settlement is not a euphemism for 'slum'. *International Development Planning Review* 43 (2): 139–50.
Dovey, K., Wollan, S. and Woodcock, I. (2012) Placing graffiti. *Journal of Urban Design* 17 (1): 21–41.
Downton, P. (2009) *Ecopolis*, Dordrecht: Springer.
DPMC (Department of Prime Minister and Cabinet) (2016) *Smart cities plan*, Canberra: Commonwealth of Australia.
Dransfeld, E. and Lehmann, D. (2008) *Temporäre Nutzungen als Bestandteil des modernen Baulandmanagements*, Dortmund: Forum Baulandmanagement NRW.
Ebert, R. and Kunzmann, K. (2007) Kulturwirtschaft, kreative Räume und Stadtentwicklung in Berlin. *disP –The Planning Review* 43 (171): 64–79.
Erismann, E. (2011) Temporary use during Kleinhüningen's harbour renewal process: A case study of characteristics, opportunities and tools for successful implementation, unpublished masters thesis, University of Applied Sciences Northwestern Switzerland.
Fabian, L. and Samson, K. (2014) DIY urban design: Between ludic tactics and strategic planning, in B. Knudsen, D. Christensen and P. Blenker (eds) *Enterprising initiatives in the experience economy: Transforming social worlds*. New York: Routledge.
Fabian, L. and Samson, K. (2016) Claiming participation: A comparative analysis of DIY urbanism. *Journal of Urbanism* 9 (2): 166–84.
Färber, A. (2014) Low-budget Berlin: Towards an understanding of low-budget urbanity as assemblage. *Journal of Regions, Economy and Society* 7: 119–36.
Farias, I. (2017) Assemblages, in M. Jayne and K. Ward (eds) *Urban theory: New critical perspectives*, New York: Routledge, pp. 41–50.
Farias, I. and Bender, T. (2009) *Urban assemblages: How Actor-Network Theory changes urban studies*, New York: Routledge.
Ferguson, F. (2014) *Make_shift city: Renegotiating the urban commons*, Berlin: Jovis.
Ferreri, M. (2015) The seductions of temporary urbanism. *Ephemera: Theory and Politics in Organization* 15 (1): 181–91.
Ferreri, M. (2021) *The permanence of temporary urbanism: Normalising precarity in austerity London*, Amsterdam: Amsterdam University Press.
Fidler, E. (2011) Temporary uses can enliven city neighborhoods, Greater Greater Washington, available at: http://greatergreaterwashington.org/post/12674/temporary-uses-can-enliven-city-neighborhoods/ (accessed 28 July 2020).
Finn, D. (2014) DIY urbanism: Implications for cities. *Journal of Urbanism* 7 (4): 381–98.
Florida, R. (2002) *The rise of the creative class and how it is transforming work, leisure, community and everyday life*, New York: Basic Books.

Franck, K. and Stevens, Q. (eds) (2007) *Loose space: Possibility and diversity in urban life*, New York: Routledge.

Gadanho, P. (2014) *Uneven growth: Tactical urbanisms for expanding megacities*, New York: MOMA.

Gale, T. (2009) Urban beaches, virtual worlds and 'the end of tourism'. *Mobilities* 4 (1): 119–38.

Gassner, S., Schmidt-Hitschler, U. and Hitschler, T. (2011) Organisers of *Strandleben*, Vaihingen an der Enz. Personal interview.

Gehl, J., Johansen, L., & Reigstad, S. (2006) 'Close encounters with buildings' Urban Design International, 11, 29–47.

Gibson, J. J. (1979) *The ecological approach to visual perception*, Boston: Houghton Mifflin.

Giedion, S. (1948) *Mechanization takes command: A contribution to anonymous history*, New York: Oxford University Press.

Gold, J. and Gold, M. (eds) (2017) *Olympic cities: City agendas, planning and the world's games, 1896–2020*, New York: Routledge.

Greco, J. (2012) From pop-up to permanent. *Planning* 78 (9): 15–16.

Groth, J. and Corijn, E. (2005) Reclaiming urbanity: Indeterminate spaces, informal actors and urban agenda setting. *Urban Studies* 42 (3): 503–26.

Guggenheim, M. (2010) Mutable Immobiles in I. Farias and T. Bender (eds), *Urban Assemblages*, London: Routledge, pp. 161–78.

Gunderson, L. and Holling, C. (eds) (2002) *Panarchy: Understanding transformations in human and natural systems*, Washington, D.C.: Island Press.

Haid, C. (2017) The Janus face of urban governance: State, informality and ambiguity in Berlin. *Current Sociology Monograph* 65 (2): 289–301.

Hall, E. T. (1966) *The hidden dimension*, New York: Doubleday.

Hall, P. (1998) *Cities in civilization: Culture, innovation, and urban order*, London: Weidenfeld and Nicolson.

Hamnett, C. (2003) Gentrification and the Middle-class Remaking of Inner London, 1961–2001. *Urban Studies* 40 (12): 2401–26.

Harvey, D. (2007) *A brief history of neoliberalism*, Oxford: Oxford University Press.

Havemann, A. and Schild, W. (2007) You can use my tights or: The phenomenon of temporary solutions. *Landscape Research* 32 (1): 45–55.

Haydn, F. and Temel, R. (eds) (2006) *Temporary urban spaces: Concepts for the use of city spaces*, Basel: Birkhäuser.

Healey, P. (2004) Creativity and urban governance. *Policy Studies* 25 (2): 87–102.

Henneberry, J. (ed) (2017) *Transience and permanence in urban development*, Hoboken NJ: Wiley Blackwell.

Holling, C. and Gunderson, L. (2002) Resilience and adaptive cycles, in L. Gunderson and C. Holling (eds) 2002 *Panarchy*, Washington, D.C.: Island Press, pp. 25–62.

Honeck, T. (2017) From squatters to creatives: An innovation perspective on temporary use in planning. *Planning Theory and Practice* 18 (2): 268–87.

Hou, J. (ed) (2010) *Insurgent public space: Guerrilla urbanism and the remaking of contemporary cities*, New York: Routledge.

Hou, J., Spencer, B., Yocom, K. and Way, T. (eds) (2015) *Now urbanism: The future city is here*, New York: Routledge.

Ioannides, D. and Debbage, K. (1997) Post-Fordism and flexibility: The travel industry polyglot. *Tourism Management* 18 (4): 229–241.

Isaac, J. (1992) Beyond the three faces of power, in T. Wartenberg (ed) *Rethinking power*, Albany: SUNY Press, pp. 32–55.

Iveson, K. (2013) Cities within the city: Do-it-yourself urbanism and the right to the city. *International Journal of Urban and Regional Research* 37 (3): 941–56.

Jacobs, A. and Appleyard, D. (1987) Toward an urban design manifesto. *Journal of the American Planning Association* 53 (1): 112–20.

Jacobs, J. (1961) *The death and life of great American Cities*, New York: Random House.

Jacobs, J. M., Cairns, S. and Strebel, I. (2012) Doing building work: Methods at the interface of geography and architecture. *Geographical Research* 50 (2): 126–40

Johnson, S. (2001) *Emergence: The connected lives of ants, brains, cities and software*, London: Penguin.

Jorg, J. (2008) *Make use: A comparison between temporary-use strategies of intermediary organizations with the goal of using vacant buildings as workplaces for social and creative entrepreneurs*, unpublished masters thesis, Amsterdam/Brussels: POLIS MA in European Urban Cultures.

Kamel, N. (2014) Learning from the margin: Placemaking tactics, in V. Mukhija and A. Loukaitou-Sideris (eds) *The informal American city: Beyond taco trucks and day labor*, Cambridge, MA: MIT Press.

Kamvasinou, K. (2011) The public value of vacant urban land. *Municipal Engineer* 164 (3): 157–66.

Kamvasinou, K. (2015) Temporary intervention and long-term legacy: Lessons from London case studies. *Journal of Urban Design* 22 (2): 187–207.

Kamvasinou, K. and Roberts, M. (2014) Interim spaces, in P. Barron and M. Mariani (eds) *Terrain vague: Interstices at the edge of the pale*, New York: Routledge.

Klanten, R. and Hübner, M. (eds) (2010) *Urban interventions: Personal projects in public spaces*, Berlin: Gestalten.

Kloos, M., Knüvener, T. and Wachten, K. (2007) *Freiräume auf Zeit: Neue Konzepte für Grünflächen in Stadterneuerungsgebieten*, Aachen: Internationales Institut für Gartenkunst und Landschaftskultur Schloss Dyck.

Krauzick, M. (2007) *Zwischennutzung als Initiator einer neuen Berliner Identität?*, Berlin: Universitätsverlag der TU Berlin.

Kreuzer, S. (2001) Temporäre Freiräume: Szenarischer Replik zum Vortrag des Soziologen Peter Arlt. *Zolltexte* 38: 18–19.

Kruse, S. and Steglich, A. (2006) *Temporäre Nutzungen: Stadtgestalt zwischen Selbstorganisation und Steuerung*, Lüneburg: Fakultät III – Umwelt und Technik, Universität Lüneburg.

Landry, C. and Bianchini, F. (1995) *The Creative City*, London: Demos.

Lange B (2007) *Die Räume der Kreativszenen. Culturepreneurs und ihre Orte in Berlin*, Bielefeld: Transcript.

Lange, B. (2007) Entrepreneurial temporary use: An Incubator for the creative economy, in SenStadt (ed) *Urban pioneers: Temporary use and urban development in Berlin*, Berlin: Jovis, pp. 135–42.

Lange, B. (2008) Accessing markets in creative industries: Professionalization and social-spatial strategies of culturepreneurs in Berlin. *Creative Industries Journal* 1 (2): 115–35.

Lange, B. (2011) Professionalization in space: Social-spatial strategies of culturepreneurs in Berlin. *Entrepreneurship and Regional Development* 23 (3-4): 259–79.

Lara-Hernandez, J. A., Coulter, C. and Melis, A. (2020) Temporary appropriation and urban informality: Exploring the subtle distinction. *Cities* 99, article 102626.

Larsen, J. L., Elle, M., Hoffmann, B. and Munthe-Kaas, P. (2011) Urbanising facilities management: The challenges in a creative age. *Facilities* 29 (1–2): 80–92.

Latour, B. (1987) *Science in action*, Cambridge, MA: Harvard University Press.

Latour, B. (1988) *The pasteurization of France*. Cambridge, MA: Harvard University Press.

Latour, B. (1992) Where are the missing masses? Sociology of a door, in W. Bijker and J. Law (eds), *Shaping technology/building society*, Cambridge, MA: MIT Press, pp. 225–58.

Latour, B. (2004) Why has critique run out of steam?. *Critical Inquiry* 30 (2): 225–48.

Latour, B. (2005) *Reassembling the social. An introduction to Actor-Network Theory*, Oxford: Oxford University Press.

Lefebvre, H. (1996) *Writings on cities*. (tranls. E. Kofman and E. Lebas). Oxford: Blackwell.

Loukaitou-Sideris, L. and Mukhija, V. (2014) Conclusion: Deepening the understanding of informal urbanism, in V. Mukhija and A. Loukaitou-Sideris (eds) *The informal American city: Beyond taco trucks and day labor*, Cambridge, MA: MIT Press.

Lydon, M. and Garcia, A. (2015) *Tactical urbanism: Short-term action for long-term change*. Washington, D.C.: Island Press.

Lynch, K. (1981) *Good city form*, Cambridge, MA: MIT Press.

MA18 (Magistratsabteilung 18 Stadtentwicklung und Stadtplanung, Stadt Wien) (2003) Urban catalyst: Strategien für temporäre Nutzungen - Entwicklungspotentiale für urbane Residualflächen in europäischen Metropolen; Amsterdam - Berlin - Helsinki - Neapel – Wien, Vienna: City of Vienna.

Madanipour, A. (2017) *Cities in time: Temporary urbanism and the future of the city*, London: Bloomsbury.

Marshall, R. (ed) (2001) *Waterfronts in post-industrial cities*, London: Spon.
Massey, D. (2005) *For space*. Los Angeles: Sage.
McFarlane, C. (2011) Assemblage and critical urbanism. *City* 15 (2): 204–24.
Mean, M., Johar, I. and Gale, T. (2008) *Bristol beach: An experiment in place-making*, London: DEMOS.
Mehta, V. (2020) The new proxemics: COVID-19, social distancing, and sociable space. *Journal of Urban Design* 25 (6): 669–74.
Mould, O. (2014) Tactical urbanism: The new vernacular of the creative city. *Geography Compass* 8 (8): 529–39.
Mukhija, V. and Loukaitou-Sideris, A. (2014) *The informal American city: Beyond taco trucks and day labor*, Cambridge, MA: MIT Press.
Müller, M., Schmid, J., Schönherr, U. and Weiss, F. (eds) (2015) *Null Euro Urbanismus: Ein Katalog von Good Practice Beispielen*, Hamburg: Null Euro Urbanismus Studien- und Rechercheprojekt, available at: http://www.null-euro-urbanismus.de/?page_id=81 (accessed 30 July 2018).
Nemeth, J. and Longhorst, J. (2014) Rethinking urban transformation: Temporary uses for vacant land. *Cities* 40: 143–50.
Novy, J. and Colomb, C. (2013) Struggling for the right to the (creative) city in Berlin and Hamburg: New urban social movements, new 'spaces of hope'?. *International Journal of Urban and Regional Research* 37 (5): 1816–38.
Oswalt, P. (2002) Die Stadt stimulieren: Standortentwicklung mit kapitalschwachen Akteuren und temporären Programmen. *Werk, Bauen, Wohnen* 6: 44–49.
Oswalt, P., Overmeyer, K. and Misselwitz, P. (2013) *Urban catalyst: The power of temporary use*, Berlin: DOM publishers.
Pagano, C. (2013) DIY urbanism: Property and process in grassroots city building. *Marquette Law Review* 97 (2): 335–89.
Park, R., Burgess, E. and McKenzie, R. (1925) *The city*. Chicago: University of Chicago Press.
PIA (Planning Institute of Australia) (2016) A new era for national city planning, viewed 12 June 2019, available at: https://www.planning.org.au/documents/item/7874
Pogoreutz, M. (2006) Urban intelligence, in: F. Haydn and R. Temel (eds) *Temporary urban spaces: Concepts for the use of city spaces*, Basel: Birkhäuser, pp. 75–80.
Polyak, L. (2016) Civic space: 'The reappropriation of vacant buildings in four European cities', unpublished PhD thesis, Central European University, Budapest, available at: www.etd.ceu.edu/2017/polyak_levente.pdf (accessed 19 July 2018).
Portas, M. (2011) The Portas review: An independent review into the future of our high streets, London: Department for Business Innovation and Skills, viewed 22 October 2020, available at: https://www.gov.uk/government/publications/the-portas-review-the-future-of-our-high-streets

PPS (Project for Public Spaces) (2018) The lighter, quicker, cheaper transformation of public spaces, available at: https://www.pps.org/article/lighter-quicker-cheaper (accessed 28 July 2020).

Pratt, A. C. (2009) Urban regeneration: From the arts feel good factor to the cultural economy: A case study of Hoxton, London. *Urban Studies* 46 (5–6): 1041–61.

Radywyl, N. and Biggs, C. (2013) Reclaiming the commons for urban transformation. *Journal of Cleaner Production* 50: 159–70.

Rapoport, A. (1982) *The meaning of the built environment: A nonverbal communication approach*, Beverly Hills: Sage.

RAW München (Referat für Arbeit und Wirtschaft, Landeshauptstadt München) (2007) *München – Standortfaktor Kreativität*, Munich: Referat für Arbeit und Wirtschaft.

Richards, G. and Wilson, J. (2006) Developing creativity in tourist experiences: A solution to the serial reproduction of culture? *Tourism Management* 27: 1209–1223.

Rios, M. (2014) Learning from informal practices: Implications for urban design, in V. Mukhija and A. Loukaitou-Sideris (eds) *The informal American city: Beyond taco trucks and day labor*, Cambridge, MA: MIT Press.

Rosic, N. and Froessler, D. (2009) *Leerstandsmanagement: Konzeptpapier zur Durchführung eines Leerstandsmanagements in Steinheim*, Düsseldorf: Innovationsagentur Stadtumbau NRW.

Sandercock, L. (2003) *Cosmopolis II: Mongrel cities in the 21st century*, London: Continuum.

Sandler, D. (2020) Grassroots urbanism in contemporary São Paulo. *Urban Design International* 25 (2): 137–51.

Sassen, S. (2013) Informal economies and cultures in global cities, in P. Oswalt, K. Overmeyer and P. Misselwitz (eds) *Urban catalyst*, Berlin: DOM Publishers, pp. 105–16.

Scheffler, K. (1910/2015) *Berlin: ein Stadtschicksal (Berlin: Psychogramme of a City)* (F. Illies, ed) Berlin: Suhrkamp Verlag.

Schlegelmilch, F. (2009) Zwischennutzen – leichter gesagt als getan. *Informationen zur Raumentwicklung* 7: 493–502.

Schulz, C. and Abele, M. (2011) Managers of *Strandbar Mitte* and *Oststrand*, Berlin. Personal interview.

Schwarting, H. and Overmeyer, K. (2008) *Suboptimale Nutzungen lieben lernen: Eine Schlüsselstrategie der integrierten Stadtentwicklung*, Wiesbaden: Hessisches Ministerium für Wirtschaft, Verkehr und Landesentwicklung.

Schwarzer, M. (1994) Myths of permanence and transience in the discourse on historic preservation in the United States. *Journal of Architectural Education* 48 (1): 2–11.

SenStadt (Senatsverwaltung für Stadtentwicklung Berlin) (ed) (2007) *Urban pioneers: Temporary use and urban development in Berlin*, Berlin: Jovis.

Smith, N. (1996) *The new urban frontier: Gentrification and the Revanchist City*, New York: Routledge.

Solà-Morales, I. (1994) Terrain vague, in C. Davidson (ed) *Anyplace*, Cambridge, MA: MIT Press.

Steffens, K. (2013) *Urbanismo Táctico 3: Casos Latinoamericanos*, The Street Plans Collaborative and Ciudad Emergente, retrieved 7 January 2022, available at: https://issuu.com/streetplanscollaborative/docs/ut_vol3_2013_0528_17

Stevens, Q. (2009) Artificial waterfronts. *Urban Design International* 14 (1): 3–21.

Stevens, Q. (2011) Characterising Germany's artificial 'city beaches': Distribution, type and design 3rd World Planning Schools Congress, Perth.

Stevens, Q. (2015) Sandpit urbanism, in B. Knudsen, D. Christensen and P. Blenker (eds) *Enterprising initiatives in the experience economy: Transforming social worlds*, New York: Routledge.

Stevens, Q. and Ambler, M. (2010) Europe's city beaches as Post-Fordist placemaking. *Journal of Urban Design* 15 (4): 515–37.

Stevens, Q. and Dovey, K. (2004) Appropriating the spectacle: Play and politics in a leisure landscape. *Journal of Urban Design* 9 (3): 351–65.

Stevens, Q., Daly, J. and Dovey, K. (forthcoming) Designing for Possibility in Public Space: Affordance, assemblage and ANT'.

Stevens, Q., Morley, M. and Dovey, K. (forthcoming) Mapping Melbourne's parklets: understanding the capacities of urban street spaces.

Street Plans Collaborative (2012) *Tactical urbanism Volume 1*, retrieved 7 January 2022, available at: https://issuu.com/streetplanscollaborative/docs/tactical_urbanism_vol.1

Street Plans Collaborative (2012) *Tactical Urbanism Volume 2*, retrieved 7 January 2022, available at: https://issuu.com/streetplanscollaborative/docs/tactical_urbanism_vol_2_final

Sweeney, J., Mee, L., McGuirk, P., and Ruming, K. (2018) Assembling placemaking: making and remaking place in a regenerating city. *Cultural Geographies* 25 (4): 571–87.

The Better Block Foundation (2019) Better Block, viewed 11 November 2020, available at: https://www.betterblock.org

Thorpe, A. (2020) *Owning the street: The everyday life of property*, Cambridge, MA: MIT Press.

Till, K. (2011) Interim use at a former death strip? Art, politics and urbanism at skulpturenpark Berlin Zentrum, in M. Silberman (ed) *After the wall: Berlin in Germany and Europe*, New York: Palgrave Macmillan, pp. 99–122.

Toffler, A. (1980) *The third wave*, New York: Bantam Books.

Tonkiss, F. (2011) Template urbanism: Four points about assemblage. *City* 15 (5): 584–88.

Tonkiss, F. (2013a) Austerity urbanism and the makeshift city. *City* 17 (3): 313–24.

Tonkiss, F. (2013b) *Cities by design: The social life of urban form*, Cambridge, UK: Polity.

Town Team Movement (2020) Town Team Movement, viewed 6 November 2020, available at: https://www.townteammovement.com/

Urban Catalyst (2001) *Analysis report Berlin study draft*, Berlin: Technische Universität Berlin.

Urban Catalyst (2007) Patterns of the unplanned, in K. Franck and Q. Stevens (eds) *Loose space: Possibility and diversity in urban life*, Abingdon, UK: Routledge, pp. 271–88.

Urban Unlimited (eds) (2004) *The shadow city, freezones in Brussels and Rotterdam*, Rotterdam: Urban Unlimited.

Valverde, M. (2005) Taking land use seriously: Toward an ontology of municipal law. *Law, Text, Culture* 9: 34–59.

Waldis, S. (2009) *Zwischennutzung urbaner Brachflächen und Nachhaltigkeit: Theoretisches Konzept zur Verbindung von Zwischennutzungen und Nachhaltigkeit*, Unpublished masters thesis, University of Basel.

Walker, B. and Salt, D. (2006) *Resilience thinking: Sustaining ecosystems and people in a changing world*, Washington, D.C.: Island Press.

Walker, D., Hampson, K. and Peters, R. (2000) *Relationship-based procurement strategies for the 21st century*, Canberra: Ausinfo.

Willinger, S. (2005) Leerstand als Möglichkeitsraum. Urbanistische Strategien zur Revitalisierung in den Innenstädten. *Informationen zur Raumentwicklung 6*: 397–407.

Yaneva, A (2012) *Mapping controversies in architecture*, New York: Routledge.

Zukin, S. (1982) *Loft living: Culture and capital in urban change*, Baltimore: Johns Hopkins University Press.

Index

Abstract machine 158
Academics, involved with t/t urbanism 5, 53, 68, 70, 74
Actor-Network analysis, of temporalities 140
Actor-Network Theory (ANT) 2, 26, 79, 180
Actors. *see also* Human actors; Intangible actors
   assembling 138–141
   non-government 140
   organisational skills and contacts of 139
   scope of 68–71
Administrative concepts, for city beaches 93
Advertising 22
Advocates, of t/t urbanism 53, 63
Agile open space projects 34
Agile urbanism 36
Agility 1, 33, 53, 55
Amsterdam, temporary beach (Blijburg aan Zee) 137
ANT. *see* Actor-Network Theory (ANT)
Artificial city beaches 11, 34, 79, 79, 110, 136–137
Assemblages
   approach and thinking 2, 47–49
   assemblage thinking 151–152, 158, 180, 182
   city beaches and 84–85
   durable 131, 182
   resilience thinking and 151–154
Assembling new actors 138–141
Austerity
   city beaches and 94
   policies 1
   urbanism 18, 60

Australia
   compared to Europe, and America 75
   parklets in 137, 138
   projects in 57–58
   t/t practices in 53–54, 73–74
   t/t projects in 69
   t/t urbanism in 53, 56, 57–58, 59, 60, 61, 62, 65–68, 83
Austria, temporary use thinking in 124
Avant-garde artist-led beaches 88
Avant-garde 'pop-up' urbanism 2

Badeschiff project, Berlin 93
Bad Ly project, Berlin 93
Beach(es). *see also* Artificial city beaches; City beach(es)
   atmosphere 85, 85f
   on Berlin Museum Island 112f
   community-run 88
   entrepreneurial operation of 89
   material, design and programming of 91–92
   projects 80, 88
   urban beaches 23
Berlin. *see also* Germany
   city beaches in 83, 89
   companies running beaches in 98
   as defined by Scheffler 146
   Haus des Lehrers 108
   informal food vending practices in 133
   open space projects in 35
   Palast der Republik 110
   projects *Bad Ly* and *Badeschiff* 93
   temporary use projects 112, 119, 145

Better Block Foundation 70
Blijburg aan Zee (temporary beach in Amsterdam) 137
Books, on t/t urbanism 4–6
Boom-bust cycles 1
Bottom-up urbanism 18, 60
Bristol Urban Beach 88
Britain, temporary urbanism and 19
Buildings, temporary and relocatable 85f

Cabins 84
Capacity(ies)
  analyzing and mapping 154–156, 155f, 157f, 158–161, 160f
  assemblage and resilience thinking 151–154
  capacity thinking 150–151, 162, 163–164
  expanding 163–165
  spaces of possibility 161–163
  for temporary and tactical change 161
  vs. tendencies 162
  understanding the concept of 149–150
  urban capacity 48–49
Carspace 159
Chair bombing 22
Chronos and *kairos* 140, 141, 169, 179
Cities in Time: Temporary urbanism and the future of the city (Madanipour) 9
City, mutables immobiles and 26
City beach(es)
  administrative concepts of 93
  as assemblages 84–85
  atmosphere 85, 85f
  austerity and 94
  creation and management of 95
  emergence of 89
  energy 89–91, 90f, 96f
  flexibility concept of 93
  form of 98–99
  in Germany 83, 85–86
  human actors and 85–89, 87f, 88, 97–98
  landscape elements and 83–84
  landscaping and furnishing 83–85, 85f, 96f
  non-profit organisations and 86–87, 87f
  profitability of 94
  public-private-led 87–88
  spaces, used for 87–88
  success of short-term 137
  as temporary use *(Zwischennutzung)*, 93
  use programs 92–93
  vacant land and 80–83, 81f, 82f
City preservation and change 43
Coexistence 142f, 143, 170f, 171
Collaboration, on t/t projects 71–72
Commercial beaches, in Germany 88
Commons 161
Community engagement 1, 37–39, 173–175
Community-run beaches 88, 90
Concepts, city beaches and 91–93, 92f, 96f
'Conditions of possibility' 161
Consolidation 142f, 143, 170f
Container Market 21f
Contexts and models 65–68
COVID-19 pandemic
  community engagement and 175
  intensity of urban space use and 168–172
  restructuring of time during 181
  social contact and density and 173
  tactical transformation of cities during 183
  temporary and tactical interventions during 169
  temporary transformation during 184
  urban spaces transformation and 1
Creative actors, vacant spaces and 107

Creative approaches to urban development 113–119, 113f
Creative businesses, old buildings and 103–104
Creative industries, temporary uses of 116–118, 124
Creative Nomads, role of 108f
Creative production 106–109, 108f
Creative rental concepts 115
Creative technical instruments 121
Creativity
   approaches to urban development 113–119, 113f
   concept of 103–106, 106t, 107t
   consumption of 109–112, 112f
   creative production 106–109, 108f
   design quality and 29–30
   key traits of 123
   in management processes 115–116
   temporary city beach projects and 88
   t/t urbanism and 39, 55
   in urban design, t/t urbanism and 25
   urban development and 113–119, 113f
Critical urbanism, assemblage thinking and 48
Crosswalks 17, 22, 185

de Certeau, Michel 18
Deck chairs, on city beaches 84
Deregulated planning regimes 1
Designers. *see also* Urban design; Urban designers
   activist 37
   challenges of 164
   creative open space ideas and 39
   parklets and 145
   temporary/tactical urbanism and 25
   t/t/ urbanism and 25

Displacement 2, 37, 62, 64, 141, 142f, 143, 170f, 171
DIY cases, Australian 60
DIY urban design 18
DIY urbanism 7, 19, 37, 58, 183
Do-It Yourself urbanism 60, 173

Ecological justice, in placemaking 64
Economic development, urban public space and 34
Economic vitality 180
Energy, city beaches and 89–91, 90f
Engagement. *see also* Community engagement actor 55
   features of community engagement 36–37
Entrepreneurs, operation of city beaches 89
Episteme 162
Europe
   temporary urbanism in 4, 19, 59, 183
   urban development and redevelopment 75
Extension, capacity and 149

Field of differences 152, 157f
Financial Crisis of 2007-2008 185
Flexibility of city beach concept 93
Football World Cup 90, 92, 145
Formation, of city beaches 98–99
France, origin of city beach in 80
Future directions 73–74

Gentrification 2, 4, 9, 33, 47, 53, 56, 62, 63, 70, 76, 171, 180
German cities 82, 94, 183
Germany
   archetypal city beaches in 80, 81f
   city beaches in 80, 85–86, 94
   commercial beaches 88
   Football World Cup 92

reunification of 104
Strandbar Mitte 91
typical city beaches in 81f
Global financial crisis 65. *see also* Financial Crisis of 2007-2208
Global North, t/t urbanism in 27, 34
Global South, t/t urbanism in 27–28, 185
Governance 27–28
    creative approaches to 117–118, 120–121
    processes, entrepreneurial reorganisations of 133
    of temporary uses 119–123
Government, proactive roles facilitating temporary use 122
Government-sector planner 69
Graffiti 22
Graffiti mapping 154–155, 155f
Grassroots actors 7, 54
Grassroots engagement 56. *see also* Community engagement
Grassroots t/t projects 56
Grassroots urbanism 60, 63
Greenspace 159
Guerilla signage 22
Guerrilla bike lanes 22
Guerrilla crosswalk 21f
Guerrilla gardening 17, 22
Guerrilla park (Rebar) 21f
Guerrilla tactics 29
Guerrilla urbanism 18, 60
Gymnastics club, demonstration by 87f

Hamburg, beach atmosphere 92f
Historic preservation 134
Human actors 85–89, 87f, 97–98. *see also* Actors
Human relationships, city beaches and 97

Identity. *See* Place, identity
Immutable mobile 26
Impulse 142f, 143, 170f, 171
Industrial brownfields, temporary uses of 110
Inequities, of neoliberal urban development 1
Informality, t/t urbanism and 43
Innovation
    creative 25, 37
    drivers of planning 117
    managerial creativity and 118–119
    spatial 177
    temporariness and 145
    temporary urbanism and 25, 144–145
    t/t urbanism and 25, 34, 175–179
    urban design projects and 25, 33, 39–40
    in urban planning and urban design 55, 176
Insurgent urbanism 18
Intangible actors 89–91
Intensification 35, 55
Intensity. *see also* Urban intensity
    capacity and 149
    of open space use 35
    policy planning and 55
    tactical open space interventions and 36
Interfaces 159
Irregularity, t/t urbanism and 43
Iterative testing, t/t urbanism and 39

Jacobs, Jane 103–104
Journals, special issues on t/t urbanism 6

Kairos 140
    and *chronos* 169
Kulturstrand, Munich's 99

Land marketing, creativity in 115–116
Landscaping and furnishings, of city beaches 83–85, 85f
Laneways 159

Literature and conceptual framing, on t/t urbanism 54–57
Local identity 1
Location, criteria for attractiveness of 111

Management processes, creativity in 115–116
Mapping and analyzing capacities 154–156, 155f, 157f, 158–161, 160f
Markets, temporary urbanism and 25–26
Massey, Doreen 80
'Matters of concern' 2–3, 10, 167
Melbourne
   street art scene in 155
   temporary transformation in 184
   t/t urbanism in 58
Memorials, spontaneous 22
Minimum-purchase scheme (Minimumverzehr) 93
Minimumverzehr (Minimum-purchase scheme) 93
Morland, City of 184
Munich 99
Mutability 26–27
Mutable immobile 26, 181
Myth of transience, maintaining 134–135

Neoliberal capitalism 46–47, 48. see also Neoliberalism
Neoliberal economic consensus 36
Neoliberalism 35, 47–48
Neoliberal urban governance 174
Nocturnal projections 22
Non-profit organisations, German city beach projects and 86–87, 87f
Non-profit-run Bristol Urban Beach 88
North America, temporary urbanism and tactical urbanism in 19, 46, 59

Old buildings 103–104
Open space
   during the COVID-19 pandemic 69, 172, 175
   designs 129
   development 59
   German government funding of 86
   temporary projects 138
   urban design practice and 79
   use 35

Parasite 142f, 146, 170f, 171
Paris Plage(s), 23, 24f, 80, 87, 91, 136
Park(ing) Day 70
Parklets 22, 23f, 137, 145, 177, 178
Pavements to Parks 22
Pedestrian space 159
The Permanence of Temporary Urbanism: Normalising Precarity in Austerity London (Ferreri) 8
Permanent open spaces 79
Perth, parklets in 137, 138
Pioneer 142f, 143, 170f, 171
Place
   concept of 153
   identity 182–184
   Massey's conception of 80
Place identity 42–44, 182–184
Placemaking 64, 69, 70
Planning
   creativity in 115–116
   of temporary use 117, 120–121
   for uncertainty 46–47
Planning Matter: Acting with things (Beauregard) 9
Pop-up 22, 29
Pop-up projects 63, 69
Pop-up urbanism 18, 44

Potsdamer Platz, Berlin 111
Power
   capacity and 149, 150
   of temporary use 143
Privatisation 10, 37, 47, 53, 56, 76
Profitability
   of city beaches 94
   and marketability of temporary uses 119
Public interests 47–48
Public life in urban spaces 35
Publicly-funded city beaches 88
Public sector, temporary use projects and 122–123
Public space 49, 161, 164. *see also* Semi-fixed elements of

RAC. *see* Royal Automobile Club (RAC)
Rebar 22
Regulations, temporary uses and 118–119
Relationships
   among various actors 113f
   temporary use projects and 131
Researching t/t urbanism 44–46
Resilience 40–42, 179–182
   definition of 153, 179–180
   key slow variables in 180
   resilience thinking 153–154, 178
   t/t urbanism and 178
Reunification of Germany 104
Revolt, in resilience thinking 153–154
Royal Automobile Club (RAC) 72
Rules, t/t urbanism and 27

Sand, city beaches and 83, 84
Sandpit urbanism 18
San Francisco, parklets in 184
Scheffler, Karl 146
Scope
   of t/t urbanism practice 20–26, 21f, 23f, 24f, 57–58 of actors 68–71
Semi-fixed elements of public space, design of 19
Sites
   temporary users of 114
   temporary and long term uses of 141, 142f
Skybeach, Stuttgart's 82f, 91, 98
Social construction, time as 132
Social justice, in placemaking 64
Social needs, t/t/urbanism and 46–47
South Pacific atmosphere, Hamburg 92f
Spaces. *see also* Urban spaces
   affordable, old buildings and 103–104
   of city beaches 87–88
   creative uses of 114
   of possibility 161–163
   temporarily unused 111
   t/t urbanism and 164
   vacant, creative actors and 107
Spatial innovations 177
Stand-In 142f, 146, 170f, 171
Strandbar Mitte, Berlin 91
Strandleben, Vaihingen an der Enz 87f, 97
Strategies 59
   Innovative planning 116
   institutionalised top-down 56
   long-term 137, 176
   official and conventional 114
   pre-pandemic urban planning 169
   in relation to agile open space projects 34
   in relation to tactics 7, 24f, 25, 33–34, 73, 156, 179 (*see also* de Certeau)
   short term and long term 62
Street art 156
Street Plans Collaborative 70
Streetspace 161
Stuttgart Skybeach 82f

Subversion 142f, 146, 170f, 171
Switzerland, temporary use thinking in 124
Sydney. *see also* Australia
Sydney, t/t of urbanism in 58

Tactical, as term 41–42
Tactical learning 18–19
Tactical open space interventions, intensity and 36
Tactical urbanism
  in Australian context 57–58
  challenges to the state 175
  contribution of 43–44
  de Certeau and 18
  description of 63–64
  in Europe, United Kingdom, and United States 4, 19, 46, 59
  as form of top-down strategic planning 33
  kairos link to 141
  long-term strategies and 34
  in North America 18
  place identity and 182
  vs. temporary urbanism 55
Tactical Urbanism (Lydon and Garcia) 4, 5–6
Tactics, tactical learning and 18–19
Tactic(s) 18, 22
  established t/t urbanism 18–19
  mapping as 163
Temporality
  assembling new actors 138–141
  benefits of the temporary 143–146
  durable but mutable 136–138
  maintaining the myth of transience 134–135
  temporariness as opportunity 135–136
  temporary exemptions 132–134
  temporary uses seen in two temporal perspectives 141, 142f, 143

Temporariness
  economic advantages and 136
  innovation and 145
  key traits of 123
  as opportunity 135–136
Temporary
  benefits of 143–146
  exemptions 132–134
  land uses in cities 103
  open space projects 138
  parklet 137–138
  transformations 19–20, 184
  urban interventions 33
Temporary and tactical urbanism. *see* t/t urbanism
Temporary beach, success of 26
Temporary café, Potsdamer Platz, Berlin, 1991 28f
Temporary city beach projects 88
The Temporary City (Bishop and Williams) 4, 5
Temporary framework, learning process and 25
Temporary/permanent 28–30
Temporary/tactical projects 20–21, 21f
Temporary urbanism
  in Australian context 57–58
  benefits of 144
  in Britain and Europe 19
  challenges to the state and 175
  demand side of 29
  in Europe and United Kingdom 59, 183
  forms of 22–23, 23f
  innovation and 144–145
  markets and 25–26
  tactical forms of 146–147
  tactical urbanism *vs.*, 55, 59
  top-down deployment by governments 134

urban space and 146
Temporary use projects 144–145
  new relationships between actors in 131
  public sector and 122–123
Temporary uses 104, 104t, 105t, 107, 111
  actors and 139–140
  concept of 138
  creative, economic liberalisation and 120
  duration of 136
  economic liberalisation and 120
  eight ways that time frames 142f, 170f
  German government guide to 116
  governing 119–123
  government as basis for 132–133
  'impetuous' creativity in 108
  limited duration of 131
  short-term arrangements of 139–140
  support for 133
  t/t projects and 171
  in two temporal perspectives 141, 142f, 143, 170f, 171
  in urban planning, role of creative 123
  urban planning and 136
  ways that time frames 142f, 170f
Tendencies vs. capacities 162
Time
  COVID-19 pandemic and 181
  as social construction 132
  t/t urbanism and 164
Town Team Movement 67, 70
Transience, maintaining the myth of 134–135
t/t projects. *see also* t/t urbanism
  in Australia 69
  benefits of 62
  collaboration, on 71–72
  design quality and 182
  experimental 62–65
  larger-scale 23
  urban planning and 56–57
t/t urbanism
  agility and innovation and 55
  in Australia 65–68
  benefits and impacts 1, 34–49, 62–65
  capacities for 150
  community engagement and 173–175
  critiquing 6–8
  diagramming 23, 24f, 25
  emphasis of 182
  enabling creativity, innovation in urban design 25
  granting designers to lower costs and risks 25
  innovation and 34, 175–179
  place identity and 182–184
  problems of 1–2
  resilience and 178
  role in reclaiming the city back from the car 26
  rules and 27
  scope of practice of 20–26, 21f, 23f, 24f, 57–58
  space and time and 164
  two concepts of 18–19
  urban design and 1, 25
Typology 158–159
  of different ways temporary uses link to long-term development of sites 5
  of potential relationships between permanent and temporary uses 142f, 170f

Uncertainty, t/t/urbanism and 46–47
United Kingdom
  tactical urbanism in 4, 19
  temporary urbanism in 183
United States, tactical urbanism in 4, 19, 46, 183

Urban artworks 22
Urban beach 23
Urban capacity 48–49
Urban Catalyst, research team 4–5, 18, 169, 171
Urban Catalyst: The Power of Temporary Use (Oswalt, Overmeyer and Misselwitz) 4
Urban character 42–44. *see also* Place identity
Urban density, t/t urbanism and 34
Urban design
  innovations in 176
  t/t urbanism and 1, 25, 53
Urban designers 8, 68, 164
Urban design theory 156
Urban development, Creative approaches to 113–119, 113f
Urban economies, creative production and 106–109, 108f
Urban intensity 64
  highlights of 168–172, 170f
  in inner-city areas 66
  temporal and spatial interstices of the city and 17
  temporary use projects and 143, 168–169, 170f, 171–172
  t/t urbanism and 34, 55, 63
Urbanism. *see also* Tactical urbanism; Temporary urbanism; t/t urbanism
  austerity and 18, 60
  Avant-garde 'pop-up' 2
  bottom-up 18, 60
  DIY 7, 37
  grassroots 60
  guerrilla 18, 60
  insurgent 18
  pop-up 18, 44
  sandpit 18
  temporary 19, 139–140

Urban land uses, entrepreneurial reorganisations of 133
Urban planning
  role of creative temporary uses in 123
  temporary and tactical urbanism and 1, 53
  t/t projects 56–57
Urban sites
  artificial city beaches in 136
  temporary uses of 110
Urban spaces
  by creative industries, temporary uses of 116–118
  flexibility of city beaches as 99
  pandemic and 176
  public 34
  temporary artistic uses of 119–120
  temporary physical interventions in 130
Use programs, in city beaches 92–93

Vacant land/sites
  city beaches and 80–83, 81f, 82f
  creative public uses of 110–111
Vaihingen's 87f, 97
Variability, of city beaches 95, 97
Vegetable Car 17, 18f

Weather, as form of energy 90–91
What/how/when/where/why analysis 156, 157f, 162–163
'What is urban character?' project 154
World Cup soccer matches 90f

Yarn bombing 21f, 22, 152
Yarra, City of 184

Zero-Euro Urbanism 94
Zwischennutzung (temporary use) 93

For Product Safety Concerns and Information please contact our EU
representative GPSR@taylorandfrancis.com
Taylor & Francis Verlag GmbH, Kaufingerstraße 24, 80331 München, Germany

www.ingramcontent.com/pod-product-compliance
Lightning Source LLC
Chambersburg PA
CBHW050534300426
44113CB00012B/2098